Higher education in the ancient world

By the same author

Rhetoric at Rome
The Roman Mind

M. L. Clarke

Higher education in the ancient world

Routledge & Kegan Paul London

First published 1971
by Routledge & Kegan Paul Ltd
Broadway House, 68–74 Carter Lane
London, EC4V 5EL

Printed in Great Britain
by Richard Clay (The Chaucer Press), Ltd,
Bungay, Suffolk

ISBN 0 7100 6916 2

Contents

Map

Preface

First I must explain and justify my title. By higher education I mean all education above the primary or elementary stage. Some of this can perhaps hardly qualify as 'higher'. Grammar, for instance, was normally studied at what one might call the preparatory school level; but it could be pursued further than that, and in view of its close relationship to rhetoric, which for many in the ancient world was the final stage of education, it seemed right to include it. The 'ancient world' of my title is the world of Greece and Rome from the fourth century B.C. onwards. I have continued the story, though briefly and rather superficially, into what are generally thought of as the Middle Ages. So far as education is concerned the ancient world might well be said to have lasted until 1453 in Byzantium, and there is at least a case for maintaining that it lasted until then, or even later, in the West. Indeed, in some respects it lasted almost to the present day. There must be men alive whose fathers had an education not very different from that of the Roman Empire, who read at school little more than Homer, Virgil and Horace, and who learned their geometry from Euclid.

Some writers on ancient education are primarily concerned to draw lessons from it for the present day (*Ancient Education and Today* is the title of a work by a former headmaster and Professor of Education). This is a legitimate approach; no doubt one can draw stimulus and inspiration from the educational theory and practice of the best teachers of antiquity, and the past would hardly be worth studying if one could learn nothing from it. My approach, however, is rather different. I think of educational history as an important part of social and cultural history. Our culture and outlook on life depend to a large extent on what we have learned at school, and this was particularly true before the invention of printing facilitated the diffusion of knowledge and ideas outside the schools. My chief concern has therefore been to describe what was taught and how it was taught. I have not said much about educational theory; what Plato advocated in the *Republic* is not what the ordinary student experienced in the schoolroom.

If there are lessons to be learned from the educational system of antiquity they may not be those we wish to find there. Those who deplore early specialization or the neglect of science will find that these are features of education in the ancient world as much as, indeed more than, at the present day. Those who think that education should be relevant to modern conditions will find little support in ancient practice; Homer, the standard textbook of the Greek grammar schools, read in fifth-century Athens, Republican Rome and imperial Byzantium, was, it might be said, equally irrelevant to all these societies. Nor does the ancient world provide much support for what we call a classical education; Greek and Latin were not dead languages for the Greeks and Romans. What we do find, and what we may well envy, is a remarkable stability in education. The ancients were not constantly devising new syllabuses and trying new methods; they were content with the established textbooks and well-tried methods. The consequence was a strong and lasting cultural tradition which united educated men of different countries and different ages and was able to survive even the challenge of Christianity.

Previous general histories of Greek and Roman education may be said to have been superseded by H.-I. Marrou's *Histoire de l'éducation dans l'antiquité*, published in 1948 and translated into English in 1956 as *A History of Education in Antiquity*. If I have made some critical references to Marrou's work, this does not mean that I do not recognize the value of his lively and informative survey. Where I cover the same ground as he did I hope that I have been able to add something. In particular I have dealt in considerable detail with the teaching of the philosophers, on which there is a good deal of evidence which Marrou did not use. For my brief section on Arab education I have had the benefit of the advice of Dr R. Walzer.

Translations except where otherwise stated are by the author.

Abbreviations

The following are the principal abbreviations used in the notes:

A.J.P.	*American Journal of Philology*
A.P.	*Anthologia Palatina*
C.A.G.	*Commentaria in Aristotelem Graeca*
C. Gloss. Lat.	*Corpus Glossariorum Latinorum*
C.I.L.	*Corpus Inscriptionum Latinarum*
C. Ph.	*Classical Philology*
Cod. Just.	*Codex Justinianeus*
Cod. Theod.	*Codex Theodosianus*
D.H.	Dionysius of Halicarnassus
D.L.	Diogenes Laertius
F. Gr. Hist.	*Fragmente der griechischen Historiker*
Gr. Graeci	*Grammatici Graeci*
Gr. Lat.	*Grammatici Latini*
I.G.	*Inscriptiones Graecæ*
J.R.S.	*Journal of Roman Studies*
O.G.I.	*Orientis Graeci Inscriptiones Selectae*
Ox. Pap.	*Oxyrhynchus Papyri*
P.G.	*Patrologia Graeca*
P.L.	*Patrologia Latina*
R.E.	*Realencyclopädie der classischen Altertumswissenschaft*
R.E.G.	*Revue des études grecques*
R.L.M.	*Rhetores Latini Minores*
Rh. Mus.	*Rheinisches Museum*
S.B.	*Sitzungsberichte*
S.E.G.	*Supplementum Epigraphicum Graecum*
S.I.G.	*Sylloge Inscriptionum Graecarum*
S.V.F.	*Stoicorum Veterum Fragmenta*

chapter 1
Introduction

The history of higher education in the ancient world begins in
the fourth century B.C. The great achievements of fifth-century
Athens were based on a very slight foundation of formal education. The young Athenian learned to read and write; he went
to the palaestra for physical training and to the music master
for instruction in lyre-playing. Otherwise he learned not so
much from schools as from the city itself, with its democratic
political institutions, its festivals and its social gatherings. In
the second half of the century, however, men became conscious
of their lack of higher education, and in response to the new
demand there appeared those itinerant lecturers whom we
know as the sophists. From their unsystematic instructions developed the ancient schools of rhetoric and other disciplines.
Similarly the conversations of Socrates led to the philosophical
schools of the fourth century. Learning became systematized,
embodied in regular courses of instruction and in textbooks.
The history of the various schools, their scope and methods of
teaching, will be considered in later chapters; by way of introduction something must be said of their relation to one another
and of the general plan of ancient education.

There was a theory in the ancient world that every seventh
year in a man's life was of peculiar significance. At seven a boy
grew his second teeth; fourteen was taken as the age of puberty
and twenty-one as that of full physical maturity; and so on,
with less and less plausibility, until the end of life.[1] Education
was linked to this theory to the extent that seven was commonly

considered to be the right age for schooling to begin,[2] and Aristotle at any rate thought that the ages of fourteen and twenty-one should mark stages in a boy's education.[3] He does not explain the significance of twenty-one, but fourteen for him meant the change from what we may call primary to secondary education,[4] though the term primary is a little misleading for a course which continued to fourteen and no doubt included some study of literature as well as reading and writing.

After the age of fourteen Aristotle assigns three years to what he calls 'other studies'. He means, no doubt, those subjects which were recognized as constituting a general education and for which the Greeks used the term *enkuklios paideia* or *enkuklia mathemata*. The Romans, who took over Greek ideas of education with very little change, called them the *liberales artes*, the subjects, that is, suited to a free man or, as an earlier generation of Englishmen might have put it, what every gentleman ought to know. It was generally agreed that the encyclic or liberal arts were seven in number: grammar, rhetoric, dialectic, arithmetic, music, geometry and astronomy. These seven, with the addition of the professional studies of medicine and architecture, were expounded in Varro's *Disciplinarum Libri* in the first century B.C.; Varro was only reproducing what was accepted in the contemporary Greek world, and there is good reason to believe that this general education was already established in the fourth century B.C.[5]

In Aristotle's scheme the 'other studies' are to be followed by a period of physical training. He has in mind the practice at Athens where the *ephebia*, or national service, at first of two years' duration, later reduced to one, began at the age of eighteen,[6] and education was therefore interrupted. Plato presumably also had the *ephebia* in mind when he fixed twenty as the age for beginning higher education.[7] His proposal involved a break with the practice current at the time, of beginning philosophy well before twenty. 'As things are,' he writes, 'those who take it up at all are adolescents, who have only just put boyhood behind them. In the interval before they set up house and begin to earn their living they are introduced to the hardest part—by which I mean abstract discussions—and then when they have done with that their philosophic education is supposed to be complete. Later they think they have done much if they accept an invitation to listen to such a discussion, which is, in their eyes, to be taken as a pastime.'[8] Though he disapproved of too early a start on philosophy, Plato himself certainly had adolescents among his pupils; a fragment of the comic poet Epicrates which describes his teaching refers to his pupils as *meirakia*, young people, that is, between the ages of fourteen and twenty-one.[9]

Plato was not greatly interested in the *enkuklios paideia*. He had little use for literary and rhetorical studies, and was more concerned to claim a place for the mathematical subjects in higher education than to require a grounding in them at a lower stage. In the *Republic* he is in favour of their being available to boys, but would not make them compulsory. He goes a little further in the *Laws*, where he says that the ordinary person who is not going to study these subjects in detail should at least acquire some knowledge of them.[10] But whatever may have been the case with Plato, the Academy after his time certainly required its pupils to have completed a course of general education before entry. Xenocrates, the third head of the school, refused to accept anyone who had not studied the *enkuklia mathemata*, and a later Academic, Crantor, was equally insistent that those studies were a necessary preliminary to philosophy.[11] Though there is no definite evidence on the point, it is likely that the Peripatetics took the same view. The Stoics would not be so particular; Zeno in his early days had rejected the *enkuklios paideia* as useless, and Chrysippus did not do more than allow that it had some value.[12] Epicurus was notoriously hostile or, if not hostile, indifferent to *paideia*, and this probably indicates that he was prepared to take younger pupils; he himself began his philosophical studies at the age of fourteen, or twelve according to another account,[13] and as a man with a gospel to preach to mankind he no doubt understood the desirability of making proselytes at an early age.[14] Cicero, who had himself studied under an Epicurean while still a boy,[15] perhaps had this school in mind when he wrote scornfully of those who accepted the first dogmatic teaching they heard at an impressionable age.[16]

Generally speaking the encyclic subjects were regarded as subordinate to philosophy; they were *propaideumata*, preparatory studies which trained one for something higher. The clearest statement of this view is provided by Isocrates. What he called philosophy others would have called rhetoric, but most of the philosophers would have shared his view of the position of the encyclic subjects. A thorough study of these, he maintains, may be of value to those who would make a living by them, but for the rest the benefit comes from the process of learning. While engaged on them and 'forced to apply their minds to difficult problems and not let their attention wander, being trained and sharpened in these disciplines they can more easily and quickly grasp and learn subjects which are more important and valuable'. Just as primary education prepares for the secondary stage (the *enkuklios paideia*), so the latter, for Isocrates, is a training and preparation for 'philosophy'.[17]

A similar view is expressed by Seneca, though he is less precise than Isocrates about the educational value of the encyclic subjects and more concerned with morality. These subjects, he says, are useful only so far as they prepare the mind as opposed to engaging it permanently. *Non discere debemus ista sed didicisse.*[18] 'Why then,' he asks, 'do we teach our sons the liberal arts? Not because they can impart virtue but because they prepare the mind for the reception of virtue.' He goes on, like Isocrates, to compare the relation of the liberal arts to philosophy with that of primary education to the liberal arts; the latter 'do not lead the mind as far as virtue but make the way to it easier'.[19] To give one more illustration of the same point of view, the author of the treatise on education ascribed to Plutarch lays down that a freeborn boy should acquire some knowledge both of rhetoric and of the other encyclic subjects but 'should learn them in a cursory manner, so as to acquire as it were a taste of them (for it is impossible to be a complete master of everything), but philosophy should have precedence. . . . Philosophy should be made the crown as it were of education.'[20]

In the Middle Ages the liberal arts were divided into the trivium and the quadrivium. The first consisted of grammar, rhetoric and dialectic, the subjects connected with the use of language, the latter of the mathematical arts, arithmetic, music, geometry and astronomy. Of the subjects in the first group dialectic, or logic, was in a somewhat anomalous position; though it was always recognized as one of the arts, it tended to lose its independent status and to be regarded as part of philosophy.[21] Rhetoric was the most important of the three. It was indeed in a position by itself among the encyclic arts. It prepared men for speaking in the law courts and in political assemblies and so was eminently useful as leading to a political career. It might be studied along with the other encyclic subjects, but it was often pursued when they had been abandoned, and it could become a rival to philosophy as the crown of education. Isocrates, though he dissociated himself from the professional rhetoricians and claimed to be teaching philosophy, in fact provided a higher education of a rhetorical character which would compete with what the philosophers offered. His course lasted for three or four years, and his pupils are described as *meirakia*;[22] as they would have already studied the encyclic subjects before they entered his school their age at entry would be about sixteen or seventeen. They would be completing their education, preparing for public life or for a career in teaching or literature. In Rome no less than in Athens rhetoric led to a political career, and for those aiming at such a career it provided, generally speaking, the final stage of education. Grammar was subordinate and preparatory to rhetoric and other subjects tended to be pushed out. Quintilian recommends the study of geometry (including some arithmetic and astronomy) and of music, but he would not allow these subjects to encroach on the time allotted to rhetoric, which he regarded as so exacting that it demanded the students' whole attention.[23] We can think of Quintilian's school as providing a course which lasted, like that of Isocrates, about three years and would be completed at the age of eighteen; this at any rate was the age at which one of his pupils, the younger Pliny, began practice at the bar.[24]

Boyhood may have ended at fourteen according to the accepted septennial scheme, but growing up is a gradual process, and the Romans seem to have felt that it was not complete until sixteen. This was the usual age for changing from the *toga praetexta* of the boy to the *toga uirilis* of the man. The assumption of the man's toga marked the stage at which a boy saw the last of his *paedagogus*, or slave tutor, and became his own master. In Republican times he entered on his apprenticeship to public life and began to learn the ways of the forum under the guidance of some distinguished political figure. At this stage of his life Cicero began to study law under Scaevola[25] and at the same time attended the forum and heard the leading orators of the day, though he did not give up his academic studies in rhetoric and philosophy. In the time of Quintilian the change of toga made little difference to the average student of rhetoric, who continued to be in effect a schoolboy until well after the official end of boyhood.

This, however, still meant something. It gave the boy the opportunity of exercising some choice as regards his education,[26] and choice might lead him to philosophy. Persius began to study under the Stoic Cornutus at the age of sixteen, after his assumption of the man's toga;[27] and the Nicander to whom Plutarch addressed his work on how to listen to lectures, who was embarking on a full-time study of philosophy, was at the same stage of his life.[28]

On the other hand there were some who started on philosophy before sixteen. Galen did so at fourteen, as did Apollonius of Tyana; Seneca was a boy when he heard Sotion.[29] There were some, too, whose philosophical study did not begin till later. Quintilian, who would certainly have been reluctant to lose any of his pupils as early as sixteen, envisages the possibility that after completing their course in rhetoric they might proceed to philosophy as an alternative to going out into the world.[30] Marcus Aurelius, though he had had some lessons in philosophy before, did not devote himself to serious study of the subject till he was twenty-five, after an elaborate training in rhetoric under Fronto.[31] Lucian's pathetic perpetual student Hermotimus began on philosophy when about forty and was still going to lectures, reading books and writing out notes nearly twenty years later.[32]

Generally speaking higher education in the ancient world was, by comparison with the practice of modern Europe, completed at an early age. To give three examples from different periods and different *milieux*, the younger Pliny, Origen and St Augustine, all men of high culture and intelligence, completed their formal education before their nineteenth birthday. The encyclic subjects, if we exclude rhetoric, were not pursued, except by a few specialists, beyond a quite humble level. The general education of the ancients corresponded more or less to the Ordinary Level work of a modern

English schoolboy. Moreover, it was often neglected. This was certainly the case at Rome, where literary and rhetorical studies tended to oust other subjects; it is clear from Quintilian that most Romans in his day thought it unnecessary to study anything but grammar and rhetoric.[33] Even among the Greeks we find complaints of premature specialization. In the first century B.C. Dionysius of Halicarnassus lamented the habit of entering on rhetoric without any knowledge of the encyclic arts, and a century or so later the rhetorician Theon said much the same.[34] According to the ironic advice Lucian puts into the mouth of a teacher of rhetoric, it is no disadvantage to a would-be rhetorician to have omitted what are generally considered the necessary preliminary studies.[35] Neglect of literary studies was less common; Galen, however, notes with regret an increasing tendency in his day to start philosophy without any previous study of grammar or rhetoric.[36]

The encyclic arts, however, continued to play their part in education, at any rate in the Greek-speaking world. To give some examples, the historian Nicolaus of Damascus had studied grammar, rhetoric, music and the mathematical subjects, and in Plutarch's day the youths of Athens were studying grammar, geometry and music.[37] Philo as a boy attended courses in the same three subjects, and in Alexandria in the early third century Origen taught dialectic, geometry, arithmetic and astronomy as preliminary studies to philosophy, from which he went on to theology.[38] In the Latin-speaking West these studies had a less secure place; it is typical of the educational situation in the later Empire, at any rate in one of the provinces, that St Augustine had to acquire his knowledge of the liberal arts, other than grammar and rhetoric, from books, without the aid of any teacher.[39] But he did acquire such knowledge; it was still recognized as part of the equipment of the educated man.

The schools of antiquity were specialist institutions in which a single subject was taught. The grammarian had his school of grammar, the rhetorician his school of rhetoric; the mathematical subjects were taught by mathematicians in their own schools and philosophy by philosophers in theirs. The schools were established as a result of private enterprise and it was only under the Roman Empire that they enjoyed some support from the state. Athens expected her citizens to have their children educated, but did not provide the schools in which they learned; state control was mainly concerned with physical and military education, with the organization of the gymnasia and the *ephebia*. In the Greek cities of the Hellenistic age endowments for educational purposes were sometimes made by individuals, as at Miletus at the turn of the third and second centuries B.C., where Eudemus gave his city 60,000 drachmae, and at Teos in the second century, where 34,000 drachmae were donated by Polythrus;[40] in the second century the kings of Pergamum, Attalus II and Eumenes II, made gifts for educational purposes to Delphi and Rhodes respectively.[41] Such endowments, however, did not cover the provision of higher education, though occasionally special benefactions were made for this purpose; at Eretria the official in charge of the gymnasium provided a teacher of rhetoric at his own cost, and another such official provided a scholar to lecture on Homer.[42] The philosophical schools of Athens, of which more will be said in a later chapter, were private foundations which owed their continuity and remarkable longevity in part to the fact that they possessed property left by the founder to his successors.

One institution of the Hellenistic age provides a partial exception to what has been said above about the lack of state support for higher education. The Museum at Alexandria was in intention an institution for research and the pursuit of learning rather than for education, but its members inevitably gathered pupils round them. It was founded by the first Ptolemy; it had its own buildings, and its members, including philosophers, rhetoricians, physicians and poets, enjoyed freedom from taxation and free meals at a common table.[43] These privileges were continued by the Roman emperors after the end of Egypt's independence, and though the later history of the Museum is obscure, it seems that common meals were still provided to men of learning at Alexandria at the end of the fifth century.[44]

The first Roman emperor to concern himself with the subsidizing of education was Vespasian, who established chairs of Latin and Greek rhetoric at Rome with salaries from the imperial treasury.[45] After Vespasian, Marcus Aurelius founded a state chair of rhetoric at Athens and gave salaries to the heads of the philosophical schools there.[46] Salaries were also provided from municipal funds. This was already being done under Augustus, when some of the cities of Gaul supported teachers of rhetoric, and in the time of the younger Pliny it was a common practice.[47] These salaries probably did not preclude the acceptance of fees; Quintilian received a salary of 100,000 sesterces as public professor at Rome,[48] but if we can trust Juvenal, who depicts the wealthy parent as grudging him his fee, he also demanded 2,000 sesterces per annum from those who attended his classes.[49] Those who did not enjoy salaries and depended on fees could, if they were successful and popular, do well for themselves; Remmius Palaemon, a teacher of grammar in the first century, made 400,000 sesterces a year from his teaching.[50] There were, however, complaints from teachers that their pupils, or their parents, defaulted or paid their fees late or not in full.[51] The usual practice was to fix an annual fee, but this was apparently not paid till the end of the year, so that it was possible to avoid payment by leaving before it became due.[52] One teacher, the rhetorician Proclus, required the payment of 100 drachmae in advance, which sum gave the right to attend at all times; another rhetorician, Scopelian, adjusted his fees to the means of his pupils.[53] The Latin grammarian Antonius Gnipho left it to his pupils to determine what fee to pay and did better by relying on their generosity than he would have done if he had followed the normal method.[54]

Rhetoricians were more highly paid than grammarians.[55] The edict of Diocletian on wages and prices lays down that a grammarian should receive 200 denarii a month per pupil and a rhetorician 250.[56] By the latter half of the fourth century the gap between the two professions had widened, judging by the emperor Gratian's law of 376 in which rhetoricians in Gaul are allotted salaries twice as high as grammarians.[57]

Apart from the salaries which they might receive teachers of the liberal arts were also subsidized indirectly by being allowed immunity from the various burdensome services to which Roman citizens, and in particular members of the city councils, were liable under the Empire. This policy was initiated by Vespasian[58] and was continued and extended by later emperors. These immunities applied to grammarians and

rhetoricians and also to physicians.[59] Philosophers also enjoyed certain immunities. But they were in a weak position
compared to other teachers, at least so far as monetary contributions were concerned; it could always be pointed out that
a desire for exemption showed a spirit of avarice alien to the
profession of philosophy or that one who claimed to be able to
meet the blows of fortune should also be able to meet the
obligations of citizenship.[60] Primary school teachers did not
enjoy any subsidies, whether in the form of salaries or by way of
immunities;[61] the state did nothing for those who provided the
foundation on which higher education was based. The favoured
teachers were those who, in the words of Vespasian's rescript of
the year 75, 'train the souls of the young to gentleness and civic
virtue'.[62] How they performed this task will be seen in the
following chapters.

chapter 2
The teaching of the liberal arts

Grammar

According to one ancient writer grammar is a discipline to which we are subjected from our earliest years.[1] This is true in that grammar (*grammatike*) is concerned with the written word (*grammata*) and in any literate society education in its earliest stages is to a large extent concerned with the mastery of words. But ancient usage commonly excluded the primary stage of education from *grammatike* and applied that term to the literary and linguistic studies which followed the acquisition of an ability to read and write. Primary education was known as *grammatistike* and was conducted by the *grammatistes*, in Latin commonly called the *ludi magister*. The *grammatikos*, the grammar school master, taught at the next stage of education.

The profession of grammar was also distinct from that of rhetoric. This distinction, according to Suetonius, had not existed originally; the old grammarians taught rhetoric as well, and many of them left works on both subjects.[2] He gives some examples from Republican Rome of men who taught the two subjects,[3] and mentions one teacher who had flourished when he was a boy who lectured on grammar in the morning and gave rhetorical declamations in the afternoon.[4] But though he may be right in general as regards Rome, his statement does not apply to the ancient world as a whole. We know of one Greek teacher, Aristodemus of Nysa, who, both in his native city and in Rhodes, taught grammar and rhetoric, the latter in the morning and the former in the afternoon.[5] But this seems to have been an exceptional case. The earliest Greek teachers of rhetoric were not also grammarians; they had the practical aim of enabling their pupils to defend themselves in the courts, and to this they confined themselves.

In the educational system which took shape in the Hellenistic age and was well-established under the Roman Empire, grammar stood between *grammatistike* and rhetoric. The grammarian's pupils came to him at the age of twelve or thereabouts,[6] and left at about fifteen to go on to the rhetorician; he conducted what might be called a preparatory school for boys. Grammarians, however, were often men of considerable scholarship, whose attainments qualified them to teach at a higher level than this. And they sometimes did. Strabo was twenty when he studied under Tyrannio at Rome,[7] and advanced teaching of this sort must have been a good deal more to the taste of a distinguished scholar like Tyrannio than the instruction, on which he was engaged in 56 B.C., of Cicero's ten-year-old nephew.[8] A Latin grammarian, Caecilius Epirota, had a select class consisting only of *adulescentes*, boys over sixteen, and would take no younger pupils except under strong pressure from parents;[9] and in the second century we find Aulus Gellius continuing to study under a grammarian after the usual leaving age, when he was an *adulescens*.[10]

The English words 'grammar' and 'grammarian', commonly used for *grammatike* and its teachers, are somewhat misleading. 'Language and Literature' would adequately represent the content of the subject as it was taught in the ancient schools. It included grammar in the modern sense, the study of language; it also included the reading and explanation of the standard works of literature, particularly the poets. In both these aspects it goes back to fifth-century Athens. The science of language, the study of the forms and meanings of words, of inflexions and the rules for correct speech, originated with the sophists; Protagoras, Prodicus and Hippias all had linguistic interests. Literary as well as linguistic scholarship begins in the period of the sophists. The reading of the poets, especially Homer, was an established part of education, and reading inevitably involved explanation. Protagoras maintained that an educated man should understand what was said by the poets and be able to explain them.[11] Hippias lectured on

Homer;[12] and as early as 427 B.C., judging by a fragment of a play of Aristophanes of that date, students were learning the meaning of those Homeric 'glosses', or obsolete words, the explanation of which was part of the regular work of the later grammarians.[13]

The philosophers, Platonist, Aristotelian and Stoic, concerned themselves with language and literature; a pupil of Theophrastus, Praxiphanes, who wrote on Homer and developed the study of *hellenismos*, or correct speech, was regarded by some as the earliest *grammatikos*.[14] But such studies became divorced from philosophy and reached their height with the great Alexandrians, Aristophanes and Aristarchus. A great deal of work was produced, largely on Homer, who held and continued to hold a secure place in education and whose poems provided a rich field for commentary, textual, linguistic and historical. This work would in due course move downwards from what one might call the university level to that of the ordinary grammar school teacher. An important figure in the history of teaching is Dionysius Thrax, a pupil of Aristarchus and author of the first systematic textbook on grammar on which all subsequent Greek grammars were based. He taught in Rhodes, and like every other grammarian he expounded Homer. An interesting scrap of information about his methods has survived. He made a reproduction of Nestor's cup, described in the eleventh book of the *Iliad*, his pupils subscribing to provide the materials.[15] Modern teachers with their visual aids can look back to him as a pioneer.

Dionysius defined grammar as 'the practical knowledge of the ways of poets and prose writers', and divided it into six parts. These were: reading with correct pronunciation; explanation of poetic figures of speech; explanation of rare words and of the subject matter; etymology; analogy (that is, the doctrine of regular grammatical forms); and the criticism of poetry.[16] Others produced other definitions of grammar and other divisions of its constituent parts. Crates and his followers of the school of Pergamum distinguished the *kritikos* from the *grammatikos*; criticism they regarded as a higher and more inclusive science than grammar, a term which they applied to the explanation of rare words, accentuation and the like.[17] The word *kritikos* was at one time in use for the teacher of literature (we find it in the pseudo-Platonic dialogue *Axiochus*, where the *kritikos* appears among the teachers to whom a growing boy is subjected),[18] but the term *grammatikos* prevailed, and the *grammatikos* dealt with both language and literature, with, to use Quintilian's words, *recte loquendi scientia*, the art of correct speech, and *poetarum enarratio*, the interpretation of the poets.[19] How he handled these in his teaching we shall see later. In the meantime we turn to Rome.

Higher education in Rome was in most respects a close copy of that of Greece. The expansion of Rome brought her into contact with the older civilization of the Greek-speaking world with its established intellectual traditions and its expert teachers in the various branches of knowledge. These teachers came to Rome and taught there, using their own language and following the methods of instruction in use in the contemporary Greek world. They continued to do so. In the case of two of their disciplines, grammar and rhetoric, the Romans developed Latin courses closely modelled on the Greek, but this did not mean that the Greek courses were superseded. The two languages and their literatures were studied side by side. The Romans were thus the first people in history to base their education on the study of a foreign language in addition to their own. The position of Greek to them was not unlike that formerly held by Latin in modern Europe, except that they recognized the claims of their own literature in education at a much earlier stage than the modern European countries did.

To speak of Greek as a foreign language to the Romans is, however, a little misleading. They did not learn Greek as a modern English schoolboy learns French or German. Many of them must have been bilingual from their earliest years. They would pick up the language in the home from Greek-speaking slaves. It was usual to employ Greek nurses,[20] as English families used to have their French or German governess or continental families their English nanny. Quintilian tells us that it was a common practice to make a child speak only Greek for a time (as Montaigne spoke nothing but Latin when a boy) and finds it necessary to warn against the danger of acquiring a faulty pronunciation of the native tongue.[21] There is an interesting piece of evidence on this point from late antiquity in the autobiographical poem of Paulinus of Pella.

He tells us that having been used to speaking and playing with Greek slaves he was imperfectly acquainted with Latin when he started his lessons in that language.[22] Paulinus was brought up in Gaul in the fourth century, a place and a time at which one might have expected Greek influence to be relatively weak; such a situation is even more likely to have existed in Roman households at an earlier date. Where it did not exist the acquisition of Greek cannot have been easy, and this is no doubt the reason why St Augustine never made much progress with the language. He did not have a Greek nurse, and he was plunged into Homer and expected to read him without any real knowledge of the language.[23]

So the Roman boy pursued what Paulinus of Pella calls the *doctrina duplex*, the double course of studies. He would learn Greek first, then add Latin and proceed with the two simultaneously,[24] first at the primary stage, then under a grammarian, or rather under two, a Greek and a Latin, for it does not appear to have been the normal practice for one person to teach both languages.[25] This scheme of study was not confined to the higher ranks of society. Echion in Petronius, one of the freedman guests at Trimalchio's dinner, who was certainly not himself a man of much education, describes how his son is getting on well in Greek and has made a start on Latin.[26]

In his account of the Latin grammarians Suetonius tells us that the earliest teachers of literature in Rome were Livius Andronicus and Ennius, *semigraeci*, as he calls them, from south Italy, who came to Rome and there set up as teachers both of Greek and of Latin literature. Then in 168 B.C. Crates of Mallos paid a visit to Rome. He was detained as a result of falling into a drain and breaking his leg, and took the opportunity to give some lectures on grammar which aroused a keen interest in the subject.[27] Suetonius is concerned only with the effects of Crates's lectures on Latin studies; but he must have lectured in Greek and on Greek language and literature, and he may be assumed to have had an influence on Greek studies in Rome as well as indirectly on Latin. Greek grammarians, no doubt, found their way to Rome in the second century as other teachers did, and they were well-established there in the first century, when Aristodemus of Nysa taught Pompey's children[28] and Tyrannio, as has already been mentioned, taught young Quintus Cicero. Cicero himself acquired his knowledge of Greek literature from a Greek grammarian in Rome, perhaps the poet Archias, whom he claimed as one of his early teachers when in later life he spoke in his defence.[29]

The history of Latin grammar was like that of Greek in that the oldest element in it was the study of literature and the linguistic element came in later. Crates's lectures were probably concerned as much with literature (he wrote on Homer and other Greek poets) as with language, and their effect at first was to stimulate an interest in the study of Roman poets, whether dead or contemporary; the development of Latin grammar in the narrow sense came later. A significant figure in both literary and linguistic scholarship was L. Aelius Stilo, who was born about the middle of the second century. Suetonius, though he mentions his work, does not include him among the professional teachers, and though Cicero and Varro studied under him, Aelius as a Roman knight who busied himself with writing speeches for others to deliver is unlikely to have kept a regular school for boys.[30] The professional grammarians were for the most part freedmen and, as their names show, of Greek origin. Suetonius was able to give brief biographies of twenty who had been distinguished teachers, most of them belonging to the Republican and Augustan periods; he mentions others, and there must have been more who did not leave a name behind them, for by the end of the Republic there were more than twenty well-attended schools in Rome and the study of the subject had spread to the provinces.[31] By that time the grammarians would be teaching language as well as literature. Varro's elaborate work *De Lingua Latina* shows the extent to which this study had progressed by the end of the Republic, and Varro no doubt built on the work of the professional teachers such as Antonius Gnipho, who taught the young Julius Caesar and is recorded as having written *De Latino Sermone*.[32] Cicero speaks of the rules of correct Latin as something learnt by boys at school;[33] it is clear that when he wrote *recte loquendi scientia* no less than *poetarum enarratio* formed part of the grammar school course.

The best source of information about the ancient grammar school is Quintilian's *Institutio*. Quintilian had been a practising teacher, and though his subject was rhetoric, he would naturally be interested in the stage of education which preceded his own. Moreover, he is as good an authority for Greek as for Latin grammar. The method, he says, is the same for both, which is another way of saying that in education the Romans slavishly followed the Greeks.[34] So with Quintilian as our main guide we follow the boy through his course of study at the grammar school, beginning, as Quintilian does, with the linguistic side of the work, with grammar in the modern sense of the word.[35]

The position of grammar in ancient education was different from what it is, or used to be, in the modern world. It was not the first stage in the learning of a foreign language. The boy who entered the grammar school was already able to read and write Greek or Latin or both; he now learned the grammar to ensure that he spoke and wrote the language or languages correctly. He began with letters, proceeded to syllables and then came to the parts of speech. He had to be sure of his declensions and conjugations (some teachers, says Quintilian, try to go too fast and omit them). He must be familiar with the genders and cases, including such nice points as whether there is a sixth case in Greek and a seventh in Latin. The study of nouns, says Quintilian, should include the origins of proper names, and when the teacher comes to verbs, he will not be content with voices and moods, persons and numbers, for these really belong to the primary school; he will deal with various perplexing forms and usages which do not come within the ordinary rules of inflexion.[36]

The virtues and faults of style were considered to come within the sphere of grammar, but here there was some over-lapping with rhetoric, and in practice the grammarians concerned themselves mainly with the virtue of correctness. They carefully classified the various types of incorrect language, which they divided into barbarism (involving individual words) and solecism (involving groups of words). In this connection there was much discussion and argument between the advocates of analogy, that is of regular declensions and conjugations, and those who defended anomaly and allowed the various irregularities sanctioned by usage. The grammarians— *custodes Latini sermonis*, custodians of the Latin language, as Seneca calls them[37]—were naturally biased towards analogy. Quintilian on the whole is in favour of anomaly and censures those pedantic teachers who insist on allegedly correct forms which are not in common use. He recognizes, however, that usage can support incorrect speaking, and chooses as his standard the agreed practice of the educated.[38]

From language we turn to literature, the reading and explanation of the poets. In the Greek schools reading began with Homer; the oldest of the Greek poets had a secure place in teaching throughout antiquity, and we know from Quintilian and from other sources that he was not only read but read before any other authors.[39] In the fourth century B.C. some teachers used anthologies of selected passages,[40] but the normal method appears to have been to work through both epics from beginning to end.[41] The *Iliad* of course would come first, and schooldays were inevitably associated with the wrath of Achilles:

> Romae nutriri mihi contigit atque doceri
> iratus Graiis quantum nocuisset Achilles.
>
> 'Twas mine at Rome in boyhood to be taught
> What woes Achilles' wrath to Greece had brought.[42]

So Horace recalls his study at a Greek grammar school. No doubt his master took him on to the *Odyssey*; when he re-read Homer at Praeneste he re-read both epics.[43] A generation before Horace, Cicero also learned of the wrath of Achilles at Rome, and his letters show how well he remembered his school lessons.[44] When a letter writer quotes poetry it can be assumed that the quotation will be known to the recipient and it is likely to be one familiar from schooldays; Atticus was at school with Cicero and Cicero is particularly fond of quoting Homer when writing to him. In his letters to Atticus and to other correspondents Cicero draws for his quotations on fifteen out of the twenty-four books of the *Iliad* and eight out of those of the *Odyssey*; he had evidently acquired from his Greek grammarian a good knowledge of both works, particularly of the *Iliad*.

Second to Homer came drama. In the time of Plato both tragedy and comedy had a place in teaching, and as in the case of Homer there were some who made use of anthologies.[45] The normal method, however, was to read whole plays; but obviously no grammarian would get through the whole of

Attic tragedy, and in due course certain plays were selected for
school reading. At an unknown date, perhaps in the third
century A.D., seven plays of Aeschylus, seven of Sophocles and
ten of Euripides were selected; the rest of the plays, apart from
nine of Euripides which happen to have survived independently,
ceased to be read and were lost. Comedy was represented in
school reading by Menander. Quintilian who, though he has
some reservations on moral grounds, regards comedy as
particularly valuable, explains that he means Menander
'though I would not exclude others'.[46] In later antiquity, however, there was a rather surprising development. Though
Menander appears to have had a secure place in the school
curriculum as late-as the fourth century,[47] he must have dropped out in favour of Aristophanes, since the latter survived in a
selection of eleven plays, with the scholia that are a sure sign of
attention on the part of the grammarians, whereas Menander
did not survive.[48] Why this should have happened is hard to
see, unless it was that the grammarians preferred Aristophanes
because he provided more scope for commentary.

In addition to epic and drama, lyric poetry would be read.
Here some selection was usual, and the final choice fell on the
Olympic odes of Pindar. Statius's father, who taught Greek
literature at Naples, expounded not only Pindar but also, if we
can believe his son, Ibycus, Alcman, Stesichorus and Sappho.
His curriculum, a comprehensive one apart from the surprising
omission of Attic drama, also included Hesiod, Theocritus,
Callimachus, Lycophron, Sophron and Corinna.[49]

In early days Rome, unlike Greece, had no recognized classics to provide the basis of literary education, and the earliest
teachers, Livius Andronicus and Ennius, used their own works
for teaching.[50] One might indeed almost say that Latin literature owed its origin to 'grammar'. Andronicus's Latin *Odyssey*
was probably written to serve as a textbook; Ennius no doubt
designed his epic to be read outside the classroom as well as
inside, but anyone who could claim to be the Roman Homer
might expect his work to hold the same place in the Roman
grammar school as Homer himself held in the Greek. The Latin
grammarians made the best of what was available in their
literature until the appearance of the masterpieces of Augustan
poetry gave Rome a new set of classics to supersede the old.

Suetonius mentions lectures or commentaries by Republican grammarians on Naevius's *Bellum Punicum*, Ennius's *Annals* and Lucilius.[51] We know that Horace when a boy had to study Livius Andronicus (presumably his *Odyssey*) under Orbilius,[52] and his list of authors whom, as he says, 'Rome learns by heart', Ennius, Naevius, Pacuvius, Accius, Afranius, Plautus, Caecilius and Terence,[53] may be taken as comprising the grammar school curriculum of his day, or at least, since it is rather a long list, those from whom the grammarians selected. These authors gave place to Virgil and Horace himself. The older writers were pushed out of the curriculum, in Rome at any rate, though they survived longer in the provinces;[54] Quintilian recognizes their value, but regards them as authors to be read in later life, not to be included in the regular school curriculum.[55]

The first grammarian to lecture on Virgil and other modern poets was Caecilius Epirota, who began to teach after 26 B.C.;[56] and by about the middle of the first century after Christ Virgil at any rate was firmly established in the schools. This seems to be indicated by the frequency with which Seneca quotes him, often without mention of his name, and by the familiarity with his works shown by Petronius's characters.[57] By the end of the first century, when Quintilian wrote, it was the recognized practice to begin Latin reading with Virgil, as Greek reading began with Homer.[58] How much of Virgil, it may be asked, was read? Probably all his works. Seneca knows, and expects his readers to know, them all.[59] Servius, who was a grammarian, as was Donatus whose work he used, comments equally on the *Eclogues*, *Georgics* and *Aeneid*, and if Theocritus and Hesiod were read in the Greek schools one would expect the Romans to include the Latin equivalents of their works.[60]

Petronius's Eumolpus, a poet who is also a teacher, couples Virgil and Horace with Homer and the Greek lyric poets, and Quintilian and Juvenal provide evidence that Horace was recognized in their time as one of the school classics.[61] As for tragedy, the relegation to obscurity of the older writers left a gap which was never filled. The Augustans tried to fill it, but in spite of Varius's *Thyestes*, so much admired by Quintilian,[62] without success. In comedy one of the older writers, Terence, could be not without justice regarded as the Roman equivalent of Menander. By the fourth century, and probably well before then, he was established as one of the classics of the grammar school, as is shown by Donatus's commentary and by the evidence of Ausonius, who mentions Virgil, Horace and Terence as the three Latin poets whom his grandson will read at school.[63] Plautus had been studied by Aelius Stilo and Varro in the Republican period, and there was some revival of interest in him, as in other old Latin writers, among the grammarians of the second century; Aulus Gellius mentions one of them who offered to answer questions on Plautus and Ennius as well as on Virgil.[64] But probably Plautus was regarded as a subject for advanced study; certainly he never acquired the same position in the school curriculum as Terence. The Roman schools did not follow the example of the Greek and substitute for their Menander an older and more difficult dramatist.

In modern Europe school curricula have been fixed by statute and ordinance, or in more recent times by Ministries of Education or, in Britain, by the requirements of external examining boards. In the ancient world they were fixed by convention and tradition. In practice this left little room for experiment; though there was no reason why any grammarian should not introduce new authors if he wished, this was seldom done. In Rome Lucan's poems were for a time read in the schools, or perhaps only in one.[65] Other authors may similarly have been used by individual teachers for short periods, but none of them attained a status comparable to that of the recognized classics already mentioned.[66]

So far no prose writers have been mentioned. Dionysius Thrax included prose writers as well as poets within the scope of grammar,[67] but other ancient authorities limited it to poetry,[68] and this limitation corresponded to scholastic practice. When Quintilian says that it is not enough for the grammarian to read the poets, but that he must be acquainted with the whole range of literature,[69] this does not mean that the school curriculum was a wide one but that the master's own studies must advance beyond those of his pupils, so that he can answer any question that may arise in connection with his teaching. Generally speaking prose writers belonged to other branches of study, the orators to rhetoric and the philosophers to philosophy. The position of historical writers was somewhat anomalous. There was no teaching of history as a subject on its own,

c

and though some reading of historical texts was done in the Greek schools of rhetoric, this was not the case in the Latin ones.[70] The Roman grammarians eventually admitted at least one historian, Sallust; Gellius describes how his teacher Apollinaris Sulpicius confuted a fellow-grammarian who claimed to be the one and only expounder of Sallust,[71] and Ausonius, advising his schoolboy grandson and recalling at the same time his own schooldays, mentions the reading not only of the standard Latin poets but also of Sallust's *Catiline* and *Histories*.[72]

Reading an author in a grammar school meant first of all reading aloud correctly and expressively, or rather reciting from memory. Memorization was the practice in the fifth century B.C., to judge by what Protagoras says in Plato's dialogue.[73] Evidence for fourth-century practice comes from Plato's *Laws*. 'We have our poets,' he writes, 'a great number of them, writers of hexameters, iambic trimeters and all the recognized metres, some with a serious purpose, others writing to amuse, and according to innumerable authorities any properly educated young person should be brought up on these and saturated with them, attending a great many reading classes and becoming thoroughly well informed on them and being required to learn whole poets by heart,' and he goes on to refer to the alternative practice of making selections and requiring whole speeches from the poets to be committed to memory.[74] No doubt memorization continued to be the practice throughout antiquity. Cicero, writing as a moralist, after commending Plato's expulsion of the poets from his ideal city, exclaims: 'And yet we, taught of course by Greece, read and learn them by heart from boyhood and think this a liberal education.'[75] How much the average schoolboy succeeded in memorizing it is hard to say. We find occasional references to men who knew the whole of Homer or Virgil by heart, but these would hardly have been mentioned if they had not been exceptional.[76] Undoubtedly a well-educated man of antiquity carried a great deal of poetry in his memory, much of it no doubt derived from school reading; but there must always have been those who found it hard to learn or who, if they learned easily, forgot easily, as Darwin did when a boy at Shrewsbury at a time when reciting Homer and Virgil from memory was still part of the grammar school routine. Moreover, it may well be that schoolboys did not always have texts of their own but had to rely on what was dictated by their masters or copied out in school; in these circumstances it is likely enough that only portions of the works read were committed to memory.[77]

Extraordinary care was taken in training boys to read correctly.[78] Three points, according to Dionysius Thrax, had to be taken into consideration in reading: expressiveness, accentuation and punctuation or pauses; and Ausonius writing to his schoolboy grandson makes the same points:

> tu flexu et acumine uocis
> innumeros numeros doctis accentibus effer
> adfectusque impone legens: distinctio sensum
> auget et ignauis dant interualla uigorem.

> With modulation and stress of voice bring out 'measureless measures' with a scholar's accent, and infuse expression as you read. Punctuation enforces the meaning and pauses give strength even to dull passages.[79]

Quintilian lays most stress on the last point. The schoolboy, he says, should learn where to take breath, at what point to make a pause in the line, where the sense ends or begins, when the voice should be raised or lowered, what modulation should be given to each phrase, where he should lessen or increase speed, or speak with greater or less energy; and in order to do this properly he must above all understand what he reads.[80] Quintilian is not much concerned with expressiveness, and deprecates an excessively histrionic delivery; reading in his view should be manly, with a combination of dignity and charm.[81]

The grammarian did more than teach correct and expressive reading: he explained and commented on the texts read. This was called in Latin *praelectio*; the word suggests an introductory lecture preceding the reading of the text, but in fact reading preceded rather than followed explanatory comment.[82] In a prelection, according to Quintilian, the class should be asked to parse and scan, and a late grammarian, Priscian, shows how this was done. He treats in turn, and in great detail, the first line of each of the twelve books of the *Aeneid* in the form of a catechism, in which the pupil is first asked to scan the line, then to say how many, and what, caesuras there are, how many feet and why, how many words the line contains, how many nouns, verbs and other parts of speech, after which there follows a study of each word in turn.[83] Apart from this the master pointed out incorrect and irregular uses (though Quintilian notes that this should not imply censure of the author, since poets were allowed certain licences) and showed the different ways in which each word could be understood. He explained rare words and expounded tropes and figures of speech and of thought. He would impress on his class the value of arrangement and appropriateness of subject-matter, and would discuss characterization and virtues of thought and expression, showing where copiousness is to be commended and where restraint.[84]

He would also deal with what the ancients called *historiae*, explanation of the subject-matter which, given the character of ancient poetry, consisted largely of mythological information. Here there was plenty of scope for a display of unnecessary and pedantic erudition.[85] It was a common game to mock the grammarians for their addiction to out-of-the-way learning or to try to catch them out by discovering their weak spots. They were expected to know whether Homer or Hesiod was the older, why Hecuba though younger than Helen showed her years, the respective ages of Achilles and Patroclus, the route taken by Ulysses, whether Penelope was chaste, why Asclepius was struck by lightning, the fact that Heracles was bald when he came out of the sea monster after rescuing Hesione.[86] Juvenal depicts them as having to answer, while on the way to the baths, such Virgilian questions as the name of Anchises's nurse and that of Anchemolus's stepmother.[87] The emperor Tiberius used to tease them by asking who was Hecuba's mother, what was the name of Achilles when he was masquerading as a girl, and what song the Sirens sang.[88] The grammarian could be represented as a self-satisfied pedant whose learning fell short of his pretensions and who was easily provoked to anger if his ignorance was exposed.[89]

It will be seen that the teacher of literature in the ancient world kept close to his texts and was primarily concerned to explain them. He had little to say on the general character of

the works he read. He would probably begin his prelections as
Servius began his commentary with a brief life of the author and
a summary of the purpose of the work. Apart from this he
confined himself in the main to explanation and noting points of
poetical technique. Though he might point to individual
beauties he did not attempt to evaluate the works he dealt with.
Dionysius Thrax had included criticism as one of the con-
stituents of grammar but, whether rightly or wrongly, this was
interpreted to mean textual criticism. The grammarian, says
one of Dionysius's commentators, does not judge poems in the
sense of saying that they are good or not good.[90] Indeed, the
classics of the grammar school were assumed to be good, if not
perfect. Among themselves the grammarians might venture to
make some slight criticisms of Virgil, but their pupils were not
allowed to do anything but admire.[91] Grammar school teaching
left the impression that Virgil had not only never made a mis-
take but had never written a line that was not admirable.[92]

The grammarian did not, as a modern teacher of literature
often does, make his pupils write essays of literary appreciation.
If this had been suggested to him he might have answered that
criticism was, in the words of 'Longinus', 'the last fruit of much
experience',[93] and his pupils were for the most part only boys.
He might also have answered that it was not his job to teach
composition at all since this was, in theory at any rate, the
function of the rhetorician.

The rhetoricians had devised a system for teaching composition from the beginning by means of a series of carefully
graded exercises known as *progymnasmata*, designed to lead up to
the practice speeches which were the main activity of the schools
of rhetoric. These preliminary exercises had originated perhaps
in the second century B.C. In the time of Quintilian there was a
tendency, in the Latin schools though not in the Greek, for
them to move downwards from the school of rhetoric to that of
grammar, a development which Suetonius attributes to the
fact that the earliest Latin grammarians had also taught
rhetoric and Quintilian to failure on the part of the rhetoricians
to do their job properly.[94] In Quintilian's scheme of education
the progymnasmata are divided between the grammarian who
has the elementary ones, and the rhetorician who handles
those which are more advanced; and since Quintilian accepts

this scheme without question, it was presumably the established practice in his day.[95] There was, however, a growing tendency, which he deplores, for the grammarians to take over all the preliminary exercises, and not only that but to start their pupils on declamation.[96] By the time of Suetonius it appears that both the rhetoricians and the grammarians had abandoned the progymnasmata altogether.[97] But if they did, their disappearance was not permanent. St Augustine describes how as a school exercise he was made to write a prose version of Juno's speech at the beginning of *Aeneid* I.[98] This is probably to be regarded as an example of the progymnastic exercise known as *ethopoiia* to the Greeks and *allocutio* to the Romans, the composition of an imaginary speech by a mythological character. As Augustine did this exercise at the grammar school it is clear that, even if such work had been abandoned by the rhetoricians, it had not dropped out of education altogether.

Since the progymnasmata properly belong to rhetoric they will be considered further in the next section. Here we will only note the remarkable specialization of the ancient schools. In spite of their wide knowledge of literature the grammarians were believed to be incapable of teaching composition, and of some of them it was said, no doubt unjustly, that they could not even put two words together competently.[99] To the modern observer it appears that the schools of grammar and of rhetoric should have been combined and composition taught concurrently with reading. The Greeks did indeed allow some overlap between the two, and a boy beginning his course in rhetoric continued to attend the grammar school for part of his time.[100] But this was not the practice with the Romans. Even the wise Quintilian would have each school stick to its own job;[101] and co-operation between the two professions or surrender of their particular functions was unlikely as long as the rhetoricians regarded themselves as superior to the grammarians and were more highly paid for their instructions.

It remains to say something about the daily routine of the schoolroom. First the school itself. This would be a single room, adorned with busts of the poets. There would be an anteroom, where the boys would leave their cloaks and tidy their hair, separated from the schoolroom by a curtain.[102] Juvenal's picture of the grammarian trying to keep an eye on a roomful of badly behaved boys[103] gives the impression of a single teacher without assistants. Cicero, however, has a reference to the *hypodidascalus*, the assistant master, and one of St Augustine's friends acted as assistant to a grammarian.[104] We hear too of the *proscholus*, who would be in charge of the *proscholium*, the anteroom; but to judge by the fact that Ausonius includes among his Bordeaux professors a man whom he describes as *proscholus siue subdoctor*, this official, like the English usher, rose from being a kind of porter with minor disciplinary functions, to the position of assistant teacher.[105] But if a single teacher was in sole charge this need surprise no one who remembers that in the old English grammar schools the normal staffing was two for a school of six forms.

The day began with recitation, as it still did in the English grammar schools until about the middle of the last century.[106] Each boy in turn recited the piece he had been set. He sat in his place with his right hand extended and delivered his lines together with a paraphrase, after which, it seems, he stood up before the master and gave an outline of the context of the passage.[107] Returning to his seat he was given a book and wrote out what had been prescribed for the day (perhaps the passage to be committed to memory and recited the next morning), and after this had been corrected he read it out.[108] The master then gave his exposition of the passage (the *prae-lectio*), and there followed some rapid reading at sight.[109] One of the tasks assigned was the recitation of nouns or of single lines of verse.[110] This could occasion remarkable feats of memory; when the elder Seneca was at school he repeated two thousand nouns, and after more than two hundred individual lines had been recited by his fellow-pupils he repeated them in reverse order.[111] The boys were divided into classes according to their abilities for their lessons in grammar, in which as well as listening to the master's exposition they were required to answer questions.[112] The day might end with dictation, followed by the reading aloud of the dictated passage, first by all together then individually.[113]

Such were the methods of the grammarians. It would be easy to condemn them as pedantic and unimaginative. But within their limits they were successful. They ensured the maintenance of a standard language, whether Greek or Latin, in different parts of the world throughout a long period of history,[114] and they imposed a standard literary culture based on a few recognized classical poets. These poets their pupils not only read but learned by heart. Perhaps, as their teachers hoped, their minds were elevated and their morals improved by their reading.[115] At any rate they got to know their classics, and this knowledge, it was hoped, would remain with them for life.[116] The answer to those who depreciated grammar was given by Quintilian: 'For this reason we should not tolerate those who run down this subject as trivial and jejune. In fact it serves as a foundation for oratory, and if this is not firmly laid any superstructure will collapse. It is a necessity for boys, a delight to the old, the sweet companion of privacy and the only type of study that has more substance in it than display.'[117]

Rhetoric

It was the general belief in antiquity, the truth of which there is no reason to doubt, that the inventors of rhetoric, the first men, that is, who professed to teach the art of speech, were two Sicilians, Corax and Tisias. Their original aim was the practical one of assisting litigants to establish their claim to property.[118] In teaching they were particularly concerned with arguments from probability; success in the courts, they insisted, was more likely to result from saying what was plausible than from the simple truth.[119] In 427 B.C. the Sicilian Gorgias came to Athens; he remained there to teach the art of speech. Like other rhetoricians he aimed at making successful speakers in the law courts and in political assemblies.[120] But he was chiefly remembered for his stylistic innovations; he developed a highly artificial style, characterized by parallelism and assonance, which he used for ornamental compositions on paradoxical themes such as the still extant praise of Helen. These compositions his pupils were made to learn by heart.[121]

Gorgias was not the only teacher of rhetoric in Athens of the later fifth century. There was Protagoras, with his claim to make the worse cause appear the better, who trained his pupils in handling general questions and commonplaces, and elaborated the rules of correct diction;[122] Thrasymachus, who specialized in the appeal to the emotions; Theodorus of Byzantium with his rules about the constituent parts of a speech; and Euenus of Paros, who was interested in the indirect approach and in methods of implying praise and blame, and who composed a verse mnemonic to assist his pupils.[123] There was Antiphon, whose model speeches, the 'tetralogies', in which forensic cases are argued on both sides, still survive.

In fourth-century Athens there was no lack of teachers of rhetoric. Textbooks were produced, a sure sign of the existence of regular and systematic teaching; Aristotle in a lost work collected together and summarized those that had been written before his time.[124] The rhetoricians mainly taught forensic oratory.[125] They had no doubt that the art of speech could be taught, just as reading and writing could be;[126] they had their rules, and the man who followed the rules would be equipped to get the better of his opponent in the law courts.

Distinguished from these professionals with their limited aims was Isocrates. He had a school in Athens near the Lyceum, open to anyone who was willing to pay the fee of 1,000 drachmae for the course.[127] It was a flourishing school, drawing pupils from abroad as well as from Athens, and its numbers, so it is said, were at one time as many as a hundred.[128] Though Isocrates wrote at some length about his educational ideas, it is not easy to say exactly what he did with his pupils during their years with him.[129] He dissociated himself from the professional rhetoricians, the 'sophists' as he called them; his teaching was more of a general education designed to fit a man for a political or literary career than a narrowly professional one. On the other hand it was essentially rhetorical in that it was based on the use of words. According to Isocrates himself there were three factors which contributed to progress in studies: natural gifts, knowledge of the theory of the subject and practice. In his own type of education the most important thing was natural aptitude; knowledge of the rules was the least important, but practice was of great value. The function of the teacher was to neglect nothing which could be taught and himself to provide a model by following which his pupils could improve their style.[130] Isocrates was said to have written a *techne*, a formal treatise on rhetoric, but there was some doubt about this,[131] and, even if he did, it is clear that what distinguished him from the contemporary rhetoricians was the relatively small emphasis he placed on rules and his belief in the importance of practice. His pupils, we may suppose, were made to write speeches and to write in imitation of their master; no doubt he carefully criticized their compositions and they, or at any rate a select few, might be invited to criticize his.[132]

The tradition of Isocrates survived in that rhetoric became a recognized part of a liberal education; it failed to survive in that the rhetoricians of the Hellenistic age for the most part lacked his wide culture and high ideals and, like the 'sophists' whom he criticized, put their faith in rules. The rules of rhetoric became standardized in main outline, though there was always room for disagreement on details and for subtle distinctions and refinements within the agreed framework. The chief rhetorician of the Hellenistic period was Hermagoras of Temnos, who flourished in the second century B.C., and who was particularly associated with the doctrine of *stasis*, or *status*, the determining of the point at issue in any forensic case. He and other rhetoricians like him presumably passed on to their pupils their rhetorical theory with all its elaborate definitions, divisions and subdivisions. At the same time Isocrates's insistence on the necessity of practice was not forgotten. It became a regular part of school routine to make practice speeches on themes of the type that might arise either in the courts or in deliberative assemblies. It was generally believed that this practice dated from the time of Demetrius of Phalerum, the Athenian statesman and orator of the end of the fourth century, and there were some who, though with inadequate evidence, ascribed the innovation to Demetrius himself.[133] Whatever the truth—and Antiphon's tetralogies suggest that something similar had been done well before Demetrius's time—it is significant that this development was associated with the end of Athenian independence and with the man who was thought to have set Greek oratory on the downward path.[134] Declamation, to use the term which became familiar in the Roman world, flourished when political oratory declined.

Rhetoric came to Rome in the second century B.C.[135] There was some opposition at first to the rhetoricians as to other Greek teachers, and in 161 the Senate empowered the praetor

M. Pomponius to expel rhetoricians and philosophers.[136] Perhaps the influence of Cato was in part responsible for this move; he was a strong opponent of Greek influences, and to judge by his recorded remarks on oratory (his definition of the orator as *uir bonus dicendi peritus* and his precept *rem tene, uerba sequentur*—hold on to the matter and the words will follow) he would have had little sympathy with the subtleties of Greek theory.

The old Roman tradition was that a young man learned the art of speaking as part of his training for a public career by a kind of apprenticeship. He attached himself to one of the leading orators of the day, accompanied him to the forum and so learned how things were done.[137] This *tirocinium fori*, as it was called, survived even when rhetoric had become a recognized part of school training. When Caelius Rufus ceased to be a boy he was entrusted by his father to Cicero; under the Empire there was a similar relationship between Quintilian and Domitius Afer and between Tacitus and the orators Aper and Julius Secundus.[138] But generally speaking the Greek method of training by professional teachers prevailed. As Cicero put it, 'At first our countrymen knew nothing of art and did not realize that there was any value in practice or that there were any rules or system, but they achieved such success as could be attained by talent and reflection. Afterwards, however, when they had listened to Greek orators, become acquainted with Greek literature and come into contact with Greek teachers, there was a remarkable burst of enthusiasm among our countrymen for the study of the art of speaking.'[139]

The Romans at first learned their rhetoric in Greek from Greek teachers, and it was not until the early part of the first century B.C. that a Latin version of the Greek art was developed. Latin treatises on the theory of rhetoric, closely modelled on Greek textbooks, were written, works such as Cicero's early *De Inventione* and the treatise of unknown authorship addressed to Herennius. A Latin school was opened in Rome in 92 B.C. by one Plotius Gallus, and here for the first time Roman boys were taught to compose declamations in Latin. Cicero as a boy wanted to attend, but was discouraged from doing so by his advisers on the ground that a better training could be obtained in Greek.[140] No doubt it was the orator

Crassus who was responsible for this advice, for he directed Cicero's early studies, and as censor, along with his colleague Domitius Ahenobarbus, he expressed his disapproval of the Latin schools of rhetoric in an edict of the year 92.[141] Crassus was criticized for what appeared to be his indifference to education, but defended himself on the ground that the Latin rhetoricians were men of little culture who taught only impudence; he did not despair of the eventual development of a Latin rhetoric, but the time had not yet come.[142]

The censors' edict cannot have had more than a temporary effect. Only a few years after it there were Latin teachers of rhetoric in Rome, though they had not the prestige of the Greeks; Cicero describes how as a young man he declaimed every day in Latin or in Greek, but more often in the latter language, because the best teachers were Greek and they were unable to correct his Latin declamations.[143] When the time came for Cicero's son and nephew to study rhetoric they were put, at a tender age, under a Greek rhetorician, Paeonius.[144] By the time of Augustus, however, Latin rhetoric had evidently advanced at the expense of Greek, to judge by the elder Seneca, who mentions about twice as many Latin declaimers as Greek.[145] As in the case of grammar the professions of Greek and Latin rhetorician were normally distinct. There were, however, exceptions, of whom the most notable was Sextus Clodius, Mark Antony's friend and instructor, who taught both Greek and Latin rhetoric and even declaimed in both languages on the same day.[146]

The bilingual character of Roman culture was officially recognized by Vespasian when he established salaried chairs of both Greek and Latin rhetoric at Rome. The Greek chair continued to be filled under succeeding emperors, and it was accounted promotion for a Greek rhetorician to move from Athens to Rome.[147] The younger Pliny studied under the Greek rhetorician Nicetes as well as under Quintilian,[148] and in the second century we hear of Romans studying rhetoric in both languages.[149] But one's impression is that under the Empire the *doctrina duplex* often ended with the grammar school; Quintilian takes it for granted that the orator will have studied Greek grammar, but makes no mention of his studying Greek rhetoric. In the Latin-speaking provinces Greek rhetoric probably never flourished much; in the fourth century there were still Greek grammar schools in Gaul, but it is doubtful whether there were any Greek rhetoricians.[150]

A school of rhetoric, like other ancient schools, would have its benches for the pupils and its raised chair or throne for the master. There would be a single schoolroom or auditorium, which in the case of a successful teacher would be well filled. Quintilian writes of teachers who take on too many pupils for the sake of their fees, and so are unable to give them individual attention.[151] One second-century Greek rhetorician, Chrestus, had at one time as many as a hundred fee-paying pupils.[152] Libanius had eighty at Constantinople; at Antioch he started with seventeen, but soon had fifty. This is a number which, considering that he had several assistants, should have been manageable, though he complains that the size of his class makes it impossible to get through the day's work before sunset.[153] Libanius was evidently one of those teachers who believed in giving his pupils individual attention.

In areas where there were a number of rival teachers numbers could fluctuate considerably; students moved about sampling one after another, or defected towards the end of the school year to avoid paying their fees.[154] The audience might also be swollen by mature-aged hearers. Even apart from those occasions when the rhetoricians gave their public declamations to admiring audiences anyone, it seems, could drop in; the younger Pliny, given the task of choosing a teacher for a friend's nephews, sampled a number of schools, sitting among the young students, and in one of them he found a number of other senators.[155] There might also be less welcome visitors like the students at Carthage in St Augustine's day who burst into classes for which they were not enrolled and made a nuisance of themselves by their rowdy behaviour.[156]

The regular students at a school of rhetoric ranged in age from about fifteen to eighteen, and in a well-conducted school the younger ones would be separated from the older. In Proclus's school the boys sat in one place and the adolescents (*meirakia*) in another, with the boys' *paidagogi* in the middle.[157] Quintilian probably had a similar arrangement in his school, since he advocates separating *pueri* from *adulescentes*.[158] The two groups would probably be separated to some extent for teaching purposes,[159] and apart from this there would be some division into classes; we hear of a boy being 'top of his form' (*ordinem* or *classem ducere*) and of a form order based on merit changing at the end of each month.[160]

There were two sides to rhetorical teaching: theory and practice. The student had to learn the rules, and he had to practise speaking. For a summary of the rules we cannot do better than use that which Cicero put in the mouth of Crassus in *De Oratore*, the 'common and hackneyed rules' which Crassus says he learned as part of a liberal education:

> First, that it is the orator's duty to speak in a way adapted to win the assent of his audience; secondly, every speech must be either on some general abstract question without reference to special persons or circumstances, or on some subject with a definite setting of special persons and circumstances; but that in either case, whatever be the point at issue, the question usually arising in connection with it is either as to the fact or, if the fact be admitted, what is the nature of the act, or may be what name is to be given to it, or, as some add, whether it is justifiable or not; further that disputes arise out of the interpretation of a document, in which there is some ambiguity of statement or some contradiction, or which is so worded that the strict letter of it is at variance with its spirit; and that to all these varieties there are attached appropriate methods of proof. Of questions, again, which are distinct from any general thesis, some are juridical, some deliberative; there is also a third class, as I was taught, which deals with panegyric and invective; and there are certain topics to be made use of in the law courts where justice is the object of our efforts; others in deliberative speeches which are in all cases modified by the interests of those to whom our advice is given; others, again, in panegyrics in which everything depends upon the personal dignity of the subject. I learned also that the whole activity and faculty of the orator falls under five heads—that he must first think of what he is to say; secondly not only tabulate his thoughts but marshal and arrange them in order with due regard to their relative weight and importance; thirdly, clothe them in

artistic language; fourthly, fix them firmly in his memory; fifthly and lastly, deliver them with grace and dignity of gesture. I was further made to understand that before we speak on the point at issue, we must begin by winning the favourable attention of our audience; then we must state the facts of the case, then determine the point at issue, then establish the charge we are bringing, then refute the arguments of our opponent; and finally in our peroration amplify and emphasize all that can be said on our side of the case, and weaken and invalidate the points which tell for the opposite side. I had heard lectures also on the traditional rules for the embellishment of style; in connection with which the first requirement is pure and good Latin, the second clearness and lucidity, the third artistic finish, the fourth suitability to the dignity of the subject and a certain elegance of form. I had also learnt special rules under each head. Besides this I had been made to understand that even those gifts which are exclusively natural may be artificially improved. On delivery, for instance, and the memory, I had been initiated into certain rules which, though short enough, involved much practice. For it is to the exposition of such rules as these that all the learning of our friends the professors is directed . . .[161]

The rules were expounded in lectures and embodied in text-books. Quintilian gave two lecture courses, a simple outline for the younger pupils, which they were expected to take down verbatim, and a longer course of several days' duration for the more advanced.[162] Simple textbooks free from the subtle elaborations of the more academic rhetoricians, were much in demand. Sometimes they took the form of question and answer. Cicero wrote a book in this form, *Partitiones Oratoriae*, for the benefit of his son; from the later Empire we have another such rhetorical catechism by Chirius Fortunatus.[163] Sometimes they dealt with only one section of rhetoric such as the figures of speech and of thought, which were listed with definitions and examples.[164] Rhetorical theory continued to be taught and studied. But probably it did not bulk very large in school teaching. In Quintilian's time there were rhetoricians who were quite happy to remain ignorant of theory and thought that all that was necessary for the training of an orator was declamation.[165]

Before we come to declamation something must be said about the exercises in composition which preceded declamation in the regular course of studies, the progymnasmata already mentioned in the first section of this chapter. These were arranged in order according to difficulty.[166] The first and most elementary was the fable, the retelling of one of the moral animal stories attributed to Aesop. Next came short exercises in narrative, the subject of which was normally taken from mythology. The third exercise was the so-called *chria*, the record of a saying or action attributed to some well-known character, for example, 'Isocrates used to say that the roots of learning are bitter but the fruits sweet.' Similar to this was the *gnome* or *sententia*, an aphoristic maxim without the name of its author prefixed. In connection with the *chria* the schoolboy was required to perform the curious exercise of 'declining' it, that is, varying it so as to display the name of the person concerned in all its grammatical forms.[167] The following is an example from a Latin source:[168] 'Marcus Porcius Cato [substituted for Isocrates for the benefit of Roman schoolboys] used to say that the roots of learning are bitter but the fruits sweet.' In the genitive case: 'A saying of Marcus Porcius Cato is current to the effect that . . .' In the dative: 'It seemed good to Marcus Porcius Cato to say . . .' In the accusative: 'They say that Marcus Porcius Cato said . . .' In the vocative: 'O Marcus Porcius Cato, it was a fine saying of yours that . . .' In the ablative: 'We are told that it was said by Marcus Porcius Cato that . . .' After this the process was repeated in the plural, and in defiance of sense the saying was attributed to a number of Catos, again in all six cases. The Greek schoolboy had to decline the dual as well as the singular and the plural; a school exercise which has survived in papyrus ascribes a saying not only to Pythagoras in the singular and the plural but also to two Pythagorases.[169]

In Quintilian's scheme the first four exercises are allotted to the grammar school and those which followed, which were more difficult and more closely related to forensic oratory, to the school of rhetoric. These were: *anaskeue* and *kataskeue*, the criticism and defence respectively of the credibility of some incident from mythology or history; commonplace (attacks,

that is, on notorious sins or sinners); praise and blame, normally of mythological or historical characters; comparison
(between, for example, Ajax and Achilles or Demosthenes and
Aeschines); *ethopoiia*, or *allocutio*, the composition of an imaginary speech put in the mouth of a mythological character;[170]
ekphrasis, or vivid description; *thesis*, that is, a general question
which could be argued either way, such as 'Should one
marry?'; and finally the commendation of a law supposedly
being introduced.

A number of Greek rhetoricians published works on the
progymnasmata in which they outlined the ways in which each
should be treated or gave specimen 'fair copies'. One of them,
Aphthonius, who flourished in the later fourth century, both
gave rules for treatment and showed how they should be applied, and his work, with its infallible prescriptions for essay
writing, proved immensely popular. It continued in use in
Byzantium, was translated into Latin in the Renaissance and
was widely used in the schools of Western Europe. Its influence
lasted even into the nineteenth century.[171]

The inventor of the progymnasmata, whoever he was, de-
serves some credit for his ingenuity in devising a scheme which,
starting with simple narrative, led on to exercises of greater
difficulty, though to the modern teacher, familiar with constant
experiment in method and constant production of new textbooks, it may seem strange that it was so long accepted as
fixed and immutable. Variations from it were slight and un-
important. Theon started with the *chria* rather than the fable,
and there were other small variations in the order in which the
exercises were taken.[172] Quintilian mentions one which falls
outside the normal syllabus; his own teacher, he records, used
to set such subjects as 'Why is Venus represented as armed at
Sparta?' and 'Why is Cupid thought of as a boy, winged, with
arrows and torch?'[173] At one time the Roman schools made use
of translation from Greek,[174] not, as would be the case in a
modern school, to improve, or to test, the pupils' knowledge of
Greek, but to improve their Latin style. Crassus, according to
Cicero in *De Oratore*, used to practise translation in his youth,[175]
and Quintilian, no doubt in deference to Cicero, mentions this
exercise with approval, but only in his tenth book, which deals
with the studies of those who have passed beyond the school

D

stage.[176] Evidently this was not one of the regular school exercises in his day.

The progymnastic exercises were written, and they would be criticized and corrected by the master. He might provide the boys with an outline in advance, or he might dictate his own fair copy.[177] The aim was not so much to encourage imagination and powers of independent thought as to develop in the learner a command of the resources of language, an ability to say the same thing in a number of different ways. The schoolboy learned not to express his own feelings and experience but to elaborate and adorn his theme on accepted lines, to paraphrase, for instance, a moral maxim and support it by simile, example and quotation. As he progressed no doubt he learned to treat his themes with greater freedom, but his writing would tend to bear the stamp of his early training, to show a high degree of fluency but a certain emptiness and conventionality in its content.

In the Greek schools the younger pupils were made to read orators and historians, this work being under the direction of assistant teachers.[178] Libanius had as many as four assistants.[179] We have a glimpse of his curriculum for those who had just joined his school in a letter he wrote to a parent whose sons had been two months with him. During the first month they had divided the time between Libanius himself, who presumably took them for composition, and the assistants with whom they read 'the ancients', the classical authors; the second month they spent on reading and did not see anything of Libanius, though he intended to resume his lessons with them shortly.[180]

Quintilian tried to introduce something similar into his school though, as the Roman rhetoricians, so far as we know, did not have assistants, he had to do the work himself. His method was to select one of the class to read aloud, to explain the background of the case and show how the orator had treated it, pointing out his virtues or—for sometimes he would choose speeches that were open to criticism—his faults; he would also ask frequent questions in order to keep the attention of the listeners and develop their powers of judgment.[181] The experiment was not a success. His pupils thought they were too old for this sort of thing, and they preferred to take Quintilian himself as a model rather than Cicero or whatever author they were reading.[182] He gave up the practice, though he remained convinced of its value and recommended it to posterity.[183]

Whether because of Quintilian's influence or not, the practice of reading authors was in use in some Latin schools after his time. We hear of one second-century rhetorician reading Cicero's *Pro Plancio* with his class and another reading a speech of Gaius Gracchus.[184] In the fourth century we find the rhetoricians lecturing not on speeches but on books of rhetorical theory. Marius Victorinus, the leading teacher of rhetoric in Rome of the mid-fourth century, published a commentary on Cicero's *De Inventione* which was presumably based on his oral teaching. This work of Cicero was evidently in general use at that time. St Augustine tells a story of how a former pupil of his was lecturing on it and while preparing his lecture for the next day came upon a passage which he could not understand; the solution came to him in a dream in which his old teacher appeared to him and solved his difficulty.[185] There is evidence too of a widening of the curriculum to include non-rhetorical texts; Augustine at Carthage read a philosophical work, Cicero's *Hortensius*, 'in the course of the ordinary school curriculum'.[186]

Having passed through the course of progymnasmata and, in the Greek schools at any rate, having read some standard prose texts, the student of rhetoric passed on to declamation. Of this there were two kinds, the *suasoria*, in which the speaker gave advice to a historical character or group of persons at some important point in their career, and the *controversia*, in which the speaker, presented with an imaginary case of the type which might come up in the courts, made a speech on one or the other side. The *suasoria* was considered the easier of the two and was commonly set to the younger pupils.[187] The *controversia* was the more advanced exercise and the one to which the rhetoricians devoted most of their energies.

The older *controversiae*, according to Suetonius, 'were based either on history, as is sometimes the case even now, or upon some event of recent occurrence in real life, and so they were usually presented with the names of the places concerned added'.[188] The Roman rhetoricians of the Republic took over some themes from the Greeks, keeping the Greek setting; for others they drew on their own history or on cases that had come up before the courts. But they also used imaginary cases without any specific setting. Cicero gives an example of the sort of easy case which was set to boys: 'The law forbids a foreigner to ascend the walls. He does so and drives off the enemy. An action is brought against him.'[189] Ingenious and obviously fictitious cases were devised such as the following:

> The law ordains that those who leave their ship in a storm shall lose everything; the ship and its cargo become the property of those who remain on it. Two men were sailing on the high seas, one the owner of the ship, the other of its cargo. They saw a shipwrecked man swimming and stretching out his hands to them; overcome by pity they brought the ship alongside him and took him on board. Some time afterwards they too ran into a heavy storm, with the result that the owner of the ship, who was also the helmsman, betook himself to a boat, from which he guided the ship as best he could with a tow rope, while the owner of the cargo fell on his sword. The shipwrecked man went to the helm, and did his best to save the ship. When the waves subsided and the weather changed, the ship was brought into harbour. The man who had fallen on his sword was only slightly wounded and his wound quickly healed. Each of the three claimed the ship and its cargo.[190]

Towards the end of the Roman Republic there was a new development. The elder Seneca, who was born about 55 B.C., could even say that declamation was younger than himself and that he had watched it from its beginnings.[191] Declamation in the sense of making practice speeches as part of the training of an orator was not of course new; what Seneca observed in his lifetime was rather a change in its character. It became an end in itself, a type of oratory in its own right, rather than a preparation for advocacy. Rhetoricians, besides the ordinary round of teaching, would declaim in public, and it was possible to win a reputation as a declaimer and be a failure as an advocate. At the same time there was a change in the subject-matter of declamation. The themes tended to become unreal and melodramatic; schoolboys and their masters exercised their eloquence and their ingenuity on those imaginary cases involving rape, disinheritance, tyrannicide, shipwreck and capture by pirates which were an easy target for the mockery of critics.

The following will serve as examples of the more fantastic themes set in the schools. The first three come from the collection of the elder Seneca; the last is found in both Greek and Latin sources from late antiquity.[192]

> The law ordains that in the case of rape the woman may demand either the death of her seducer or marriage without dowry. A certain man raped two women in one night; one demanded his death, the other marriage.

> A man was captured by pirates and wrote to his father asking to be ransomed. The father refused. The daughter of the pirate chief made the young man swear to marry her if he was set free. He did so. She left her father and followed the young man. He returned home and married her. An heiress appeared on the scene. The father ordered him to leave the pirate chief's daughter and marry the heiress.

> The law requires that children support their parents or be imprisoned. A certain man killed one of his brothers as a tyrant. The other he caught in adultery and, in spite of his father's entreaties, killed him. He was captured by pirates and wrote to his father to be ransomed. The father wrote to the pirates promising to pay double if they cut off his son's hands. The pirates let him go. He refused to support his father when the latter was in need.

> A young man saved his father when his house caught fire, and lost his sight when attempting in vain to save his mother. The father remarried. His new wife one day told her husband that the son had some poison on him and had offered to share his father's property with her if she administered the poison to him. The father asked his son whether this was true and he denied it. He found the poison on him and asked for whom it was intended, to which the son said nothing. The father then altered his will and left his money to the stepmother. That night the father was found dead, with his wife apparently asleep by him and the son's bloodstained sword on the pillow while the

blind son was standing at the door. The blind man and
his stepmother each accused the other of murdering the
father.

Themes of this sort were treated in both Greek and Roman
schools, but the Greeks had a greater liking than the Romans
for historical subjects. In the later Roman collections of
declamations (those ascribed to Quintilian and that of Calpurnius Flaccus) *controversiae* with a historical setting are
extremely rare and *suasoriae* non-existent; in the Greek collections these types are well represented.[193] In the second century
Greek rhetoricians would give advice in the character of Solon
or Pericles, would re-enact debates from the Peloponnesian
War, would impersonate Demosthenes or his opponents.[194] A
papyrus of the third century contains the following subjects for
declamation: 'Cleon is accused of demagogy for proposing to
put to death the male population of Mitylene.' 'Euripides is
tried for impiety for showing Heracles going mad in a play.'
'After he has sacked Thebes Alexander offers its land to the
Athenians.' 'Demades advises . . .' at which point the fragment
ends.[195] The Greek rhetoricians tended to live in the past,
recalling the great days of Athenian history. 'Bring in Marathon
and Cynaegirus,' says the rhetoric teacher in Lucian, 'they are
indispensable. Don't fail to have Athos crossed by ship and the
Hellespont on foot, the sun hidden by the arrows of the Persians, Xerxes in flight, Leonidas performing marvellous deeds,
Othriades writing his dispatch with his own blood, Salamis,
Artemisium, Plataea—plenty of all that.'[196]

The procedure at a school declamation was as follows.[197]
The master would announce the theme and then proceed to
analyse it and discuss the method of treatment. This preliminary discussion was in Latin variously known as the *divisio*,
praelocutio or *praefatio*, and in Greek as the *protheoria*.[198] It was
delivered seated, after which the master would stand up and
deliver the complete declamation; one Greek rhetorician
describes himself as making two speeches every day, one from
his chair and the other standing up.[199] On certain days—every
sixth day, according to Juvenal—the students themselves declaimed.[200] The famous Augustan rhetorician Porcius Latro
claimed that he was not a teacher but a model, and refused to

hear his pupils declaim; but it was only an exceptional person who could get away with this.[201] For most rhetoricians it was part of their regular duties to listen to their pupils' performances; apart from anything else this was expected of them by the parents, who thought that the more often their boys declaimed the better.[202]

The practice, it seems, was for the boy to read his composition aloud from his seat and then deliver it from memory standing before his master.[203] This could be something of an ordeal. St Jerome in old age used to dream that he was back at school, dressed in his best, declaiming before his rhetoric master, and Libanius has a picture of the rhetorician sitting frowning on his high throne while his pupil approaches in fear and trembling to pronounce his declamation.[204] Yet the rhetoric school seems to have been generally enjoyed. Pliny looks back to schooldays as the happiest period of his life and congratulates the aged rhetorician Isaeus on being privileged to carry on into old age one of the pleasantest occupations of youth.[205] The students took a lively interest in their teachers' declamations; they applauded, noted down their best remarks and passed them on by word of mouth or in their letters home.[206] Their own performances gave them the opportunity of displaying their cleverness and, since they normally impersonated the litigant rather than an advocate, their histrionic ability.[207] Their fellow-students formed an appreciative audience. They would applaud, jump up from their seats and rush forward with excited cries, though responsible teachers like Quintilian disapproved of this and insisted that the young declaimer and his fellow-students should keep their eyes fixed on the master and judge the success of the declamation by the latter's reactions.[208]

If the ancient schools of rhetoric are regarded as providing a professional training for advocates they can hardly, at any rate in the imperial period, be counted a success. They dealt often enough with cases unlikely ever to occur, based on laws sometimes Greek, sometimes Roman, sometimes imaginary.[209] No attempt was made to reproduce the atmosphere of the courts. Each speech was self-contained, delivered on one side or the other and answering only imaginary objections.[210] Even in Republican times Cicero remarks that most students of rhetoric learned little more than verbal fluency from their school exercises.[211] After the rise of the new style of declamation criticism was more severe. Declaimers, it was said, aimed at pleasing rather than convincing, at commending themselves not their case, and when they came to practise in the courts they were unable to shake off the follies that had been encouraged by the schools.[212] It is hard to say, according to Messalla in Tacitus's *Dialogus*, 'whether the actual place or the fellow-pupils or the character of the education does more harm to the young mind'.[213] Teachers might blame the parents, whose ambition was that their sons should become great orators at as early an age as possible,[214] but the teachers, convinced that speech was the greatest gift of the gods to men and proud of their own accomplishments, did little to disabuse them.

The wisest Roman teacher of rhetoric, Quintilian, did his best to make declamation what it had originally been and what he thought it should be, a preparation for advocacy. He regarded it as a valuable exercise which could be and often was mis-used. But he had to compromise. Though he would not accept the view that its object was simply display, he admitted that there was an element of display in it. He would have liked if possible to get rid altogether of incredible themes involving 'magicians, plagues, oracles and stepmothers more cruel than any in tragedy', but he evidently found this impossible, and he was willing to allow his pupils occasionally to handle the wilder themes.[215] His comments on the treatment of *contro-versiae* show that in his teaching he handled them in a sober and sensible manner, subjecting them to careful analysis and doing his best to make them a serious and profitable exercise. The same sobriety and common sense is found in the collection attributed to Quintilian known as the *Declamationes Minores*. This consists of what appear to be notes made by a pupil of his master's teaching, and it is at least possible that the master was Quintilian himself. It originally comprised as many as 388 *controversiae*, and if all of them were recorded by one pupil during his school career, we can take it as the record of a com-plete course in this type of declamation. The showiness and bad taste which were commonly associated with declamation were certainly not encouraged in this school; but one cannot help pitying those who had to submit to so monotonous a curriculum.

If declamation was not a preparation for pleading, says Quintilian, it could only be compared to a stage display or to the ravings of a lunatic.[216] Yet the view that it was an end in itself prevailed. The oratory of display flourished, and the rhetorician, the *sophistes* as the Greeks called him, the teacher and public performer, was admired, applauded and honoured. The schools aimed at producing men with a ready command of words, who could delight and entertain their listeners by their elegant style and mellifluous delivery. They had their successes, but they had their failures too. The schools of rhetoric, St Augustine remarked, throughout the world were crowded, but there were few who attained to the highest eloquence.[217] There were dull boys who made little progress; the parents blamed the teachers, the teachers blamed the boys' nature.[218] Even Quintilian, in general so optimistic about the potentialities of the young and the power of education, evidently failed to make much headway with some of his boys.[219] Perhaps the fault did not lie wholly with their nature. He writes of students looking up to the ceiling in the vain hope of getting inspiration, of an anxious self-criticism which reduced some of them to silence.[220] It looks as if a too intensive training in the art of speech could defeat its own ends; perhaps the boys would have profited by a little relief from endless speechmaking.

Mathematics and music

The term *quadrivium* for the 'mathematical' arts of arithmetic, geometry, astronomy and music is not found earlier than Boethius, but the Greek phrase from which it is derived was in use well before then,[221] and the four subjects had long been associated in education. They had been taught in Athens of the fifth century B.C. by Theodorus of Cyrene and Hippias,[222] and before that by the Pythagoreans. According to the Pythagorean Archytas the mathematicians had handed down knowledge 'about geometry, arithmetic and sphaeric (astronomy) and last but not least music; for these subjects seem to be sisters'.[223]

According to Proclus, Pythagoras transformed the study of geometry into a liberal education.[224] The phrase may be anachronistic, but it expresses the important fact that Pythagoras made mathematics into an intellectual study pursued for

its own sake independently of its utilitarian applications. This
was what gave the subject its place in a liberal education.
Voices were occasionally heard in antiquity urging the practical
importance of mathematics; among them, rather surprisingly,
is that of Plato who, in his *Laws*, holds up as an example the
Egyptians, with their interesting and amusing methods of
teaching the young practical arithmetic and mensuration, and
castigates his fellow-countrymen for their ignorance of such
matters.[225] But the characteristic view was that of Isocrates,
who regarded mathematics as simply providing mental training.[226] This is repeated by Cicero, who maintains that the value
of the subject lies in its power to sharpen and stimulate the
minds of boys and so make it easier for them to learn more
important things; and the same view is said by Quintilian to be
the generally accepted one.[227]

Some mathematics was no doubt included in primary education throughout antiquity, even if it was only, in Plato's words,
'to tell the difference between one, two and three'.[228] Evidence
on this point is meagre, though we know at least that in St
Augustine's day the hateful chant 'unum et unum duo, duo et
duo quattuor' was part of primary education.[229] There must
also have been many who needed some arithmetic for business
purposes, but these were outside the scope of liberal education.
At Rome they were catered for by the *calculator*, the teacher of
practical or commercial arithmetic.[230] It is his school no doubt
of which Horace gives us a picture:

>   'dicat
> filius Albini, si de quincunce remotast
> uncia, quid superest? poteras dixisse.' 'triens' 'eu.
> rem poteris seruare tuam. redit uncia, quid fit?'
> 'semis'.

> 'Can Albinus's son tell us: if one twelfth is subtracted
> from five twelfths, what is the remainder? Come on, you
> ought to be able to answer that.' 'One third.' 'Good.
> You'll be able to look after your property. And if you add
> one twelfth, what's the result?' 'A half.'[231]

It would be from the *calculator* too that the freedman Hermeros
in Petronius learned to do his percentages. This was not a

liberal education; Hermeros prided himself on knowing nothing of 'geometry, literature, and all that nonsense'.[232] Though Hermeros classes geometry as useless knowledge its position was a little different from that of arithmetic. Here there was not the same difference between the liberal and the illiberal. Geometry was of use not to shopkeepers and merchants but to respectable professional men like architects and surveyors.[233] None the less the teachers of geometry tended to depreciate its practical utility. 'What shall I get by learning this?' asked one of Euclid's pupils; at which Euclid summoned a slave and told him to give the pupil three obols 'since he must gain something out of what he learns'.[234]

Plato, although he was alive to the practical uses of mathematics, believed that they had a further value. They turned the soul from the world of becoming to truth and reality.[235] So he proposed that the Guardians in his Republic should spend the years between twenty and thirty in the study of mathematics, including arithmetic, plane and solid geometry, astronomy and music, after which they would proceed to dialectics. Though this programme can hardly have been carried out in its entirety in the Academy, Plato certainly gave mathematics an important place in his teaching. The geometer and astronomer Eudoxus was among those who studied in his school and we hear of Plato setting his students problems in astronomy and mathematics generally.[236] 'Philosophy nowadays has become mathematics,' wrote Aristotle, thinking no doubt of the Academy under Plato's immediate successor Speusippus.[237]

Mathematics, however, soon parted company with philosophy. After the fourth century it developed as an independent discipline in Alexandria, where Euclid taught at the beginning of the third century and founded what may be called a school of mathematics.[238] Under the Roman Empire there was a revival of interest in the subject on the part of the philosophers. Lucian describes how when he called on the Platonist Nigrinus he found a board with geometrical figures on it in the centre of the room, and a model of the celestial sphere.[239] Theon of Smyrna's textbook of mathematics was professedly designed to assist in the reading of Plato. Hypatia, who had evidently inherited the ability of her father the mathematician Theon of Alexandria, wrote commentaries on Apollonius of Perga's work on conic sections, and on the *Arithmetica* of Diophantus.[240] Mathematical works were also written by the neo-Platonists Iamblichus, Proclus and Domninus, that of Proclus (a commentary on Euclid) being evidently based on lectures given in his school at Athens.[241]

Though Platonists might regard mathematics as preparatory to, or forming part of, philosophy, for most people it was part of their general education, the *enkuklios paideia*. Hippocrates of Chios, a geometer who flourished in the late fifth century B.C., was the first to write an elementary textbook, a sure sign that his subject was becoming part of regular teaching.[242] At the end of the fourth century Arcesilaus, the head of the Academy, studied mathematics in his native city of Pitane in Aeolia before he went to Athens and took up philosophy; and in the third century it was taken for granted that arithmetic and geometry would be among the subjects which a boy would have to study.[243] An inscription from Magnesia of the second century B.C. gives the name of the winner in an examination in arithmetic, and we hear of a geometer at Callipolis.[244] Inscriptions of the later second century show that the Athenian ephebes engaged in mathematical studies.[245]

Mathematics was thus a recognized part of education in the Hellenistic world, and like other disciplines it passed to Rome. There is a well-known passage of Cicero in which he contrasts the honour accorded to the subject among the Greeks with its neglect by the Romans: 'we have limited it to the utilitarian purposes of mensuration and calculation'.[246] This is, however, misleading if it is taken to imply a complete neglect on the part of the Romans of all but the practical aspects of the subject; some of them at any rate had a full liberal education including the mathematical arts. Cicero himself mentions Sextus Pompeius, uncle of the famous Pompey, as an example of one who had studied mathematics;[247] Pompeius would not have been aiming at a career in commerce or surveying. The Stoic Diodotus, who had taught Cicero in his early years and lived on in his house, gave lessons in geometry although he had lost his sight;[248] Quintilian requires some mathematical study as part of the training of an orator, and had evidently had experience of such study himself.[249] Some instruction in astronomy would be included in the normal mathematical course.

Cicero's translation of Aratus made early in life suggests that he had had such instruction, for Aratus, as we shall see later, was regularly used as a school textbook. Vitruvius had certainly studied astronomy, since he himself refers to his teachers in the subject.[250]

It is true, however, that the Romans did not add anything to the development of mathematical science, nor did they, if we exclude the 'commercial' schools of the *calculatores*, produce teachers of the subject. They learned it, so far as we can tell, from Greeks and in Greek.[251] Though the mathematical arts had been included by Varro in his *Disciplinarum Libri* and a Latin technical vocabulary must therefore have been available after the appearance of his book, the absence of Latin textbooks (other than astronomical) suggests an absence of Latin teachers; there is no evidence that Euclid was translated into Latin before Boethius.[252]

The fact that geometry is more often mentioned than arithmetic and astronomy should not lead us to suppose that the latter two subjects were neglected. Geometry was sometimes taken to include the other two,[253] and the title *geometres* was no doubt often given to a mathematical teacher who did not confine himself to the subject from which he got his name; the *geometres* appears in the edict of Diocletian, but there is no mention of the arithmetician or the astronomer.[254] A *geometres* could also be a teacher of music. Nicomachus of Gerasa and Theon of Smyrna both wrote on music as well as mathematics, and the Diodotus whom we have already mentioned as a mathematical teacher could play the lyre and so may well have also taught music.[255]

Mathematics is an impersonal subject, and we do not know much about the personalities of the ancient mathematicians or about their methods of instruction. No doubt most of them did teach (we know that Euclid did), and we can assume that they taught on the lines of their written works. Arithmetic meant the theory of numbers. Geometry after Euclid's day would follow in his footsteps, starting with definitions and, after setting out certain postulates and axioms, proceeding to prove a series of theorems.

Astronomy might seem to be the most specialized of the mathematical arts, and no doubt in the hands of men like

Aristarchus and Hipparchus it was specialized. But it was also a popular study. The stars were familiar to all. The sailor used them for navigation, the farmer's calendar was based on them. Literature was full of them; as Quintilian said, it was impossible to understand the poets without a knowledge of the stars.[256] There were many too in later antiquity who believed that their destinies were determined by the stars, and this may have contributed to the popularity of the subject though, whatever might be said by critics of the liberal arts like Seneca and Sextus Empiricus, who professed to regard astronomy as no more than astrology, the schools confined themselves to description of the heavenly bodies and did not teach how to cast horoscopes.[257]

For the beginner in astronomy there were simple introductions like that of Geminus, written in the first century B.C. There was also a metrical textbook in the shape of Aratus's *Phaenomena*. Aratus was not an astronomer, but a man of letters; what he did in his poem was to versify a prose treatise of Eudoxus at the instigation of the Macedonian king Antigonus. His work proved immensely popular, not only in Greece but also in Rome, where it was translated by Cicero, Varro of Atax and Germanicus. This popularity is not really surprising. The subject itself had a wide appeal and in the ancient world verse was probably more attractive and easier to read than prose; as the astronomer Hipparchus wrote, 'the charm of the poetry gives a kind of credibility to the matter'.[258] What is perhaps surprising is that this second-hand and not entirely accurate work of an amateur was used as a textbook by the professionals, as is shown by the fact that commentaries were written on it by astronomers and mathematicians, including Attalus of Rhodes, Hipparchus, Ptolemy and Theon of Alexandria.[259]

It was usual to preface the exposition of Aratus with an introduction. Some of these survive, the longest being adapted from a work by an astronomer called Achilles,[260] of the third century after Christ. Another, which survives only in excerpts,[261] begins with definitions of sphere, circle, point, pole, axis, and proceeds to further questions with their answers; evidently the writer or his excerptor used the method of catechism. This introduction is followed by a lengthy explanatory commentary on the text of Aratus, in the course of which we can now and again hear the voice of the teacher asking such questions as, 'What is the difference between a star and a constellation?', 'What is the heaven?', 'What is the axis?'[262]

A mathematical teacher, we may suppose, would have among his students a few specialists who would follow him into the higher reaches of the subject; he would also have a larger number of boys who would follow a short course as part of their general education. How much the latter would get through it is hard to say. Quintilian, who was certainly no specialist in mathematics, knew the first theorem of Euclid and had been exercised in detecting numerical fallacies.[263] He explains at some length that when the lines bounding two figures are equal in length it does not follow that the areas within the lines are equal, and he shows an acquaintance with certain other problems which would require a more advanced knowledge.[264] The student of astronomy who worked through Aratus would learn of the various constellations; the Milky Way, the tropics, the equator and the ecliptic; the rising and settings of the stars; and finally weather signs. For the movements of the planets, which Aratus omitted, he would have to go to prose treatises like that of Geminus, or rely on his master's oral exposition. The planets were certainly included in some courses not designed for specialists; Vitruvius specifically states that he had learned of them from his teachers.[265]

The teaching of mathematics, whether geometry, arithmetic or astronomy, required somewhat different methods from those of the grammarian or the rhetorician. The mathematician needed to illustrate his expositions, and this he did on the table or board known as the abacus. The symbols of the mathematician's trade were 'the dust and the rod'.[266] The dust, or sand or ash, was spread on the flat surface of the abacus, and the rod was for drawing figures on it. In the absence of blackboard and chalk this was the method in use throughout antiquity, from the fifth century B.C. when Socrates, according to Aristophanes, sprinkled some ash on a table and used a bent spit as a compass,[267] to the fifth century after Christ when in Martianus Capella's allegory Geometria carries a rod and is preceded by some attendants bearing 'a kind of little table' with sand sprinkled on it.[268] It has been supposed that for the Roman student of geometry it was enough to memorize the definitions and propositions.[269] Such evidence as there is suggests rather that demonstration on the abacus always formed part of teaching. Perhaps the only account of a geometry teacher in action at Rome is that which Cicero gives of Diodotus; as he was blind, he was unable to use the rod himself, but he managed by telling his pupils what lines to draw (presumably on the abacus) from what point and in what direction.[270]

For the astronomer an indispensable aid to teaching was the sphere or globe.[271] He would not normally have at his disposal a planetarium such as that devised by Archimedes showing the movements of sun and moon and planets, but a solid globe, normally of wood, showing only the fixed stars.[272] This would be fastened at the poles to a vertical ring or circle, which was attached to a horizontal one resting on pillars. The surface was of a dark colour, like that of the sky at night: on it the stars were marked, with the outlines of the constellations more faintly indicated; the signs of the zodiac might be represented in a reddish colour, and the Milky Way in white, though the latter was often omitted.[273] These spheres were regularly used for the exposition of Aratus and were consequently known as Aratean spheres.[274]

Music, as we have seen, was regarded as allied to mathematics. It was not, however, this aspect of the subject that originally gave it its place in ancient education. Music, instrumental and vocal, was part of the life of the Greek cities. It was a feature of festivals, religious rites and social gatherings; there were contests, with prizes, in playing the lyre and the *aulos* and in singing to the accompaniment of the lyre. In Athens of the fifth century every free citizen was expected to learn both singing and playing; Themistocles, it was said, was considered uneducated because he declined to play the lyre at a party.[275] In Aristophanes's 'old education' the boys walk in good order, in all weathers, to the school of the lyre player, singing some fine old songs as they go.[276]

When Hippias and Theodorus taught music along with mathematics in the fifth century they presumably dealt with the theoretical side of the subject rather than the practical. Yet Aristotle's careful and rather inconclusive discussion of music in education is concerned with the latter aspect. By then the professional was ousting the amateur, and there was a general belief that the activity of the executant was degrading and unworthy of a free man.[277] The *aulos*, a wind instrument similar to the clarinet or oboe, which was considered unduly exciting in its effects, had already been given up, and Aristotle rejects all training in instrumental playing which is directed towards performance in competitions.[278] He is, however, prepared to allow a place to music in early education on the ground that some practical experience in youth makes one better able to appreciate the performances of others in later life.[279]

Instruction in playing and singing continued to be given to boys in the Greek cities of the Hellenistic world. We hear of competitions at Chios and Magnesia in playing the lyre both with the fingers and with the plectrum or in singing to the lyre,[280] and the school regulations at Teos provide for the teaching of the lyre as well as for instruction in letters and physical and military training.[281] Instrumental music was still part of the education of a well-born boy in the Greek-speaking world of the second century after Christ, to judge by Lucian's picture of the adolescent with his slaves carrying tablets and books or, when he had to go to his music master, 'a well tuned lyre'.[282]

At Rome in the year 129 B.C. Scipio Aemilianus discovered that young Romans were learning to sing and condemned the introduction of a study which 'our forefathers would have considered a disgrace for the freeborn'.[283] He did not succeed in stopping it. Cicero, contrasting the professional approach with that of the amateur, writes: 'Valerius used to sing every day; that was only to be expected as he was an actor. But our friend Numerius Furius sings when it suits him; he is the head of a household and a Roman knight; he learned as a boy what he ought to learn.'[284] We remember too the boys and girls of the best families who took part in the singing of Horace's *Carmen Saeculare* and Quintilian's claim that a musical education is of value for the training of an orator's voice.[285]

There is some evidence too for the study of instrumental music at Rome other than by professionals. The emperor Titus could not only sing but also play the lyre.[286] Nero's activities as a musician were notorious, but as he started to learn singing to the lyre only after he became emperor, the 'music' which he

E

studied as a boy was probably theoretical rather than practical.[287] Music as one of the liberal arts meant primarily the
study of theory. As St Augustine says, executants rely not on
knowledge but on practice, whereas music as a liberal art
necessarily involves knowledge.[288]

According to the ancient theorists there were two sides to
music: rhythm (including metric) and melody.[289] But in later
antiquity the former was taken over for teaching purposes by
the grammarians, and the musicians were left with melody.[290]
They discussed notes and intervals and scales, and the charac-
teristics of the different 'modes'. Their writing, and presumably
their teaching too, was dry and technical; one of them, Bac-
chius, uses the method much favoured in later antiquity of
question and answer. They liked to think, however, that they
were not only producing instructed connoisseurs but also training character. It was commonly believed in antiquity that
music had an effect on the emotions and on conduct. Plato
discussed musical education from this point of view. He rejected certain types of music as too mournful or as relaxing and
effeminate, and approved only those types (the Dorian and
the Phrygian modes) which he considered promoted courage
and self-control.[291] He wrote, too, of a more general and in-
tangible influence exerted by music, of rhythm and melody
producing a corresponding grace and orderliness in life.[292]
Such ideas persisted, even though with changes in music and in
the part it played in life they lost much of their validity. To
quote the treatise on music attributed to Plutarch: 'If a man
has diligently studied music as part of education and has
given it the necessary attention in early years, he will commend
and embrace what is noble and condemn what is not, in music
and in other matters too; and one so educated will be free from
all ignoble action and reaping the greatest benefit from music
he will prove of the highest value to himself and his city, since
all his actions and words will be well tempered and always and
everywhere he will maintain a sense of fitness, self-control and
orderliness.'[293]

chapter 3
Philosophical teaching

The schools of Athens

The history of ancient philosophy is commonly held to begin
with Thales; that of philosophical schools begins with Pythagoras in the sixth century B.C. In the Greek colony of Croton
in south Italy Pythagoras taught his disciples and organized
them into a society. This society had its distinctive discipline
and way of life. There were two grades of disciples. There was
the inner circle, the *mathematici*, who were in full possession of
the master's doctrine, and the *acousmatici* or *acoustici*, to whom
only a summary without explanation was imparted.[1] Disciples
were not admitted except after a period of probation, which
included a silence of five years or, according to another version,
of a length which varied with each pupil but was not less than
two years.[2] The Pythagorean abstained from animal food and
from beans, and drank no wine.[3] He used clothes and bedding
made from flax and not from wool.[4] He cultivated control over
the tongue; he was enjoined not to reveal the secrets of the
master's doctrines and to practise silence as part of his self-
discipline.[5] He engaged in self-examination at the end of the
day before retiring to bed, and on rising in the morning would
consider carefully what he should do during the coming day.[6]

The Pythagoreans lived in an atmosphere of peace and
serenity. Music, they held, had the power of healing the diseases of the soul, banishing sadness and allaying anger and
desires. On retiring to bed they would purify their minds by the
music of the lyre from all the disturbances of the day and on

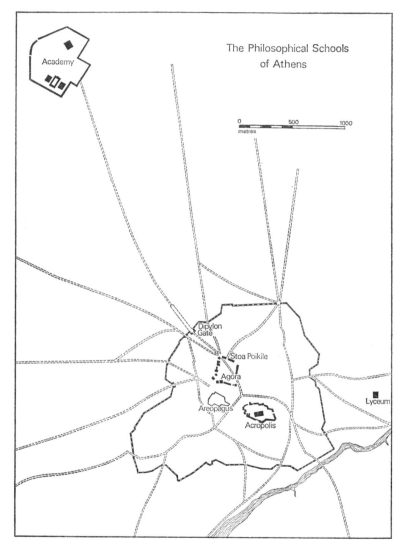

Sketch map of Athens showing the location of the philosophical schools.

rising would dispel by the same means the effects of sleep.[7]
In a Pythagorean community the day began with solitary walks
in quiet places. After the morning walk the group met together,
if possible in a temple, and devoted themselves to study. There
followed a time for recreation and exercise. After a light
luncheon of bread and honey they engaged in affairs of state.
In the evening they went for another walk in groups of two or
three, after which they dined, and after dinner there were
readings by the youngest members of the group under the
presidency of the oldest.[8]

Such is the picture of the Pythagorean school given by our
sources. They are far removed in date from Pythagoras himself.
But there is no need to doubt the general reliability of the
picture they give; the peculiar features of the Pythagorean
discipline are only explicable as based on the directions of a
revered master whose commanding personality impressed itself
on his followers. In one respect, however, the picture may be
misleading. Apart from the reference to affairs of state it gives
the impression of a kind of monastic community withdrawn
from the world; in fact Pythagoras himself took a leading part
in the political life of Croton, and his followers gained a position of influence and authority in the south Italian cities which
led to opposition and revolt and to the eclipse of the school.
About the middle of the fifth century B.C. there was a major
attack on its members in which its meeting houses were des-
troyed and its leaders killed. Many Pythagoreans emigrated to
Greece; some stayed behind, but finally all left Italy, so it is
said, except Archytas of Tarentum.[9] The exiles noted down the
traditional doctrines and left them behind to be handed down
in their families; they were a dwindling band, living in isola-
tion and not attempting to spread their doctrines, and finally,
in the fourth century B.C., they died out.[10]

Pythagoreanism was the philosophy of the West and never
obtained much of a footing in Athens.[11] The Athenian schools
derived from a different source, from the conversations of
Socrates. Plato was familiar with Pythagorean doctrines and
he made the acquaintance of Archytas on his visit to Italy in
387, but it was in Athens that he founded his school on his
return from the West, and whatever influence Pythagoreanism
may have had on his thought, he remained essentially an

Athenian, one who had associated with Socrates in his youth and who owed to him the inspiration to devote his life to philosophy.

No two teachers could be more unlike in their methods than Pythagoras and Socrates. Pythagoras's disciples were united in a strictly organized community; those of Socrates were not organized at all. The doctrines of Pythagoras were given forth as a kind of revealed truth; Socrates had no doctrines to impart and claimed that he knew nothing except the fact of his own ignorance. The followers of Pythagoras were content to accept the authority of the master, and if challenged to answer: '*Autos epha*', 'The master said it';[12] those of Socrates, if they learned anything from him, learned to think for themselves.

Socrates was an unusual type of teacher; indeed he himself said that he was not a teacher at all.[13] He was the midwife who brought other people's thoughts to birth, the gad-fly who stimulated his sluggish contemporaries.[14] He had no school; he did not give regular classes, and he took no fees. His conversations were conducted in public. 'Early in the day he went to the public walks and gymnasia; when the agora filled up he was to be seen there, and for the rest of the day he would be wherever he was likely to find most company.'[15] Everyone who was prepared to submit to his questioning could hear him, whatever their age and status. But it was the young who heard him most willingly, and over them he exercised a remarkable fascination. He was, if we can believe Plato, susceptible to the youthful charms of those good-looking boys who were to be seen in palaestra and gymnasium surrounded by admirers; but, as Alcibiades says in the *Symposium*, in his relations with them the positions of lover and beloved were reversed as they found themselves irresistibly attracted by his personality.[16]

There were those who thought his was a bad influence. He was accused of corrupting the youth, and the charge was sufficiently plausible to secure his condemnation by an Athenian jury. But his followers remembered him, in Plato's words, as the best and wisest and justest man they had known,[17] and the later philosophical schools, with the exception of the Epicurean, all derived from him. As the emperor Julian put it, 'To him I ascribe the wisdom of Plato, the generalship of Xenophon, the fortitude of Antisthenes, the Eretrian and

Megarian philosophies, Cebes, Simmias, Phaedo and a host of others; not to mention the offshoots derived from the same source, the Lyceum, the Stoa and the Academies. . . . All who now find their salvation in philosophy owe it to Socrates.'[18] The Socratic belief that virtue is knowledge implied that it could be taught and it was on this assumption that the later schools were based. Their regular courses of instruction were very different from the conversations of Socrates. But so far as they insisted on the Socratic message that the most important thing in life was 'to care for the soul and make it as good as possible', so far as the philosopher continued to be the friend of his young charges, the master who guided and helped them on the path to virtue, something of the Socratic tradition survived.

When Plato began to teach shortly after his return to Athens he chose as his headquarters the Academy, a gymnasium on the outskirts of Athens three-quarters of a mile from the Dipylon gate.[19] A gymnasium as one of the chief places where the young congregated was a natural choice for a teacher. Socrates had frequented the gymnasia; a little before Plato settled at the Academy Antisthenes had begun to teach in another gym-nasium, the Kynosarges,[20] and the third of the suburban gymnasia, the Lyceum, was to be Aristotle's headquarters. What was new about Plato's teaching was that he gave it a permanent centre. He acquired a property nearby. Our sources speak of a garden or a little garden, and describe it as near the gymnasium, or as by Colonus, which was within easy reach of the Academy.[21] There must have been a house as well as a garden, since Plato had his residence there. It was a small estate bought, we are told, for 3,000 drachmae.[22]

We have little information about the organization of the Academy during Plato's lifetime. Much has been made of the fact that he erected a *Mouseion*, a shrine of the Muses, in the gymnasium.[23] The Academy, it is said, was a *thiasos Mouson*, a religious corporation for the service of the Muses, and this was its basis in law.[24] The importance of the *Mouseion* has perhaps been exaggerated. Other schools besides those of the philo-sophers had their statues of the Muses and acts of worship in honour of them;[25] nor need we look for a legal basis for an organization which, so far as we know, did not hold any cor-

porate property in Plato's time. Plato's will as recorded by
Diogenes Laertius contains no provisions such as we find in
those of Theophrastus and Epicurus for the continuance of the
school, and no mention of the property at the Academy.[26] On
the other hand, he could hardly have spent forty years in teaching without giving some thought to the future of the school, and
though he can have had no idea that it would last some nine
hundred years, the fact that he chose his nephew Speusippus
to succeed him suggests that he made some further provision
for the future; it is a reasonable assumption that the property
where he had lived for so long was made over to Speusippus
in his lifetime. As it happened, Speusippus did not live there
but in the city, but his two successors Xenocrates and Polemo
occupied Plato's old home,[27] so that, however the property
was conveyed, it belonged in effect to the school.

For some time teaching continued to be conducted in the
Academy gymnasium; Speusippus, Xenocrates and Polemo all
taught there. Cicero describes himself as visiting the Academy
and observing the actual seat where Polemo sat;[28] elsewhere we
are told that Polemo taught in the garden, while his pupils
built small huts to live in near the *Mouseion* and the *exhedra*.[29]
Lacydes, head of the school in the second half of the third
century B.C., is said to have taught in a garden laid out by
Attalus of Pergamum,[30] but this was apparently part of the
Academy. The school clearly remained in its old home, for a
century or so later Carneades was teaching there.[31] With
Sulla's siege of Athens there came a break. Sulla cut down
trees in the Academy to assist his siege operations, and when the
Athenians joined Mithridates, Philo, then head of the school,
fled to Rome.[32] In 79–78 B.C., when Cicero was studying at
Athens, Philo's successor, Antiochus, taught in the gymnasium
of Ptolemy.[33] If we can take literally Horace's description of
his student days in Athens—*inter siluas Academi quaerere uerum*,
to seek for the truth amid the groves of the Academy[34]—the
trees cut down by Sulla had grown again by then and the school
had returned to its old haunts. But it is more likely that Horace's
phrase is no more than a sentimental tribute to the past and
that the grove of Academe had been finally abandoned.[35] Only
a few years before Horace went to Athens Cicero was there
staying with Aristus, Antiochus's brother and successor, and

Aristus apparently lived in a house in the city.[36] Nor is there any evidence in later writers that Plato's successors taught in the Academy.

To the east of the city, and nearer to its walls than the Academy, was the Lyceum. It was here that Aristotle established his headquarters when he returned to Athens in 335–334 B.C. and set up as a teacher on his own. The gymnasium contained a *peripatos* or walk, which he used for his teaching and which gave the school its name. He taught here until 323 B.C. when he handed the school over to Theophrastus and left Athens. From Theophrastus's will we learn something about the premises. As in the Academy there was a *Mouseion*; Theophrastus directed that certain trust funds should be devoted to its completion and to furnishing it with statues of the goddesses. A bust of Aristotle and other offerings were to be replaced 'in the temple', a little stoa by the *Mouseion* was to be rebuilt, and tablets containing maps were to be placed in the lower stoa. An altar was to be repaired and a statue of Aristotle's son Nicomachus to be completed. The garden, the *peripatos* and the houses adjoining the garden were bequeathed to ten of his friends, or rather to those of them who should wish 'to share the school and the pursuit of philosophy', since it was not possible for them all to be always in residence; they were to 'hold it in common as a temple and to live in friendship and amity with one another'.[37] The will reveals a well-organized body with a considerable property, and this in spite of the fact that both Aristotle and Theophrastus were not Athenian citizens, and so were unable in ordinary circumstances to own landed property. Aristotle perhaps only rented the property; through the good offices of Demetrius of Phalerum Theophrastus acquired a garden of his own,[38] and a whole complex of buildings, houses, *peripatos*, *Mouseion* and stoas, appears to have been at his disposal.

The references in his will to rebuilding and repair remind us of the disturbed state of Athens at the time of his headship, and it may well be that the buildings of the school had suffered in the siege of Athens in 296–294 B.C. The school itself had earlier been threatened with suppression when Demetrius of Phalerum surrendered the city to Demetrius Poliorcetes in 307 B.C. and freedom was, or was thought to be, restored. Sophocles of

Sunium proposed a law forbidding philosophers to teach without the permission of the council and people.[39] This was evidently directed against the Peripatetics, who had close associations with the pro-Macedonian party and who numbered Demetrius of Phalerum among their pupils. Theophrastus along with other philosophers thought it wise to withdraw from the city. Soon, however, there was a reaction in favour of the philosophers and in the next year Sophocles was successfully indicted by one Philo under a *graphe paranomon*, an action to annul the measure as contrary to existing law. The incident is of some interest in connection with the legal status of the philosophical schools. A law of Solon had laid down that any ordinances made by the members of a *thiasos* and other such bodies with regard to their own members were valid unless they were contrary to the laws of the state,[40] and it has been suggested that it was on the basis of this law that Philo made his case against Sophocles, and that as a philosophical school had the status of a *thiasos*, to infringe its rights was to be guilty of impiety, *asebeia*.[41] But a *graphe paranomon* was not necessarily based on purely legal considerations. We know that in this case a speaker defending Sophocles recalled various pupils of the Academy who had made themselves tyrants.[42] Clearly this was primarily a political case, and it is unlikely that much consideration was given to such nice questions as the rights of corporations.

The repeal of Sophocles's law meant that the philosophers could now look forward to security, and a year afterwards Epicurus moved to Athens and established himself as a teacher there. Unlike Plato and Aristotle he did not attach himself to a gymnasium; he preferred a comparatively small circle of friends to a public place and a general audience. He chose a garden, and though the Academics and the Peripatetics also had their gardens, that of Epicurus was particularly associated with his school. The *kepos*, the garden, meant the school of Epicurus. The garden was a small one within the city boundaries, and there was of course a house attached to it, or not far distant.[43]

Epicurus duly made provision in his will for the continuance of his school. He left his property on trust to two of his friends for its benefit. They were to make over 'the garden and what goes with it' to Hermarchus, the new head, and his fellow-philosophers, and to Hermarchus's successors, who were to maintain and carry on the school there. The house was to be assigned to Hermarchus and his associates as a dwelling-place.[44] The garden was evidently kept up; Atticus used to frequent it when he studied under the Epicurean Phaedrus.[45] But the house had fallen into ruin by the year 51 B.C., when Cicero got involved in an attempt to mediate between Patro, who had succeeded Phaedrus in the headship, and the Roman Memmius who, though he was the friend of Lucretius to whom the *De Rerum Natura* was addressed, showed so little respect for the feelings of the Epicureans as to plan buildings on the site of their founder's house—*nescio quid illud Epicuri parietinarum*, some ruined walls or other once Epicurus's, as Cicero puts it.[46] Evidently the house, though ruinous, had remained in the hands of the Epicureans and, as Cicero's letter to Memmius shows, they attached importance to its possession. The Areopagus, it seems, had granted Memmius the site. When Cicero was first approached by Patro he refused to get involved. But when he arrived in Athens on his way to his province he was approached again by Patro, whose appeals were reinforced by Atticus. Memmius had now given up the idea of building but he was annoyed by Patro's insistence, and as it was clear that the Areopagus would do nothing against his wishes, Cicero wrote tactfully to him asking him to have the decree of the Areopagus repealed. Whether he was successful or not is not known.

The fourth school, the Stoic, unlike the other three, had no recognized headquarters and little organization. Its founder Zeno taught in the Stoa Poikile, a colonnade overlooking the agora from which the school took its name, but Chrysippus, the 'second founder' of the school, taught at the Lyceum and, at the end of his life, in the Odeum.[47] We hear nothing of Zeno bequeathing property or making provision for the future of his school. None the less it survived, and the fact that it had a regular succession of heads suggests that it acquired some degree of organization.[48]

The head of a school normally held office for life, though in the Academy two heads, Socratides and Lacydes, are recorded as having resigned.[49] The method of election varied; either the existing holder bequeathed the headship in his will, or it was conferred by vote of the members of the school. In the early history of the Academy the choice was more than once made by vote, and it is interesting to note that it was not the senior members who were responsible for the choice but the younger pupils. It was they who elected Xenocrates on the death of Speusippus, Menedemus and Heracleides being defeated by a few votes.[50] It was they, too, who on the death of Crates chose the senior member of the school, Socratides, as his successor, though he soon resigned in favour of Arcesilaus.[51] Later on selection by vote seems to have been abandoned in the Academy; Crates of Tarsus, who succeeded in 131–130 B.C., was nominated by his predecessor.[52]

In the Peripatetic school the headship appears to have been determined by bequest. Theophrastus's will does not distinguish Strato, who in fact succeeded him, from the other 'friends' to whom he left the school, but that of Strato specifically leaves the school to Lyco, with the explanation that the rest are either too old or too busy.[53] Lyco left it to certain members of the school to choose their head, but the fact that this was a specific provision of his will indicates that he had the right to dispose of the headship.[54] Of the Stoic method of selection we know nothing. Among the Epicureans appointment was made by will; Epicurus bequeathed his school to Hermarchus, and indicated that Hermarchus would in due course follow the same method.[55] We have evidence from the imperial period which shows that this method was still in use then, though it was possible in the case of an unsatisfactory choice for the will to be set aside and a new head chosen by the members.[56]

While many who studied philosophy were youths completing their education and destined to leave after a year or two, some would stay on and devote their lives to philosophy. Aristotle spent twenty years in the Academy. There would be senior members attached to the schools, the graduates, to use the terminology of the modern university, as opposed to the undergraduate students. Theophrastus bequeathed the property of the Peripatetic school to ten of its members, as did Lyco, the fourth head;[57] it is tempting to think of something like an English collegiate foundation consisting of ten fellows, or rather, since the ten included the head of the school, a master and nine fellows.

Under Xenocrates an arrangement was made in the Academy by which members of the school, presumably senior members, held in rotation a position of responsibility as *archon*, and this system was imitated by Aristotle in his school.[58] At first the *archon* held office for ten days at a time; later, in the Peripatetic school at any rate, the period was thirty days.[59] If the nine senior members referred to above successively filled the office of *archon*, and if we can assume that there was, as in other types of school, a 'long vacation' of three months, each would serve for one month in the year. The *archon* had to look after the religious rites and superintend the *Mouseion*.[60] He also had charge of the symposia. These parties were a feature of the two older schools. The philosophic drinking party, as Plato's *Symposium* shows, goes back to the time of Socrates, and Plato's solemn discussion of drinking in the *Laws* shows that he believed such parties could have an educational value. Xenocrates in the Academy and Aristotle in his school laid down rules for the conduct of symposia, and Theophrastus bequeathed money towards them.[61] Under Lyco their luxurious character had become something of a scandal and the expense a burden to the *archon*. On the last day of his monthly period of office he had to give an entertainment. He collected a contribution from the students, but senior members, so it was alleged, also attended, as did guests invited by Lyco, and there were complaints that the contributions did not go far towards meeting expenses. The original purpose of these gatherings, relaxation and learned talk, had, it was said, been forgotten and they had become merely an occasion for eating and drinking.[62]

In the Academy Plato's personality was evidently a powerful influence during his lifetime, for it is recorded that his disciples even imitated his stoop.[63] But he does not seem to have attempted to promulgate any particular doctrine and it is not easy to say for certain how he taught. Whereas the teaching of other ancient philosophers is reflected in their written works, Plato's dialogues are clearly not derived from lecture notes or (though they were so used by later Platonists) designed as textbooks. He is known to have given at least one public lecture, and it was not exactly a success. The subject was The Good, and most of the audience came expecting to hear about one of the recognized goods of life, such as wealth, health and strength; they were disappointed when Plato's lecture turned out to be concerned with mathematics, with numbers, geometry and astronomy.[64] Clearly Plato did not put his views over very successfully; a number of his pupils who attended recorded what he had said, but the record was as enigmatic as the lecture. Plato dissociated himself from such publications, and declined to publish his doctrine himself. It was not, he said, something that could be written down; it was a kind of sudden illumination, like a flame leaping up from a spark, which resulted from much discussion and a common life.[65] These being his views, one would not expect him to have taught by means of formal lectures, and that on The Good may have been his only one. His teaching appears to have been mainly of an informal nature; he was the director of studies rather than the lecturer. He would offer advice and criticism. In particular he suggested problems in mathematics. We know that one of the problems which he set was to determine what uniform and ordered notions would account for the apparent movements of the planets, and it was to solve this problem that Eudoxus worked out his theory of concentric spheres.[66] The history of the Academy found at Herculaneum describes Plato as setting problems and 'acting as architect', that is, as planner and organizer of the work.[67]

Of Plato's methods with his younger pupils we have an interesting picture in a fragment of the comic poet Epicrates.[68] The scene is the gymnasium of the Academy, and a band of youths is engaged in defining and classifying animals, trees and vegetables. In particular they are trying to determine to what species a pumpkin belongs. They had made several attempts when a doctor from Sicily made a derisive noise. This had no effect on them, and Plato, who was present, gently and without getting annoyed told them to try again. Though the evidence of comedy should not be taken too seriously, something can be learnt from the fragment. The method of division and classification which Epicrates parodies was presumably a well-known feature of Academic teaching; and it is significant that Plato is shown leaving the students to themselves and confining himself to encouragement. It is pleasant too to find that, though his Second Letter gives the impression of a somewhat arrogant, even irritable, personality, he had the reputation of being a kindly and sympathetic teacher.

Plato's informal methods of teaching did not survive, and if we can judge by the story of Polemo bursting into the school in a state of intoxication while Xenocrates was lecturing on self-control,[69] it was the practice for the head of the school to give formal disquisitions on moral topics. Arcesilaus, head of the school in the mid-third century, gave a new character to the Academy. He was the first, says Diogenes Laertius, to disturb the doctrine handed down by Plato and by the use of question and answer to give it a more eristic character.[70] Yet his methods could be, and were, represented as a return to those of Socrates. Socrates, says Cicero, never held school, but by questioning and cross-examining used to draw out the views of those he talked to and himself reply to their answers. 'This practice was abandoned by those who followed him, but was revived by Arcesilaus. He arranged that his would-be hearers should not ask questions of him, but should say what they thought; and when they had done so he spoke on the other side. But his hearers defended their point of view as far as they could.'[71] Cicero goes on to say that the Academy had now fallen into line with the other schools, where the hearers contributed nothing, but simply put forward a thesis to be demolished. The man who wanted to hear a philosopher would announce 'I hold that pleasure is the highest good', and the philosopher would proceed to argue on the other side in a continuous speech, 'so that it is obvious that those who express a particular point of view do not really hold it, but want to hear the opposite'.[72] Cicero himself gives us an idea of how the professional philosophers taught in his *Tusculan Disputations*, where he professes to record a series of discussions in which he argues against an unnamed interlocutor. Each discussion opens with the interlocutor announcing a proposition which Cicero then demolishes. As the philosophers used to invite suggestions for discussion,[73] so Cicero at the beginning of one of the disputations announces: 'Dicat si quis uolt qua de re disputari uelit.'[74] The hearer in the *Tusculans* does a little more than simply announce the thesis and then relapse into silence: he keeps up the argument for a time, though he soon abandons it. It is clear that Cicero is trying to reproduce the methods of the earlier Academy rather than those of the contemporary schools.[75]

As regards Aristotle's teaching our evidence is somewhat confusing. On the one hand we have the extant treatises, believed to be his notes of the lectures given in the Lyceum; on the other hand there is a strong ancient tradition which presents him as a popular teacher of rhetoric. The two aspects of his work are combined in the story that he gave two different kinds of instruction, in the morning the 'acroatic' lectures for the select few, dealing with the more difficult problems of philosophy, and in the afternoon the 'exoteric' lectures, of a more popular character, dealing with rhetoric.[76] When he began his rhetorical teaching is not clear. He is said to have been induced to do so by the success of Isocrates and, adapting a line of Euripides, to have exclaimed: 'It is a shame to remain silent while allowing Isocrates to speak.'[77] If this is correct, his teaching began before the death of Isocrates in 338 B.C., and as he was away from Athens from 347 to 336 B.C. it must date from before 347 B.C., during his first Athenian period, when he was still attached to Plato's school. In view of Plato's hostility to rhetoric which, to judge by the *Laws*, did not diminish with years, this is surprising; moreover, the afternoon lectures with which the rhetorical teaching is associated are assigned in our sources to Aristotle's second Athenian period, when he had founded his own school, and according to one version the name in the parody of Euripides was not Isocrates but Xenocrates, head of the Academy when Aristotle returned to Athens.[78]

Whatever may be the truth about the origin of Aristotle's rhetorical teaching we can hardly doubt that it took place and that it did not consist only of lectures on the lines of his extant *Rhetoric*. Cicero looks back to him as a pioneer of a method of which he himself approved, that of treating theses, or general questions, and arguing them on both sides; his method differed from that of Arcesilaus in that he did not argue against everything but elicited the arguments that could be produced for and against every proposition, and that he used not the subtle argumentative style of the philosophers but a fuller and more oratorical manner.[79]

This kind of teaching presents a rather marked contrast with the scientific and historical researches undertaken in the

Lyceum and with the methods of study reflected in Aristotle's extant works. After Aristotle's death the scientific and scholarly side of his work was continued by Theophrastus and his successor Strato; but later the arguing of theses became the main occupation of the school. If we can believe Strabo's circumstantial story[80] this was because Aristotle's works (those, that is, which we have today as opposed to the early published works now lost) were for some time not available to the school. Theophrastus bequeathed them, and his own books, to Neleus. Neleus took them away to Asia Minor and left them to his heirs, who were men with no philosophic interests and who kept them in hiding for a time for fear that the kings of Pergamum would appropriate them. About 100 B.C. one Apellicon, a bibliophile rather than a philosopher, brought the books to Athens and published them.[81] Until then the Peripatetics had had only a few books, and according to Strabo were unable to engage in serious philosophy but could only elaborate theses. When the books were available the school was better able to develop Aristotle's doctrine, though they were hampered in its interpretation by the faulty nature of the copies made by Apellicon. From that time onwards commentary on Aristotle was the main activity of the school and earlier methods of education died out.

Epicurus's school differed somewhat from the older schools. It was essentially a community. The Academy and Lyceum had their acts of worship, their common meals and symposia, but can hardly have had so close a community life as that associated with the garden of Epicurus, the 'community life of initiates' as an Epicurean renegade called it.[82] The Epicureans made a cult of friendship. The community of friends actually lived together in Epicurus's house, and the same tradition was kept up after his death. 'What a large band of friends,' says the Epicurean spokesman in Cicero's *De Finibus*, 'and how closely united in friendly agreement and unanimity did Epicurus have in a single house and that a small one; and this is still the case with the Epicureans.'[83] Both during his lifetime and after, Epicurus's birthday was celebrated and there was a gathering on the twentieth of each month, established in memory of Epicurus himself and his disciple Metrodorus.[84] In no other school was there so strong a veneration for the founder.

F

His followers pledged themselves to be obedient to him; they revered him as saviour, even as god; his portrait was to be seen in their houses, even on their cups and rings.[85] Nowhere else was there so rigid an orthodoxy. As a non-Epicurean of the second century after Christ put it, the Epicureans 'never speak in opposition to one another or to Epicurus in any respect worth mentioning, but innovation to them is an act of law-lessness, or rather impiety, and is condemned, and for that reason no one even ventures on it. Their doctrines rest un-changed in perfect peace as a result of the harmony they main-tain one with another. Epicurus's school is like a city wholly un-disturbed by faction, with one mind and one opinion.'[86]

Epicurus had no wish to give open lectures to large audiences. The wise man, he said, would establish a school, but not in such a manner as to become leader of a rabble; he would give readings in public, but only by request.[87] His doctrine of living unobtrusively was applied to teaching as well. He was, however, remarkably successful in securing and retaining the allegiance of those who came to him. He had the art of simplify-ing. He produced conveniently short and easy summaries of his doctrine, in particular the *kuriai doxai*, a series of forty articles of belief which the Epicurean would learn by heart.[88] A member of the school called Philonides, known to us from one of the mutilated rolls discovered at Herculaneum, made epitomes of the letters of Epicurus and of others of the school for the benefit of his less industrious pupils.[89] Attention was given to methods of education and to the art of correcting faults. The philosophic teacher was recommended to be frank without being bitter or abusive, not to get angry but to be gentle and sympathetic, to use irony rather than mockery, to avoid cor-recting in the presence of others who need not be there and to take account of the nature of the person under correction.[90] The Epicurean philosopher evidently regarded himself as trainer of character no less than of intellect; like the Stoics of the Empire he was the guide and counsellor, the spiritual director.

The Stoics like the Epicureans were a dogmatic sect, and like them they had a message for mankind. They did not, however, develop the community spirit that was characteristic of the Epicureans. Not for them such harmless but trivial expressions of unity as celebrating the birthday of their founder or having his portrait on their rings; they confined themselves to preaching and argument, and they were noted for their skill in dialectic, which must have made them more formidable than attractive.[91] A more genial and humane manner of exposition was introduced by Panaetius, who unlike the earlier Stoics had some feeling for literary style. 'The usual Stoic harshness and austerity he avoided. He disapproved of rigour in doctrine and hair-splitting in argumentation; he moved in the direction of mellowness of doctrine and clarity in argument, and, as his writings show, Plato, Aristotle, Xenocrates, Theophrastus and Dicaearchus were always on his lips.'[92] In the time of Cicero there was a Stoic called Dionysius who was given to quoting poetry, though he did so with little taste.[93] This suggests that the Stoics were trying to make their teaching more attractive, and that the dry forbidding dialectic for which they had been noted was giving way to the more popular method of moral exhortation which was used in the early Empire. But though we are adequately informed on Stoic doctrine in the first three hundred years of the school's history, we have no such evidence for that period as is available from the imperial period about their methods of teaching.

Philosophy in the Graeco-Roman world

Men came from all over the Greek-speaking world to study in the Athenian schools, and they went out from the schools to put into practice what they had learned or to impart it to others. The Academy sent out would-be philosopher-kings, advisers and constitution-makers. Two of Plato's pupils settled at Assos in the Troad under the patronage of the local despot Hermias and, joined after Plato's death by Aristotle and Xenocrates, formed a Platonist colony which, however, broke up with the arrest and execution of Hermias in 341.[94] Zeno's pupil Persaeus went to Macedon as tutor to the son of Antigonus Gonatas, and another Stoic, Sphaerus, assisted Cleomenes II of Sparta in reforming education and social institutions.[95] The Epicurean Philonides was in Syria under Antiochus Epiphanes and his nephew Demetrius I Soter, trying to convert them (successfully in the case of Demetrius) to Epicureanism.[96] Another

Epicurean, one Diogenes, established himself at the court of Alexander Balas, successor to Demetrius. Alexander, though himself inclining to Stoicism, tolerated him; his successor, Antiochus VI, had him executed.[97] Less dangerous was the work of those who aimed not at converting or advising rulers but at instructing the ordinary citizen. Such teachers were to be found in cities other than Athens in the Hellenistic period, for example the Peripatetic Epicrates of Heraclea, who settled in Samos about 200 B.C. and was given citizenship in recognition of his services to education.[98]

The Epicureans were perhaps more successful than the other philosophers in propagating their doctrines. It was not only members of the school who prided themselves on the spread of their philosophy;[99] their critics and enemies also admitted their success. Cicero describes Epicurus as a philosopher whose influence extended not only to Greece and Italy but also throughout the barbarian world;[100] people asked why there were so many Epicureans, or why Epicureanism made so many converts, whereas there were no examples of the reverse process.[101] Yet this advance was made in the face of some hostility; Epicureans were banished from various Greek cities, and the first Greek philosophers recorded as teaching in Rome were two Epicureans who were expelled from the city in 173 B.C.[102]

It is in Rome that we can follow most clearly the spread of philosophy. The Romans, after some initial resistance shown in the expulsion of the two Epicureans followed in 161 B.C. by a decree banishing philosophers and rhetoricians,[103] willingly learned from the Greeks, and from the middle of the second century B.C. Greek philosophy played an important part in forming the Roman mind and character. In 155 B.C. three leading Athenian philosophers, Carneades the Academic, Critolaus the Peripatetic and Diogenes the Stoic, came to Rome on an embassy. Their business was not transacted immediately, and they took the opportunity presented by the delay to give some lectures. These were attended by large numbers of young Romans and, if we can believe Plutarch, the older generation generally speaking approved.[104] In the later second century it was the Stoics who were most influential, at any rate with the governing classes of Rome. In 144 B.C. Panaetius came to Rome and became the trusted friend of

Scipio Aemilianus, who took him with him on his prolonged embassy to the East when he settled relations with Egypt, Syria, Pergamum and Greece.[105] Other Roman pupils of Panaetius were Laelius, Q. Mucius Scaevola, C. Fannius, M. Vigellius and P. Rutilius Rufus, whom Cicero described as an all but complete master of Stoic doctrine and who carried his philosophy into practice with rare consistency.[106]

In the time of Cicero Stoicism, though it had a distinguished and uncompromising adherent in Cato, does not seem to have exercised a wide appeal.[107] The Academy perhaps gained ground at the expense of the Stoa. It was to the Academy that Cicero adhered after a philosophic education which also included study under Epicurean and Stoic masters. His earliest philosophical teacher was the Epicurean Phaedrus, and, surprising though it may seem in view of his decisive rejection of Epicureanism in later life, he was for a time attracted by Phaedrus's doctrine.[108] His Epicurean phase did not last long. In 88 B.C. Philo arrived in Rome; Cicero became his enthusiastic disciple and from then on counted himself an adherent of the Academy.[109] The Academics did not object to their pupils studying in other schools (indeed Philo advised one of his to attend the head of the Epicurean school in Athens in order to see how easily he could be refuted)[110] and Cicero studied under the Stoic Diodotus at about the same time as he attended Philo's lectures.[111] Later, when he went abroad in 79 B.C., he continued his philosophic studies; at Athens he resumed the study of Epicureanism under Phaedrus and Zeno and of Academic doctrine under Antiochus, an influential figure who, besides Cicero, numbered Lucullus, Piso and Brutus among his Roman pupils.[112] In 78 B.C. Cicero was in Rhodes, and there he attended the lectures of the leading Stoic of the day, Poseidonius, whom he mentions as one of his teachers and often refers to as a friend.[113]

The Epicureans do not seem to have made much headway in Rome before the first century B.C. In the later part of the previous century there was Titus Albucius, a thoroughly Hellenized Roman who had been in Athens as a young man and had emerged a complete Epicurean.[114] In Cicero's day there were plenty of Roman Epicureans, not only among his friends and acquaintances but also among the common people.

As he regretfully observed, 'somehow or other they have the people on their side'.[115] They were first in the field in providing a philosophical literature in Latin. In addition to Lucretius's fine poem there were a number of prose expositions of the doctrines of the school by men who are merely names to us (Amafinius, Rabirius and Catius) which had a wide circulation. On the publication of Amafinius's books, says Cicero, the multitude was won over to his doctrine, and after Amafinius 'many zealous adherents of the same system wrote a great deal and took possession of the whole of Italy'.[116]

These Roman Epicureans must have studied under Greek masters, whether in Italy or in Greece. One of them, Saufeius, was like Cicero a pupil of Phaedrus, and erected a statue to him in Athens.[117] Two Greek Epicureans, Philodemus and Siro, settled in the region of Naples; they were on close terms with the Roman Epicureans of the day and were known to and respected by Cicero.[118] Philodemus, who was born in Gadara and had studied in Athens, is known to us from his elegant epigrams and his less elegant prose treatises which have been recovered from Herculaneum. He was a close friend of L. Calpurnius Piso, whom he invites in one of his epigrams to an Epicurean celebration and who, if the villa where Philodemus's treatises were found was his, was a diligent student of his master's writings.[119] Siro taught the young Virgil, and in the *Appendix Vergiliana* there are two poems, generally considered to be authentic, which throw some light on his relations with his pupil.[120] In one of them Virgil bids farewell to the school of rhetoric and looks forward to hearing the 'learned words of the great Siro'. In the other he writes of a little villa with a meagre estate which had once belonged to Siro, in which Virgil and his family are to take refuge if there is bad news from his home country. Virgil, it seems, had acquired Siro's property, bequeathed to him perhaps on the death of the philosopher.

There is little clear evidence from the Republican period of public teaching by philosophers in Rome, apart from occasional lectures such as those of the envoys in 155 B.C. The large number of Romans recorded as having studied under Panaetius might suggest that he established something like a philosophic school in Rome, but it could also be that they heard him while he was head of the Stoa in Athens. As head of the Academy

Philo probably continued his normal teaching activities in exile; others besides Cicero heard him in Rome.[121] But the usual position of a Greek philosopher among the Romans at this time seems to have been that of a member of the household, a kind of domestic chaplain, living in his patron's house and in some cases accompanying him on his travels. Lucullus took the Academic Antiochus with him when quaestor in Alexandria and later as commander in the East, and Brutus had Antiochus's brother Aristus as his 'friend and companion',[122] though as both these philosophers also taught in Athens as heads of the Academy their association with their Roman patrons cannot have been a permanent one. Crassus used to take his philosopher, the Peripatetic Alexander, with him on his travels, and another Peripatetic, Staseas of Naples, lived for many years in the household of M. Piso.[123] Diodotus, Cicero's Stoic teacher, continued to reside with him as a respected friend, and when he died left him a substantial amount of money.[124]

The position of Diodotus seems to have been that of the old family tutor allowed to go on living in the household rather than that of the guide and counsellor. It was otherwise with the Stoics associated with Cato of Utica. His first teacher was Antipater of Tyre. Later, in the year 67 B.C., he sought out another Stoic, Athenodorus, then in Pergamum, who had hitherto remained independent, and persuaded him to join him in camp and to remain in his household after his return from military service.[125] Two other philosophers, Apollonides the Stoic and Demetrius the Peripatetic, were with him discussing philosophy on the evening before his suicide at Utica.[126]

Though some Greek philosophers settled in Italy, Athens remained the headquarters of philosophy, though not necessarily the city which produced the best philosophers. Tarsus, for instance, could claim to produce better students, but they tended to leave to complete their studies elsewhere.[127] Athens attracted men from outside; the Athenians were no longer intellectual leaders, but their city remained the centre to which foreigners were drawn by its name and reputation.[128] Many Romans studied there, though it might be only during a brief visit such as that of Crassus on his return from his quaestorship in Asia or of Antonius on his way to Cilicia as proconsul.[129]

Cicero's period of study there has already been mentioned. It was evidently a memorable experience for a sensitive young man to live in the intellectual centre of the ancient world, and many years later he recaptured something of this experience in the pleasant scene with which he introduces the fifth book of *De Finibus*. He tells how he himself, his brother Quintus, his cousin Lucius, M. Piso and Atticus walked out one afternoon to the Academy, and recalled the associations of various places in or near Athens. 'There is no end to it in this city,' says Lucius; 'wherever we tread we plant our steps on some historic spot.'[130] Perhaps these memories were revived by the fact that Cicero's son, now a young man of twenty, had just gone to Athens to study. When he addresses his son at the beginning of *De Officiis* he refers to the influence of Athens and its traditions as likely to inspire him no less than his teacher, the Peripatetic Cratippus.

The young Cicero was provided with an ample allowance, and evidently was not as conscientious a student as his father would have liked him to be. Cicero anxiously awaited reports from certain Greeks who appear to have exercised some sort of tutorial supervision,[131] and from Romans like Trebonius, who stopped at Athens on his way to his province and had some idea of taking the young Cicero with him, accompanied by Cratippus, so that study should not be neglected.[132] The young Cicero himself, writing to Tiro in the autumn of 44 B.C., claims to be a reformed character; at his father's request he had broken with his Greek rhetoric teacher, who had led him into bad ways. His relations with Cratippus were those of a son rather than a pupil. He had a warm affection for him and spent whole days and often part of the night with him. He had invited him to dine as often as he could, and Cratippus would drop in on him informally and share the jokes of the young men.[133] It is pleasant to read of this friendly informal relationship between the philosopher and his pupil, but it may be that such a relationship had its dangers. There would be some temptation to flatter and compromise with the son of a wealthy and important Roman, even when the father had as strong and genuine an interest in his son's intellectual and moral progress as Cicero had.

Such embarrassments would not be likely to arise in the case of Marcus's contemporary and fellow-student, the freedman's son Horace, though as he had mixed with the sons of senators and knights when at school in Rome he may well have attended the young Cicero's dinner parties. Horace, who tells us so much about himself, is tantalizingly brief in his account of his student days at Athens:

'adiecere bonae paulo plus artis Athenae
scilicet ut uellem curuo dinoscere rectum
atque inter siluas Academi quaerere uerum.
dura sed emouere loco me tempora grato . . .'

'Athens added a little to my education. It gave me the desire to distinguish right from wrong and to seek the truth in the groves of the Academy. But troublous times dragged me away from that pleasant spot . . .' [134]

But brief though it is, the passage is not wholly unrevealing. It shows us that Horace studied philosophy and that he studied it in the Academy. It shows too that he had warm feelings for Athens; it was a congenial place from which he was dragged away by the civil war.[135]

The two students of philosophy, one known to history only because he was the son of a famous father, the other destined to be one of the leading poets of Rome, both left their studies to fight with the Republican forces. About the end of August 44 B.C. Brutus arrived in Athens. He was welcomed as a tyrannicide and inspired the young Roman students with enthusiasm for his cause. While making preparations for war he was to be seen at the lectures of Cratippus and of the Academic Theomnestus,[136] and these philosophical studies were not merely a cover for his military preparations. He had always been a follower of philosophy; he had written a book on Virtue and no doubt he wished to strengthen himself for the task before him. It was in vain, if we can believe the story that he died exclaiming that virtue was only a name and not the reality he had taken it for.[137]

In the imperial period philosophy continued to flourish. The philosopher was a familiar figure, distinguished from his fellow-men by his beard and the rough cloak (*tribon*) which had first been adopted by the Cynics but came to be the characteristic garb of all philosophers, the uniform, one might call it, of their profession. There was little development of doctrine, little new or creative thinking, at any rate before the rise of neo-Platonism, but there was an extensive educational activity which must have influenced a considerable proportion of the population. Even those unaffected by the teaching of the philosophers would be conscious of what they had missed; Petronius's Trimalchio thought it worth while to mention in the epitaph which he devised for himself that he had never attended a philosopher's lectures.[138]

On the organization of the schools in the period from Augustus to Marcus Aurelius we are not well-informed. We learn something of the affairs of the Epicurean school from an inscription of the year 121. It appears that the head of the school then had to be a Roman citizen, and Plotina, widow of Trajan, who professes herself a sympathizer with Epicureanism, intercedes successfully with Hadrian on behalf of the Epicurean Popillius Theotimus for permission to relax this rule in future, on the ground that it limits the field unduly.[139] Under Marcus Aurelius the four schools, the Academic, the Peripatetic, the Epicurean and the Stoic, were each allotted a chair at Athens with a salary of 10,000 drachmae.[140] They had evidently maintained their separate identities and they had probably kept up their successions of heads, though the evidence on this point is meagre. Lists of successions existed in antiquity, as the Herculaneum indexes show, but there seem to have been none for the period after the end of the Roman Republic. The entry in Suidas on the Epicureans gives the number of heads of the school only as far as the beginning of the Roman Empire, and Numenius, to judge by the extract from his work on the Academy given by Eusebius, traced the succession in that school only as far as Antiochus.[141] It would, however, be unsafe to assume from such evidence that continuity was broken after the time of Augustus. This can hardly have been the case with the Epicureans, for Diogenes Laertius, answering calumnies against the school, claims that their succession has remained unbroken whereas that of almost all other schools has not.[142] This passage at first sight appears to throw doubts on the continuity of the other schools; but it could be that Diogenes, or his source, was thinking of schools such as the Megarian and the Cyrenaic which had failed to survive, rather than of the Academy, the Peripatos and the Stoa. Seneca writes of the disappearance of a number of philosophic schools;[143] he includes among them the old and the new Academy, but as Ammonius, Plutarch's Academic master, was teaching in Seneca's lifetime, we must assume that Seneca regarded the old Academy of Plato and his immediate successors and the new Academy of Arcesilaus as separate and now extinct schools. The Academy at least has a good claim to have had a continuous history; the Athenian Platonists of the fifth century evidently believed that there had been an unbroken succession, that 'Golden Cord' of which Proclus spoke, from Plato downwards.[144]

The heads of the different schools were known as *diadochoi* (successors), and the same term was applied to the holders of the imperial chairs instituted by Marcus Aurelius, who evidently took the place of the heads previously appointed by the schools themselves.[145] Independence was now lost. The task of selecting the first occupants of the chairs was entrusted to Herodes Atticus,[146] and thereafter the occupant was elected by vote of the leading Athenian citizens, the 'best' men.[147] Lucian has a satirical sketch of a contested election to the Peripatetic chair between two candidates, one of whom was a eunuch; the selectors were unable to decide whether this was a disqualification and referred the matter to Rome.[148]

There is evidence of continued imperial support for philosophers in the early third century, when Alexander of Aphrodisias refers to Septimius Severus and his son Caracalla as having appointed him, or confirmed his appointment, as teacher of the philosophy of Aristotle.[149] There are references to Platonist *diadochoi* in the third century,[150] but the use of the term cannot be taken to imply the continuance of Marcus Aurelius's endowment, and it is probable that this lapsed in the course of that century.

Athens maintained its position as the chief centre of philosophical study. Philostratus has a pleasant picture of the young students there sunbathing, studying their books, making practice speeches and disputing with one another,[151] and Lucian contrasts the freedom and simplicity of the philosophic city with the luxury and pleasure-seeking of Rome.[152] Athens was the home of plain living and high thinking, and a man who offended by an ostentatious display of wealth was educated by gentle mockery and made to conform to the Athenian code of behaviour.[153] We do not, however, hear much of Romans going to Athens in the first century. Perhaps there were enough teachers in Rome itself to make a journey elsewhere unnecessary; and when Domitian deprived Rome of philosophers men might prefer to go across the Adriatic to hear Epictetus at Nicopolis rather than seek instruction further afield. But probably there were always some Roman students in Athens; there was certainly a group of them there in the second century when Gellius was studying under the Academic Taurus.[154] Apart from Athens there must have been a number of cities in the Greek world where it was possible to get a good and varied philosophical education. In the first century Apollonius of Tyana studied at Aegae under masters of all four schools as well as under a Pythagorean;[155] in the second century Galen heard representatives of the four schools in his native city of Pergamum, and all of them were Pergamenes except the Epicurean, who came from Athens.[156] In the west there was Massilia, with its combination of Greek refinement and provincial simplicity, where the young Agricola acquired his early enthusiasm for philosophy.[157]

In Rome there were still those who kept philosophers in their households to give advice and comfort as well as instruction. Such was probably the position of Egnatius Celer, the Stoic who to the indignation of Tacitus and Juvenal gave evidence against his pupil and patron Barea Soranus.[158] Julius Canus, who was put to death under the emperor Gaius, was accompanied as he went out to his death by 'his philosopher',[159] and Demetrius the Cynic was with Thrasea during his last hours discoursing on the nature of the soul as Apollonides and another Demetrius had talked with Thrasea's model Cato before his suicide.[160] There were some Roman magnates who supported philosophers in their households without any real desire to learn from them or to see that they were treated with respect. Lucian paints a vivid picture of the indignities to which Greek intellectuals, philosophers among them, might be subjected in the household of a wealthy Roman. Even women, according to Lucian, had their philosophers, though they only had time to hear their lectures while they were dressing, doing their hair or eating, and sometimes interrupted the lecture to write a reply to a note from a lover.[161]

If the question were to be asked which of the schools was most influential in the first two centuries of the Christian era, there could be only one answer so far as Rome is concerned. For the Romans during this period philosophy meant in effect Stoicism; no other school produced teachers as influential as Musonius and Epictetus, writers as powerful as Seneca and Lucan, or a disciple as devoted as Marcus Aurelius. Epicureanism, which had been so popular at the end of the Republic, had lost ground, and little is heard of the Academic and Peripatetic schools. The Romans may have been particularly attracted to Stoicism, but there is evidence that it was also popular in the Greek-speaking part of the Empire. Lucian's Hermotimus joined the Stoics because he thought they were the most numerous sect,[162] and it may be significant that Sextus Empiricus, assuming for the sake of argument that one school has more adherents than any of the others, chooses the Stoics.[163] The Epicureans, however, seem to have had a considerable following in Asia Minor. Plutarch tells of a governor of Cilicia who had some of them in his entourage;[164] according to Lucian they were numerous in Paphlagonia and were particularly strong in their opposition to the impostor Alexander of Abonuteichus,[165] and from Lycia we have the inscription put up by the devoted Epicurean Diogenes of Oenoanda, which also provides evidence for the existence of Epicurean groups in Rhodes and elsewhere. The two older schools were, so far as we can judge, very much in the background in the first century, even in the Greek world; when St Paul visited Athens he was challenged only by the Stoics and the Epicureans.[166] After that the school of Plato began to gain ground, until finally it became virtually the only philosophy.

The third century saw a decline in the philosophical schools, of which we have interesting evidence in some remarks of Longinus, who lived from about 213 to 273.[167] As a boy he travelled a good deal with his parents, and so was in a good position to observe the philosophic scene. There was then, he says, no lack of philosophers, but when he wrote towards the end of his life there was a great dearth. He mentions nine

Platonists, three Peripatetics and eight Stoics as having flourished in his youth. He does not mention any Epicurean. The Epicureans had always stood apart from the other schools, and the fact that Longinus does not mention them could mean only that he did not think them worth mentioning. But it would not be surprising if the school had in fact died out, or was moribund by this time. It is true that at the beginning of the fourth century Lactantius still thought it worth while to argue against it, and to do so at considerable length, but there is nothing in his arguments which clearly shows that the Epicureans were an active sect.[168] The emperor Julian, writing in 363, says that most of the works of Epicurus have perished, which would hardly have been the case if there had still been a living Epicurean school.[169]

The Stoics did not survive much longer than the Epicureans. According to St Augustine, writing in 387, there were then virtually no philosophers to be seen other than Platonists, Peripatetics and Cynics,[170] and some years later he says that the Epicureans and Stoics have now been so completely silenced that it is scarcely thought worth while to recall their views in the schools of rhetoric.[171] This is certainly true of the Epicureans. The Stoics had not been completely silenced, for their works were still studied in the neo-Platonist schools; but they had ceased to exist as an independent school. The two philosophies, Epicurean and Stoic, which had made so strong an impression on the world in the Hellenistic period and under the early Empire, showed less power of survival than the older and more intellectual schools of Plato and Aristotle.

Although Augustine mentions Peripatetics as still to be met with towards the end of the fourth century, there is some doubt whether the school at that time still maintained its separate identity. There is evidence from the mid and later third century of Peripatetic schools in Athens and Alexandria.[172] But from the days when Ammonius Saccas reconciled the doctrines of Plato and Aristotle,[173] the Platonist school tended to absorb the Aristotelian. Aristotle continued to be studied, but by philosophers who were primarily Platonists.

The school of Plato also absorbed the Pythagoreans. Pythagoreanism, as we have seen, had died out in the fourth century B.C., but it came to life again in the first century. This appears to have been one of the rare cases of an intellectual movement originating in Rome if, as Cicero believed, the man responsible for reviving Pythagoreanism was his learned contemporary Nigidius Figulus.[174] It may be that in spite of what our authorities say about its extinction it had continued to exist underground and had passed to Rome from south Italy. Whether it was a case of survival or of revival, Pythagoreanism certainly had some, though a limited, influence in Rome from the time of Nigidius Figulus. Sotion was expounding the Pythagorean doctrine of transmigration of souls in Rome when Seneca was a boy.[175] The conversations about Pythagoreanism recorded by Plutarch are represented as taking place in Rome, and the Pythagorean who is present at the discussion is a Lucius from Etruria.[176] Pythagoreanism, however, was not confined to the West; though Lucius's teacher Moderatus came from Spain, Euxenus, from whom Apollonius of Tyana learned his Pythagoreanism, was from Heraclea in Pontus.[177]

The Life of Apollonius of Tyana by Philostratus, though it contains a considerable element of fiction, gives us what is presumably a fairly reliable picture of the Pythagorean life under the Empire. It depicts Apollonius as a wandering ascetic and wonder worker with a varying number of followers, at one time seven, at a later stage thirty-four, who were subsequently reduced to eight.[178] He himself had been taught by a Pythagorean of mediocre attainments whom he soon outgrew.[179] Thereafter, it seems, he was his own master. He gave up eating flesh and drinking wine, and wore garments of linen.[180] He resolved to remain celibate, in this respect going further than Pythagoras himself, who had been married and had allowed and indeed recommended marriage to others.[181] He also observed the five years' silence, but evidently as a self-imposed discipline rather than as part of a probationary training.[182]

Some features of the Pythagorean discipline were adopted by those who would not have described themselves as Pythagoreans. Diodotus, Cicero's Stoic teacher, used to play the lyre, 'in the manner of the Pythagoreans'.[183] Sextius, an independent Roman philosopher of the Augustan age, whose position was closer to Stoicism than to any other school, refrained from animal food, though without accepting the Pythagorean doctrine of transmigration of souls.[184] He also used to practise self-examination each night, and would ask himself what fault he had committed during the day, what vice he had resisted and in what way he had improved. Seneca followed the same rule. When the light had been removed and his wife, knowing his habits, had stopped talking, he would review the past day and examine all his acts and words.[185]

There were also close relations between Pythagoreanism and Platonism. The doctrines of the two schools were combined and harmonized in the writings of Numenius, and the lives of Pythagoras by Porphyry and Iamblichus provide evidence of the interest in his teaching and way of life shown by the neo-Platonists. Pythagoreanism was in fact absorbed into neo-Platonism. Pythagoreans, as we can see from Justin Martyr's account of his philosophical pilgrimage, were to be met with in the second century;[186] by the next century Pythagoreanism as an independent school had probably died out.

Finally there were the Cynics. Cynicism can hardly be described as a school of philosophy and is only of slight relevance to the subject of higher education; yet it can hardly be passed over in any account of the philosophers of the Empire. Cynicism was a way of life. Its adherents cultivated poverty and self-sufficiency, rejected the values of conventional society and preached a gospel of reducing wants to the minimum. They lived the life of wandering beggars, trained to endure hardship, 'naked', as Epictetus puts it, 'without home or hearth, squalid, without slave, without city'.[187] Marked out by staff and wallet in addition to the usual beard and worn cloak of the philosopher, they were to be seen throughout the Greek-speaking world in the imperial period, at once admired and scorned by their fellow-men. They had no organization or central direction. There was some continuity throughout the ages from the time of Diogenes and Crates, and no doubt in any period a leading figure among the Cynics would attract disciples and to some extent assume their direction, as Peregrinus did in the second century. Cynics, however, were essentially independent, and normally each of them would go his own way as free from direction and organization as he was from other ties.

With one of the philosophic schools, the Stoic, the Cynics had a close relationship. Zeno had originally been a pupil of Crates. Panaetius, it is true, had no use for the Cynic way of life;[188] it was wholly alien to the aristocratic Roman society in which he moved, and it made no headway in Rome of the Republican period. But later on, in the first century after Christ, we find a much more sympathetic attitude in the Stoa. The Cynic Demetrius was closely associated with the Roman Stoics Seneca and Thrasea. Epictetus was well disposed to Cynicism, and presents it as a worthy and exacting ideal in the advice he gives to one of his pupils who had thoughts of adopting it.[189]

The Cynics were teachers in the sense that they lectured or preached, and sometimes wrote. But they did not hold school like the professors of the other sects. Some are recorded as having pupils, and Aulus Gellius heard 'many useful and noble precepts' from Peregrinus; this, however, was not in a lecture hall, but in a hut which cannot have accommodated many visitors.[190] Apart from receiving individual visitors the Cynics taught in the open. Instead of instructing a band of pupils within doors they held forth to the ordinary people wherever they could collect an audience. In Epictetus's phrase the Cynic was the common educator of mankind as a whole.[191]

These would-be educators were not themselves always well educated. Julian counts it to the credit of Cynicism that it does not require any special study or the reading of numerous books.[192] Critics of the Cynics represented them as men of little learning or culture, humble artisans who gave up their work and took up the wallet and staff and with no preparation changed from tanners or building craftsmen to wandering preachers.[193] According to Dio Chrysostom, who was influenced by Cynicism and for a time followed the Cynic way of life himself, many of them were ignorant men interested only in begging their bread, who collected an audience of children or sailors in some public place and entertained them with jokes and vulgarity; they achieved no good, and only made foolish people laugh at philosophers.[194]

The schools of the Empire

Ars est enim philosophia uitae, says Cicero.[195] Philosophy is the art, or science, of living. The word *ars* meant something that could be and was expounded systematically by professional

G

teachers. The art of living no less than the other arts, grammar, rhetoric, geometry and the rest, could be taught. If all could live with nature as guide, to quote Cicero again, there would be no need for learning. As it is, the sparks of virtue within us are extinguished by bad customs and mistaken opinions or, to use Cicero's other metaphor, the seeds of virtue are not allowed to grow.[196] But teaching, it was believed, could remove these hindrances, so that man could attain to that state of blessedness which was potentially within the capacity of everyone. The art of living then had its teachers, the philosophers. They trained the minds of the young and taught them morality, comforted and sustained those in trouble and healed the diseases of the soul. They combined the functions of the priest, the professor and the psychiatrist of the modern world.

They had their schools, or lecture rooms, with a chair for the master and benches for the pupils, and they held forth at regular times.[197] Sometimes they gave open lectures, and we hear of public disputations between members of different schools,[198] but normally teaching was carried out within the school walls for the benefit of the regular students. In most cases fees were charged. In theory, no doubt, the philosophers should have followed the example of Socrates and taught free of charge, and there were some who did so;[199] but philosophers like other men had to live, and it is not surprising that they did not usually teach for nothing and that sometimes their interest in their fees seemed out of keeping with their professed indifference to money.[200]

Plutarch's treatise on listening to lectures, or 'Students' Guide', as it might be called, gives us a picture of the inside of a philosopher's school. We read of the lecturer with his grey hair and serious brow, his formal manner and air of self-approbation which may unduly impress the inexperienced; of students who show signs of boredom and inattention, who are indifferent or even laugh when rebuked, and who look cheerful and hum a tune when leaving the school though they should be pondering their faults. We get the impression of an audience less orderly and more demonstrative than that which a modern lecturer commonly faces. They shout their approval of a popular lecturer, and use outlandish or inappropriate expressions of admiration; they have to be advised not to get excited and interrupt with objections, not to be excessive in their expressions of approval, but to listen quietly and attentively.[201]

Teaching would involve the reading of texts, formal lectures and informal discussions. The texts read would be the writings of the masters of the school to which the teacher adhered. The school of Plato, which had shown signs of forgetting its founder under Arcesilaus and Carneades, returned to him and to the reverent study of his writings. The Peripatetic school, which at one time had seemed likely to do little but cultivate the art of speaking on set themes, became primarily a school for the study of Aristotelian texts. The Stoics studied Chrysippus and the Epicureans, of course, Epicurus. While each school expounded the doctrines of its founder, or in the case of the Stoics its 'second founder', the Academy was not so exclusive as the others and was ready to admit Aristotle, whose *Problemata* Aulus Gellius read with his master Taurus.[202] Among Plato's works Taurus found that his students showed a preference for the more entertaining works, particularly those with an erotic interest; he used to complain that they wanted to read the *Symposium* because of the passage where Alcibiades comes in drunk and the *Phaedrus* because of Lysias's speech on how a youth should behave to his lovers.[203] But though he may have disapproved, the *Symposium* was one of the works which Taurus himself read with his pupils.[204]

The method followed would be similar to that known in the Roman grammar schools as *praelectio*, the reading of a text with explanatory commentary. Epictetus draws the parallel between himself and the *grammaticus* expounding his poetical texts, but is careful to point out the difference. The philosopher must not only understand his author, but must also carry out his precepts:

What is my object? To understand Nature and to follow her. I look then for someone who interprets her, and having heard that Chrysippus does, I come to him. But I do not understand his writings, so I seek an interpreter. So far there is nothing to be proud of. But when I have found the interpreter, it remains for me to act on his precepts, and that alone is a thing to be proud of. But if I admire the mere power of exposition, it comes to this—

that I have turned into a grammarian instead of a philosopher, except that I interpret Chrysippus in place of Homer. Therefore when someone says to me 'Read me Chrysippus', when I cannot point to actions which are in harmony and correspondence with his teaching I am rather inclined to blush.[205]

The students themselves read from the texts in class and the master explained them. The procedure is described in slighting terms by Fronto, who as a rhetorician by profession thought his discipline better than that of the philosophers. 'Yes, you would read a book to your philosopher; you would listen in silence while the master explained it; you would nod to show you understood; while others read you would generally go to sleep.'[206] Epictetus describes himself as waking up in the morning and thinking what author he has to expound that day. Then he says to himself: 'But what business of mine is it how so-and-so reads?'[207] From another passage we gather that he used assistants, presumably more advanced students, to set texts for reading. A pupil was studying a work on hypo-thetical arguments and was disconcerted by Epictetus's criti-cisms. The man who had set the passage laughed, at which Epictetus said: 'You are really laughing at yourself; you did not train the lad first and discover whether he could follow the passage; you merely used him as a reader.'[208]

Some written work was apparently demanded, and there were exercises in logic, whether oral or written.[209] The student was also expected to know something of what may be called the literature of the subject and, as always in education, there were those who were content with second-hand information and did not read the original sources or, if they did, did not form their own opinion.[210] Some time too was given to confuting the doctrines of other schools.[211] But on the whole there was not much interest in philosophical scholarship or in controversy, at any rate in the Stoic school, of which thanks to Epictetus we know most; the important thing was the training of character.

Formal lectures (and here again the evidence comes mainly from the Stoic school) were in the nature of moral exhorta-tions; one might well call them sermons. These discourses may have arisen out of the reading of texts, or they may have been prompted by questions, whether genuine or inspired, on the part of the students. But however they were introduced they gave the opportunity for impressive and eloquent performances, not unlike the declamations of the rhetoricians. The younger Pliny sings the praises of Euphrates, a dignified figure with his long white beard, whose eloquence had something of the Platonic breadth and sublimity, and whose style of speaking was so attractive that even the unwilling were forced to listen. 'You would listen to his admonitions attentively and in eager anticipation, and you would long to be convinced, even when he has convinced you.'[212] Seneca's teacher Attalus was a man of great eloquence.[213] When he denounced the vices and follies of mankind, Seneca felt pity for his fellow-men; when he praised poverty, he wished he was a poor man.[214] There were dangers in the cult of eloquence, and the more earnest philosophers warn against being more interested in the language than in the matter, against lecturing merely to win applause or attending lectures merely to applaud.[215] Some people, says Seneca, go to the lecture room as if to a theatre, not to learn but to be entertained. They merely want to enjoy the pleasures of the ear, and if they bring their notebooks with them it is to take down not the matter but the words. Seneca makes it clear, however, that eloquence has its value; people are impressed by words, and there is some hope that the impression may be more than momentary. We learn too from Seneca that the philosophic preacher used to introduce lines of verse with the hope of bringing his message home more effectively. One listens carelessly to prose, whereas the sentiment is more forceful when expressed in verse:

> Much is said about despising money, and this is the theme of speeches in which men are urged at great length to believe riches to lie in one's mind, not in one's patrimony, and the wealthy man to be him who adapts himself to his poverty and makes himself rich on a small sum. Yet our minds are struck more forcibly when lines like these are added:
>
> > 'His needs are least who least desires.'
> > 'He has his wish who can his wish confine
> > To that which is enough.'

. . . Even those for whom nothing is enough express
admiration and applaud and declare their hatred of
money. When you see them so disposed, press on, strike
home, lay it on, abandon ambiguities, syllogisms,
hair-splitting and other trivialities of futile cleverness.
Speak against avarice and luxury. When you see you have
made progress and touched the hearts of the listeners,
attack more strongly; it is hardly credible what a speech
of this sort can do when it is aimed at curing the hearers
and directed towards their good.[216]

As a reaction perhaps from the charm and eloquence of the
popular preachers some Stoics cultivated an almost brusque
and forbidding manner. Musonius used deliberately to dis-
courage his pupils in the hope of weeding out the unsuitable.
His discourses were directed towards making his hearers conscious of their weaknesses; 'he spoke', says his pupil Epictetus,
'in such a way that each of us sitting there thought that someone had told him of our faults'.[217] It seems to have been from
Musonius that Epictetus derived his habit of addressing his
pupils as 'slave'.[218] Epictetus himself could seem brusque and
unsympathetic, 'an old man with no kindness in him'.[219] This
mode of teaching, however discouraging it might seem, was
certainly effective; Musonius and Epictetus made a stronger
impression on their pupils and on posterity than did the other
philosophers of the day.

The asking of questions by the students was encouraged,
though only within limits. As Plutarch puts it, just as a guest at
dinner has to eat what is put before him, so one who attends a
lecture must listen in silence and not interpose questions and
raise difficulties, except when the lecturer invites him to. And
the questions should not be petty or quibbling or designed only
to show off the speaker's knowledge. Account should be taken
of the lecturer's limitations; the moral philosopher should not be
faced with problems in physics or mathematics or the natural
philosopher with logical difficulties.[220] Questions might be
asked in class, when invited, but there were also opportunities
for putting them privately after the class was finished.[221] Thus
Attalus was always ready to enter into discussions with his
pupils.[222] Taurus used to give his hearers the opportunity of

putting any question they liked to him after his daily discourses, and Gellius recalls how he once asked whether a wise
man got angry, and received in reply a lengthy exposition of
his master's views on the subject.[223]

The discourses of Musonius and Epictetus provide a number
of examples of the questions asked by those who attended their
schools. These are sometimes of a general nature, sometimes
concerned with personal problems. Musonius is asked whether
philosophy is suited to women, whether sons and daughters
should be given the same education, what is the best provision
for old age.[224] One inquirer asks Epictetus how one can eat in a
manner pleasing to the gods, another how one can be convinced
that everything one does is overlooked by God.[225] Other
questions put to Epictetus are what is meant by 'general
perception' and how it is that in spite of all the work done on
logic at the time greater progress was made in earlier days.[226]
More personal questions are those of the youth prevented by
his father from engaging in philosophy who asks Musonius
whether one should always obey one's father,[227] or of the man
who asks Epictetus how he can stop his brother from being
angry with him and, when told to send the brother to Epictetus, puts the further question how he can be in accord with
nature even if his brother refuses to be reconciled to him.[228]
The man who is contemplating becoming a Cynic puts his
question in a general form—what sort of man a Cynic ought to
be—but the answer shows that he is really asking for advice
about his own course of action.[229] In Epictetus's school questions were evidently not disallowed while the master was discoursing. Epictetus is holding forth on 'how a man can preserve his proper character in all circumstances'. He tells of an
athlete who chose to die rather than have his private parts
amputated; someone asks whether he did this as athlete or as
philosopher, and a little later there is a further question, how
each of us can become aware of what is appropriate to his own
character.[230]

Epictetus did not merely use a question as a peg on which to
hang a lecture; he would often proceed in the Socratic manner
by interrogating the inquirer.[231] He spoke frankly to those who
consulted him, and was prepared to risk offending them. The
philosopher's business was to correct the faults of those who

came to him, and those who had faults must be prepared to have them pointed out. The elegantly dressed young student of rhetoric has to listen to a long disquisition on the care of the body. 'If I say what I think,' says Epictetus, 'I shall hurt your feelings and you won't come to me again.' But if he does not say what he thinks he will be doing no good at all. 'You have come to me as to a philosopher, and I shall have said nothing to you as a philosopher. And from your own point of view is it not cruel to leave you unreformed?'[232] The middle-aged man who attended Epictetus's classes with his son resents being questioned at his time of life. Epictetus tells him that the things he has hitherto been concerned with are not the things that matter in life, that he knows nothing of God or man, good or evil, or of himself, and expects him to go away offended. He compares himself (it is a common comparison) to a physician; the patient does not object to being told by his physician that he has a fever, but if the philosopher tells a man that he is mentally ill the man immediately walks out and says, 'He has insulted me.'[233] Since these exchanges are recorded by Arrian they presumably took place in the presence of other members of the class. The physician of the soul, it seems, did not see his patients privately; they had to submit to being corrected and cured in public.

We have seen how in the early days of the Academy the study of philosophy was fostered and sweetened by social gatherings. This tradition was not forgotten. Plutarch tells of celebrations of the birthdays of Socrates and Plato, and as we find the neo-Platonists also observing these anniversaries we may assume that they were traditional in the school of Plato.[234] Plutarch describes a dinner given by Ammonius, and Gellius was invited with some other students to Taurus's house for a meal followed by wine and discussion. Each of Taurus's guests brought with him some tricky problem, not to be taken too seriously but suited to after-dinner discussion, such as When does a dying man die, when he is already dead or when still alive? When does a man get up, when he is standing or when still sitting? When does a learner become proficient in some subject, when he is proficient or before?[235] The social gatherings with learned conversation which Plutarch records were often attended by philosophers, and at one of them an Epicurean, Boethus, was the host.²³⁶ Stoics, at any rate the more austere members of the school, would be less likely to engage in social activities of this sort. Persius, however, recalls pleasant evenings spent with Cornutus:

> With you I wore away long hours of light,
> With you for feasting snatched the uncoming night.
> Both work and relaxation did we share,
> Tempering our gravity with modest fare.²³⁷

The morality which the philosophers taught was one of self-restraint and self-discipline, and a certain asceticism of life was expected of those who followed their precepts. The importance of self-control in food and drink was a frequent theme with Musonius.²³⁸ Attalus demanded chastity and sobriety, and recommended the use of a hard cushion that did not give when one sat on it.²³⁹ Some believed in harsher forms of discipline than this, and used beating or scraping the skin with a knife blade, and their critics claimed that some of their pupils had died as a result of these rigours. Such methods were, however, repudiated by the Platonist Nigrinus, who held that endurance was more a matter of the soul than the body and that account should be taken of age and previous training.²⁴⁰ The gentlemanly pupils of the Academy would perhaps not be disposed to submit themselves to much discipline. Ammonius devised for them a kind of vicarious punishment. Observing that some of his students had fed too well he ordered a freed-man to beat one of his slaves in the presence of the class on the ground that he could not lunch without wine, and while this was going on he looked pointedly at his class, hoping that they would draw the moral.²⁴¹

Serious-minded youths were susceptible enough to the ex-hortations of the philosophers to put their precepts into prac-tice. Marcus Aurelius began to practise the ascetic life in his twelfth year and slept on the ground until he was persuaded by his mother to change to a bed strewn with skins.²⁴² Seneca took to heart the exhortations of Attalus, and kept up some of his early practices later. He continued as an old man to use a hard cushion; he abstained from eating oysters and mushrooms; he did not drink wine, and avoided bathing. Other youthful austerities did not last. Under the influence of Sotion he became a vegetarian for a time, but was persuaded by his father, who was not well disposed to philosophy, to give it up; 'nor did he find much difficulty in persuading me to dine better'.[243]

Philosophy might also have some influence in keeping the young from sexual indulgence. In one of Lucian's sketches a young man gives up his mistress on the orders of his philosophy teacher, who says that virtue should be preferred to pleasure.[244] Musonius insisted that sexual intercourse should be confined to the begetting of children in wedlock, and Dio Chrysostom, if he can be counted among the philosophers, made an effective attack on the sexual laxity of his contemporaries in his Euboean oration.[245] It is rather surprising to find Epictetus more tolerant than his master Musonius on this point. Preserve chastity, he says, before marriage as far as you can, and if you do not, confine yourself to what is lawful; but do not be censorious about those who indulge and do not keep referring to the fact that you abstain.[246]

As is obvious from what has been said already, philosophy was looked on as providing moral just as much as intellectual education. The theory was that when a boy grew up and discarded the masters and guardians of his childhood, he had to learn to guide himself by reason. 'You have often heard,' writes Plutarch, 'that following God is the same as following reason, and so you should realize that the transition from childhood to manhood does not for those who think aright mean the casting off of discipline but a change of master; instead of some hired person or bought slave they take a divine guide to life, namely reason, whose followers alone deserve to be considered free.'[247] The lessons of reason imparted by a respected teacher kept the adolescent from the temptations with which he was surrounded when he became his own master. So Persius describes the influence of Cornutus. After assuming the garb of manhood, when he was free to do as he liked and to sample the pleasures of the town:

> When life's perplexing maze before me lay,
> And error, heedless of the better way,
> To straggling paths, far from the route of truth,
> Woo'd, with blind confidence, my timorous youth,

I fled to you, Cornutus, pleased to rest
My hopes and fears on your Socratick breast,
Nor did you, gentle sage, the charge decline:
Then, dextrous to beguile, your steady line
Reclaim'd, I know not with what winning force,
My morals, warp'd from virtue's straighter course;
While reason press'd incumbent on my soul,
That struggled to receive the strong control,
And took like wax, temper'd by plastic skill,
The form your hand imposed; and bears it still![248]

Parents sent their children to philosophers in the hope that their characters would improve. As Epictetus puts it, young men leave their home and their parents and go to philosophers in order to become forbearing, ready to help one another, tranquil, with a mind at peace.[249] That the philosophers' lessons did not always bear fruit is only what was to be expected. Lucian tells of a young man who, according to his uncle, a simple countryman with no knowledge of philosophy, so far from improving as a result of his lessons had got worse. He had seduced his neighbour's daughter, beaten his mother when she found him stealing some wine, and was more prone to anger, shamelessness and lying than before. He argued at meal-times, confused his family with logical puzzles, told them that God was not in heaven but pervaded everything and that he himself would eventually be the only wise man and the only king of the Stoic paradoxes. His teacher's answer was that the boy would have been much worse if he had not attended his classes. In other respects he was a good pupil; he had read the books and could answer questions correctly. 'If he has beaten his mother and seduced virgins, what is that to me?'[250]

Philosophers were naturally unwilling to admit that their instructions were of no avail. As Seneca put it, those who attended philosophers must, unless they were wholly recalcitrant, derive some benefit, as a man who exposes himself to the sun gets sunburnt even if he does not want to.[251] Others would have claimed more than this. Musonius considered that the young man who was forbidden by his father to study philosophy would be justified in disobeying him. If the father was not persuaded to change his mind, his son's conduct would surely win him over. For as a student of philosophy he would do his best to treat his father with consideration, would be well-behaved and gentle, never quarrelsome or selfish, self-controlled and not prone to anger, would willingly give up all pleasures and accept all hardships for his father's sake. What father would not pray for such a son?[252] Through philosophy, according to the treatise on education attributed to Plutarch, one can learn 'what is honourable and what is dishonourable, what is just and unjust, in short what is to be chosen and what avoided, how one should behave towards the gods, one's parents, one's elders, the laws, strangers, those in authority, friends, women, children, servants; that one should reverence the gods, honour one's parents, respect one's elders, obey the laws, submit to those in authority, love one's friends, be chaste with women, affectionate towards children and not insolent towards slaves; and most important of all, not to rejoice excessively in good fortune or grieve excessively in ill fortune, not to be unrestrained in pleasure or passionate and wild in anger'.[253] This hardly suggests the syllabus of a philosophy department in a modern university; much of it reminds one rather of what the Church catechism teaches about man's duty towards his neighbour.[254] A philosopher's school indeed had something of the character of a Confirmation class.

Some, however, remained unimpressed by the claims of philosophy. Cornelius Nepos refused to allow that it could be the guide to life when most of its teachers themselves needed a master, and when men who preached continence in the schools generally gave way to every lust in private life.[255] A friend of Seneca's, whom he was trying to reform, met his attempts with jests, and pointed to philosophers who took money, kept mistresses, and enjoyed the pleasures of the table.[256] The failings of the professional teachers of morality were an obvious target for the satirist. Lucian has an account of a dinner given in honour of the betrothal of the host's daughter to a young student of philosophy. The host's son is also studying philosophy, and the philosophers are there in force. They misbehave disgracefully. First the Stoic and the Epicurean quarrel over the seating, then the Stoic is observed eating with disgusting greed. A Cynic comes uninvited and launches into an attack on the host's luxury until he is silenced for a time by a large cup of strong wine. Later on a slave comes in with a letter from another Stoic complaining that he has not been invited and hinting at improper relations between one of the philosophers and his pupil, the host's son. The Peripatetic, the Stoic and the Epi-curean begin to abuse one another; the Peripatetic takes the Stoic by the beard and is about to strike him when the host steps in and separates them. But they soon start quarrelling again, and end by fighting. Tables are overturned and cups are thrown. The lamp is knocked down, and when light is brought again the Cynic is found trying to seduce a flute player.[257]

When the absent Stoic's letter was read out, the philosopher and his pupil who were mentioned in it showed evident signs of embarrassment. The incident is of course fictitious, but it has some plausibility, for the Stoic had touched on a point where the philosophers were vulnerable. The circle in which Socrates moved and which had been so brilliantly described by Plato was one in which paederasty was accepted, and in the early days of Athenian philosophy there was often a strong element of emotion in the relation of master and pupil.[258] Even the Stoics, for all their rejection of the emotions, held that 'the wise man would love young men whose good looks indicated their dis-position to virtue'.[259] As time went on public opinion became less favourable to paederastic love but, as the treatise on education ascribed to Plutarch shows, the Platonic tradition was not forgotten. The author approaches his subject with evident embarrassment, conscious that many fathers would not allow their sons to have lovers. But, he says, 'when I consider Socrates, Plato, Xenophon, Aeschines, Cebes, and all that band of men who approved of love between males and who brought up the young to learning, political leadership and virtuous conduct, I change my mind'. He goes on, however, to distinguish the man who is attracted by physical beauty only from the true lover, the lover of the soul, the only sort that should be allowed.[260] This embarrassing ghost haunted even the school of Plotinus, the man who was ashamed of his body. There was an occasion when, during a celebration of Plato's birthday, a speech was delivered, prompted by the account given in the *Symposium* of Alcibiades's relations with Socrates, in praise of the physical *eros* which the philosophers had always in theory rejected. Plotinus was not amused, and he commissioned Porphyry to write and deliver a reply.[261]

The idealized love of the philosophers was regarded with a certain cynical scepticism by those outside the schools, and it was suspected that the teachers' interest in their pupils was less purely intellectual than they liked to maintain.[262] Perhaps there was some ground for these suspicions, which were certainly widespread; but if, as is likely enough, some philosophers abused their position, there is no reason to suppose that they were the only teachers to do so.

We should not, however, take the gibes of satirists too seriously. In all ages men have resented the pretensions of those who claim to be better than their fellow-men and have delighted in displaying them as subject to human weaknesses. Philosophers in the ancient world were regarded much as monks and friars, Puritans, Methodists and Evangelicals have been regarded in more recent times. One would not judge the Jesuits from a sentence in *Candide* or the friars from a chapter in *Roderick Random*, nor would one assume that all Evangelical clergy were like Trollope's Mr Slope. Similarly we should not take as serious evidence all that is said about the morals of philosophers in the writers of antiquity. It may be that some were as greedy, quarrelsome and licentious as their critics maintained, and it would certainly be surprising if they all lived up to the exacting standards which they set themselves. But at the least we can say of the philosophers what Zeus says to Dike in Lucian's *Bis Accusatus*: 'Most of them have gained no small benefit from philosophy; if nothing else, respect for their cloth makes them moderate their wrongdoing.' There were some bad ones and some who were a mixture, but 'they are not all bad; it's enough if you meet with some good ones'.[263]

The philosophers, though often mocked, were on the whole respected. Parents sent their children to them to learn how to live aright, and no doubt they expected that the boys would profit by what they learned; but in their hearts perhaps they did not want the lessons to be taken too seriously, much as a modern parent who would think it only right to give his son a religious education might not be too pleased if the boy decided to be ordained, much less if he wanted to enter a religious order. As for the boys, they might well be impressed, as the young Seneca and the young Agricola were, by the teaching they received and resolve to guide their lives by it. A few persisted in their resolve. With others, even apart from possible parental discouragement, early enthusiasm might fade. As they grew up they would find that they could get on well enough without the ministrations of the physicians of the soul, at any rate while things went well with them; if faced with bereavement or loss of possessions they would be more inclined to welcome the consolations of philosophy.[264] Self-righteousness and arrogant claims to be above human weaknesses were naturally resented, but the philosophers were the only teachers of wisdom and morality, and the ancient world could not do without them until Christianity provided a new way by which to attain to the good life.

The neo-Platonist schools

We have seen in an earlier chapter how Longinus lamented the decline of philosophy in his lifetime. This decline, however, was more one of quantity than of quality, for it was in this period that philosophy attained a new lease of life with Plotinus, who studied under Ammonius Saccas in Alexandria, came to Rome in the middle of the third century and taught there for twenty-five years. Though there had been teachers of philosophy in Rome before then, most of them Greeks and teaching in Greek, as Plotinus did, this otherwise barren period in the history of Roman culture was, strangely enough, the only one in which Rome was the most important philosophical centre of the ancient world.

When Plotinus died in 270 after retiring to Campania in the previous year, his chief pupil Porphyry was in Sicily.[265] His school might have died with him if Porphyry had not returned to Rome and carried on his work. He gave public lectures, and succeeded in popularizing his master's doctrines and making them intelligible to the ordinary listener;[266] but we have no information about his later years and he is not known to have left any successors in Rome.[267] His influence lived on there in Christians such as Manlius Theodorus and Marius Victorinus and pagans such as Macrobius, and we hear of one neo-Platonist teacher, Celsus son of Archetimus, in Rome in the later fourth century;[268] but whether there was any continuity in the teaching of philosophy there we do not know.

It is to the East that we must turn for the history of philosophical teaching after Porphyry. We turn first to Syria, where Porphyry's pupil Iamblichus taught, probably at Apamea.[269] Pupils flocked to him from all quarters. His popularity is attributed to his close contact with the gods; for with Iamblichus neo-Platonism merges with mysticism and magic and the philosopher becomes the seer and wonder worker, the hierophant of paganism. His disciples believed, though he himself did not encourage the belief, that when alone at his devotions he soared aloft into the air and his body and clothing were turned to gold. Stories were told of how he manifested his divine nature, how on returning from a sacrifice he turned aside from the road because he divined that a dead body had been carried that way, and how from two springs of water he conjured up the mysterious apparitions of Eros and Anteros.[270] Iamblichus left no permanent school behind him. His pupils dispersed after his death, and Aedesius, who was considered to be his successor, opened a school in Pergamum, while one of Aedesius's pupils, Maximus, migrated to Ephesus.[271] It was Maximus whom Julian invited to Constantinople in the winter of 361–2 and who had his brief period of fame and influence as the emperor's philosophic adviser. He was with Julian at the moment of his death, and like Demetrius with Thrasea before his death, discoursed with him on the nature of the soul.[272]

Julian's revival of pagan worship and neo-Platonist beliefs died with him, and it is useless to speculate how the philosophers might have fared as the official theologians of an established pagan church. As it was they continued to teach, but their direct influence on the world in which they lived was small. The main centres of teaching were Athens and Alexandria.

Athens had the greater prestige, as the home of the *diadochoi*, the successors of Plato. The school had long ceased to occupy the Academy; in Proclus's time its headquarters was a house in the city, close to the temple of Asclepius and that of Dionysus near the theatre, which before Proclus succeeded to the headship had been occupied in turn by his two predecessors, Plutarchus and Syrianus.[273] But it was conscious of its long history going back to Plato. It was probably not large, but it was a fairly flourishing institution and in process of time had acquired property of its own. No fees were charged. The younger Olympiodorus, who taught at Alexandria in the sixth century, believed that this practice went back to Plato; 'perhaps', he says, 'Plato was able to teach free of charge because he was well off, and this is why up to the present time the property of the Platonic succession has been preserved in spite of the fact that there have been a number of confiscations'.[274] Damascius, on the other hand, states that Plato was a poor man, and that the property of the succession did not date from his time; the school, however, acquired a considerable revenue as a result of legacies.[275]

It remained a stronghold of paganism in a largely Christian world. Philosophical study was combined with religious practices and wonder working. Plotinus, for all his asceticism and mysticism, was essentially rational and intellectual; Proclus as depicted by Marinus is a kind of semi-divine figure. He was assiduous in his religious observances, and his devotions were directed equally to the gods of Greece and those of other peoples. Every month he practised the ritual purifications of the cult of Cybele; he observed the unlucky days of the Egyptians and added days of fasting revealed to him in visions. The new moon was celebrated with all solemnity. The day was punctuated by acts of worship to the sun at its rising, at midday and at sunset. Feast days were observed with prayer and hymns and sacrifices.[276] He is credited with having brought an end to a drought by his magical arts and having stopped an earthquake. He cured the daughter of his master Plutarchus by prayer to Asclepius; he uttered prophecies and received revelations in dreams.[277] His person was surrounded by an aura of divinity; on one occasion a visitor to the school saw his head haloed with light and at the end of the lecture prostrated himself in worship.[278] At the same time Proclus led a strenuous life as teacher and writer; he lectured five times a day or more often, besides writing about seven hundred lines and engaging in discussions in the evenings.[279]

After Proclus's death in 485 there were troubles in the school the exact nature of which it is not easy to discover,[280] and Aeneas of Gaza, writing towards the end of the fifth century, states that philosophy is quite unknown in Athens.[281] This no

H

doubt is an exaggeration. The succession was kept up, and the school continued. It continued until 529, when the emperor Justinian forbade heretics and pagans to teach, decreeing that only those of the orthodox faith should engage in teaching and receive support from the authorities;[282] there was also a specific rescript directed against the Athenian school, forbidding the teaching of philosophy there.[283] Damascius, the last head of the school, and six others, including the Aristotelian commentator Simplicius, had hopes of finding a greater sympathy for philosophy elsewhere. They believed that in Persia, under its king Chosroes, they would find a virtuous community living in accordance with the precepts of philosophy, and there they took refuge. They had some ground for their hopes. Chosroes was a patron of learning; Nestorian scholars from Edessa had taken refuge at his capital of Jundīshāpūr, and at his instance Persian translations were made of Plato and Aristotle.[284] The seven philosophers were, however, soon disillusioned. They found that Persia was no better than anywhere else, and they returned to Athens in 532 or 533. Chosroes, however, proved a good friend to them; in a treaty of peace which he made with Justinian it was specifically laid down that the philosophers should be allowed to live unmolested in spite of their opinions.[285] At least one of them, Simplicius, continued to write and remained faithful to his pagan beliefs. Indeed it may well be that the school of Plato did not come to an end in 529 but continued to function for a time after the return of the philosophers.[286]

Little is known of the Alexandrian school between Ammonius Saccas at the beginning of the third century and Hypatia, who was killed by a fanatical mob in 415. Among her pupils was the Christian bishop Synesius, who expresses a certain resentment at the pretensions of Athens. He complains of the arrogant attitude of the Athenians; though they were no better versed in Plato and Aristotle than the Alexandrians, they thought themselves superior simply because of the traditions of their city. They had nothing to boast of but the famous names of Academy, Lyceum and Stoa; the former home of philosophy was now noted only for honey.[287] Whatever may have been the case when Synesius wrote, in the later fifth century Athens had something more to offer than its honey, and its close contact with Alexandria is likely to have removed any feelings of rivalry and resentment that the Alexandrians may have once felt. Hermeias of Alexandria was a pupil of Syrianus, head of the Athenian school, who was himself an Alexandrian by origin. Proclus studied under the elder Olympiodorus at Alexandria, and he was in turn glad to receive as pupils the two sons of Hermeias, who were brought to Athens by their mother Aedesia, who was herself a relative of Syrianus.[288] One of these sons, Ammonius, became a teacher at Alexandria, and numbered Damascius, head of the Athenian school, among his pupils.

In the fifth century the school of Alexandria flourished. Hierocles adorned it 'by his lofty spirit and his sublimity of language and combined solemnity and grandeur with an exceptional richness of invention, and excelling in fluency and abundance of fine words never ceased to astound his hearers, rivalling Plato in beauty of language and depth of thought'.[289] Later in the century, if we can believe one of Hierocles's old pupils, the school declined; those enrolled as students had no desire to learn, the teachers were incompetent and the schools were deserted.[290] The prestige of Alexandrian philosophy was, however, high under Ammonius. We have a glimpse of the inside of his school in the dialogue on the Creation of the World by his pupil Zacharias Scholasticus. The scene is his lecture room in summer when the Nile is in flood and a pleasant breeze is blowing, and Ammonius, sitting on a high platform, expounds Aristotle with the pompous manner of a sophist. His subject is Aristotle's physical theory, and this leads to a discussion between him and his Christian pupil on the controversial subject of the Creation.[291] Ammonius himself was a pagan, but he came to an agreement with the patriarch of Alexandria which apparently enabled him to take Christian pupils. Damascius is bitter about what he evidently regarded as a betrayal of principle, and in a harsh sentence attributes Ammonius's action to his love of money.[292] But at any rate he ensured the survival of the Alexandrian school which was not, like that of Athens, committed to an attitude of opposition to Christianity. Philosophy became if not Christian at least neutral. Ammonius's pupil John Philoponus was a Christian; the younger Olympiodorus was a pagan, but his pupils David and Elias, who continued the Alexandrian tradition of Aristotelian commentary, were, as their names show, Christians.[293] The school continued to exist after the Arab conquest. It moved from Alexandria to Antioch, where it remained for over a century; it migrated in the mid-ninth century to Harrān, and from there towards the end of the century to Baghdad.[294]

Having traced the history of the neo-Platonist schools we turn to their teaching. Plotinus's school gives the impression of being something like the original Platonic Academy, a community of seekers after truth, but a Platonic community with something of the Christian monastery about it, for parents used to entrust their children to Plotinus on their death and bequeath property to him.[295] He did, however, teach. His biographer distinguishes between his hearers and his followers, or associates.[296] The former were numerous. Presumably they included youths such as those who attended the schools in the earlier Empire, though one might well suppose that Plotinus's lectures would be above the heads of the average young student; they certainly included older men, among them senators and professional men, and there was no restriction on entry to the lecture room.[297] The followers or associates, who included some women, were adults, and some of them remained for long periods. Porphyry, who joined Plotinus at the age of thirty, remained with him for six years, and another disciple, Amelius, stayed for twenty-four.[298]

Plotinus based his teaching on Plato and Aristotle, and no doubt he thought of himself as their interpreter rather than as an original thinker. He presumably read their works with his pupils, and we know that they studied commentaries by other Platonists and Aristotelians.[299] He examined the problems arising from the interpretation of certain passages, and it can be assumed that the substance of his discourses on these problems is preserved in the Enneads.[300] He was not dogmatic in his teaching; he encouraged questions, and engaged in friendly discussion rather than disputation. When Porphyry first attended the school he wrote a criticism of Plotinus's views; Amelius was made to read it and told that he must solve Porphyry's difficulties. Amelius then wrote a lengthy answer, to which Porphyry replied. There followed a reply from Amelius, after which Porphyry at last understood Plotinus's views, was convinced by them and wrote a palinode which he recited in the school.[301] Once three days were spent in the discussion of a question by Porphyry, much to the annoyance of a hearer who had been expecting a connected discourse by the master; 'but', said Plotinus, 'if Porphyry did not ask questions, I should have nothing to say which could be written down'.[302] Plotinus's method of encouraging questions had its disadvantages; it resulted in some disorderliness and lack of system.[303]

The main activity of the later neo-Platonist schools was lecturing on texts. They did not confine themselves to Plato. Philosophy now embraced the doctrines of what had previously been separate sects, and whereas it had once been a source of reproach to the philosophers that they could not agree among themselves, we find the emperor Constantine at the time of the Arian controversy contrasting the dissensions of the church with the unity of the philosophers.[304] When the emperor Julian drew up a programme of reading for his pagan priests, he advised the study of Pythagoras, Plato, Aristotle and the Stoics, but not the Epicureans and Pyrrhonists, whose works had in any case fortunately disappeared.[305] The philosophers he recommended were all represented in neo-Platonist teaching.

Plato had pride of place, but Aristotle was regarded as almost as important, and at Alexandria perhaps as more important. There the elder Olympiodorus expounded his doctrines eloquently but to the average student unintelligibly, and Ammonius devoted particular attention to him.[306] Nor was Aristotle neglected at Athens, though he was rated below Plato. Syrianus read the whole of his works with Proclus, and after thus initiating him in the preliminary and lesser mysteries, as Marinus puts it, passed on to Plato; Isidore regarded Aristotle as one of the most gifted of the older philosophers, but inferior to the divine Plato.[307] Teaching was not confined to these two philosophers.[308] Eugenius lectured on Pythagoras, Plato and the Stoics in addition to Aristotle.[309] Theosebius read from Epictetus's discourses and Isidore regarded Chrysippus as on a level with Aristotle.[310] But the neo-Platonists probably found Stoicism less sympathetic than the mystical doctrines associated with Orpheus and Pythagoras and the so-called Chaldaic Oracles, a poem in Greek hexameters which appeared about the year 200 and became a kind of sacred text for the neo-Platonists. Chrysanthius, a pupil of Aedesius, was thoroughly versed in Pythagoreanism;[311] Hierocles wrote the still extant commentary on Pythagoras's Golden Verses. Syrianus offered his pupils Proclus and Domninus the option of being instructed either in Orphism or in the oracles. When each made a different choice, Syrianus decided on the oracles, but he was prevented by death from completing his exposition; Proclus then studied all the existing commentaries on Orpheus, and the works of Porphyry and Iamblichus on the oracles.[312]

The various commentaries on Plato and Aristotle which survive from late antiquity obviously reproduce the oral teaching given in the schools. Some were published by their authors, others by pupils from lecture notes. Ammonius's lectures were published some by an anonymous pupil, others by John Philoponus; John duly acknowledges the source of his commentary, and in some cases claims to have made contributions of his own.[313] The commentaries of the younger Olympiodorus were also published by a pupil, who acknowledges his source in the phrase 'notes from the oral teaching of Olympiodorus the great philosopher'.[314] The publishing of lecture notes by pupils was a recognized practice, and when Plutarchus lectured to Proclus on the *Phaedo* he encouraged him to take notes by telling him that he could become known as the author of a commentary on it.[315] In fact Proclus's commentaries are his own work, and they appear to have been published by himself. That on the *Parmenides* is in the form of a treatise addressed to a pupil; those on the *Alcibiades*, *Republic* and *Timaeus* appear to be as delivered in the lecture room.[316]

In lecturing on Aristotle the philosophers began with the logical works and proceeded to ethics, physics, mathematics and theology.[317] The first work to be studied was the *Categories*. Porphyry wrote an introduction (*Isagoge*) to this for the benefit of a friend who found it difficult to understand; this introduction itself became a school textbook and was the object of commentaries by Ammonius and others. In dealing with Plato it was usual to make a selection from the dialogues. Iamblichus pronounced that the whole of Plato's philosophy was comprised in ten dialogues.[318] Which these were is not recorded, but the usual list was: *Alcibiades I, Gorgias, Phaedo, Cratylus, Theaetetus,*

Symposium, Timaeus, Parmenides and *Philebus*, to which some added the *Republic* and the *Laws*.[319] It was generally agreed that the *Alcibiades* provided the best introduction to Plato, and commentaries on it by Proclus, Olympiodorus and an anonymous writer still survive. Thus Plato's works were adapted to scholastic purposes and made the object of systematic exposition. But though teaching concentrated on a selection of his writings, this did not mean that the rest were completely neglected. The more advanced students would no doubt read them on their own; a system of instruction based on selection did not, as in the case of the Greek tragedians, lead to the disappearance of works other than those selected.

The reading of texts was preceded by a general introduction which might include a life of the author, and there would be an introduction to each dialogue. This, according to the Alexandrian school, should deal with six points: the intention of the work, its usefulness, where it came in the order of the author's works, its title, its genuineness, and the division of the work into chapters or headings.[320] In the commentaries of Olympiodorus, which give the clearest picture of procedure in the lecture room, the material is divided into separate lectures (*praxeis*).[321] The length of these varies, though the variation may be due to the notetaker rather than to the lecturer. Thirty-eight lectures are given to the *Alcibiades* and fifty-one to the four books of Aristotle's *Meteorologica*. In the commentary on the *Phaedo*, to judge by the extant parts, Olympiodorus got through on an average rather over one of Stephanus's pages in each lecture. In the lectures on the *Alcibiades* the material is divided into *theoria*, an exposition of the ideas, and *lexis*, a commentary on individual sentences; usually each lecture begins with *theoria* and then proceeds to *lexis*. Proclus seems to have varied his method. In lecturing on the *Republic* he dealt with a number of selected themes; otherwise his method was that of the sentence-by-sentence commentary. His commentaries ran to excessive length. That on the *Alcibiades*, which covers rather over a third of the dialogue, extends to 158 large pages in the most recent edition.[322] That on the *Timaeus* is no less ample. It deals with a third of Plato's work, about twenty-eight of Stephanus's pages, in over 1,100 pages of Teubner text.

A different method was followed by Themistius at Constantinople, a more popular and less academic expounder than the philosophers of Athens and Alexandria. His method was not to explain difficult passages, but to give a paraphrase of the argument. 'It seemed to me,' he writes at the beginning of his paraphrase of the *Analytica Posteriora*, 'a novel method and one likely to be of some use, to select from the ideas to be found in the text and to expound them briefly, preserving as far as possible the conciseness of the author.'[323] Themistius was less of a man of the schools than most of the philosophers of the period. He believed in philosophy as a training for public life; he went on embassies and delivered public orations. He might indeed, though he repudiated the title, be called sophist rather than philosopher. In spite of his activities, and although he and other fourth-century writers describe the city as a centre of philosophy,[324] it cannot be said that the schools of Constantinople were of much importance in this period.

chapter 4
Professional education

There is a well-known passage of Cicero in which, writing of
the various means of livelihood and classifying them as 'mean'
or 'liberal', he mentions three which are commended by their
intellectual content or by their value to society and which are
therefore honourable for those to whose rank they are suited.[1]
They are medicine, architecture and teaching. These may be
called the 'learned professions' of his day. The last, teaching,
required no specific training; a teacher of one of the liberal
arts, whether of grammar, rhetoric or mathematics, needed no
qualifications other than a knowledge of his subject. Of medicine and architecture there is more to be said; these were arts
in which the master combined professional practice with teaching and the pupil had to acquire not only theoretical knowledge
but also practical experience.

At first, according to Celsus, the science of medicine was considered a part of philosophy and philosophers, among them
Pythagoras, Empedocles and Democritus, were also skilled in
medicine; the first to separate the two studies was Hippocrates
of Cos.[2] The separation was not quite complete; medicine and
philosophy were never entirely divorced. But it is certainly
true that from the later fifth century B.C., when Hippocrates
flourished, medicine was an independent discipline with its
own methods and traditions. By the fifth century it was also a
recognized profession. We find a physician, Eryximachus,
among the guests at Agathon's party described in the *Symposium*;
we find medicine mentioned as a possible career for young

friends of Socrates such as Meno and the Hippocrates, name-sake of the physician, who appears at the beginning of the *Protagoras*.[3]

Hippocrates the physician lived and taught in Cos, and the island continued for some time to be a medical centre. Cnidus in Asia Minor was another such centre. Athens inevitably attracted medical men, such as Diocles of Carystus, who was accounted the second most famous Greek physician after Hippocrates.[4] After the foundation of Alexandria that city became the most important home of medical science and teaching. Distinguished medical men such as Herophilus, Erasistratus and Serapion worked there, and the city was the home of a noted school of surgery. There were other centres; schools of medicine flourished at Laodicea and Smyrna in the first century B.C.,[5] and in the second century after Christ Galen studied in his native Pergamum, in Smyrna and in Corinth before proceeding to Alexandria. But Alexandria maintained its reputation. Galen urges the student of medicine to go there, if only for the sake of anatomical study; and in the fourth century it was sufficient recommendation to a doctor if he could say that he had studied at Alexandria.[6]

Greek medicine like other branches of Greek learning came to Rome and the precise date of its arrival has been recorded. In 219 B.C. one Archagathus from the Peloponnese established a surgery in Rome. In spite of the obscurantism of Cato, to whom Greek medicine was simply part of a conspiracy to kill the Romans, he was followed by others. But the Romans themselves did not take to medical practice; generally speaking they left it to the Greeks. This was the only art, according to the elder Pliny, left untouched by the Romans, and the few of them who did practise it did their best to turn themselves into Greeks; Greek remained the language of medicine, and even those who did not understand the language would not trust a doctor who did not use it.[7]

In early days medicine was handed down from father to son. Throughout antiquity sons followed their fathers in medicine perhaps a little more than in other professions,[8] and the idea of a filial relationship between master and pupil persisted. The physician, according to the Hippocratic oath, regards his teacher with no less affection than his own parents; he looks on his teacher's children as his brothers and engages to teach them, if they wish it, without fee.[9] This implies that pupils were taken from outside the family in return for a fee, and passages in Plato's dialogues show that this was a common practice in the Athens which he depicts.[10]

The doctor then had what may be called his articled pupils, and the tradition was that the apprenticeship began at an early age; the Hippocratic work 'The Law' speaks of *paidomathia*, learning in boyhood.[11] In later antiquity, when a medical student was expected to have had a general education before he entered on his professional studies, the latter were begun at a rather later age, at or a little after the end of boyhood. Galen was sixteen when he began his medical course; the pupil addressed in Rufus's work on the names of the parts of the body is still a boy, but is assumed to have studied grammar and geometry, and so may be thought of as about fourteen.[12] This is the age recommended for beginning medical training in the late Latin treatise known as 'pseudo-Soranus', which requires the beginner to be intelligent, strong and of good character, in addition to having a knowledge of grammar, rhetoric, geometry and astronomy.[13] How long the training would last it is difficult to say. Galen's medical studies were not completed until the age of twenty-eight; on the other hand Thessalus of Tralles, a leading physician at Rome in the time of Nero, claimed to be able to turn out qualified practitioners in six months.[14]

The physician's pupil would begin by getting to know the surgery and making himself useful there.[15] He would accompany his master on his rounds and might be left with the patient to see that the doctor's orders were carried out and to report on what had happened between the visits.[16] When Apollonius of Tyana was accused of murdering an Arcadian boy he called as witnesses two physicians, who came accompanied by more than thirty pupils who had been present at the boy's death-bed; Martial, no doubt with some exaggeration, writes of a doctor bringing a hundred pupils with him on a professional visit.[17]

If these pupils, like old-style apprentices, lived in their master's house (and in view of the tradition of a filial relationship one would expect this to have been the case), we can think of the doctor as conducting something like a boarding school.

Though his pupils would learn much by accompanying him and observing and assisting him at his work, they would also receive some formal instruction. The Hippocratic oath speaks of precept, oral teaching and other methods of instruction; there was a medical literature from the fifth century B.C., and one of the Hippocratic writings refers to the study of written works.[18] As time went on the academic element in the doctor's training increased. The elder Pliny writes of the practice of 'sitting in schools listening to lectures' which had become more popular than going out to look for herbs for medicinal purposes, and Galen notes that manuals of anatomy became necessary as the old family system of training died out and the practical knowledge picked up in the course of a long apprenticeship was lost.[19] There was probably never a clear dividing line between the practising physician with his pupils and the medical school; but the schools already mentioned at Laodicea and Smyrna are described as teaching institutions (*didaskaleia*),[20] and we should no doubt think of those at Alexandria as having a similar status. During Galen's first stay in Rome he taught publicly and gave open lectures, or demonstrations, the chief centre for such teaching being the temple of Peace.[21] Anatomical demonstrations formed part of the training; the teacher used a slave in order to demonstrate the visible parts of the body, and dissected a monkey to display the inner parts.[22]

The medical literature of antiquity no doubt reflects the oral teaching of the schools. The works attributed to Hippocrates, of various dates and authorship, represent the pre-Alexandrian tradition. They were still being lectured on when Galen was a student,[23] and he himself wrote commentaries on some of them. Of Galen's many treatises some were specifically designed as textbooks, and after his death his writings became the recognized authorities in the medical schools, though the survival of the Hippocratic works shows that they were not regarded as superseded. From an Arab source we get a picture of medical teaching at Alexandria in the period after Galen. Twenty of his works formed the prescribed curriculum, and they were read in a fixed order. Each day the students assembled to read these and hear their teacher's commentary on them; after this course was completed they would turn to the rest of Galen's works, reading them individually and not in class.[24]

The architect in the ancient world, like the doctor, was recognized as a professional man, distinct from and superior to the builder.[25] In early days perhaps, as was the case in medicine, the art was handed down from father to son; Vitruvius tells us that the old Romans valued an architect primarily for the reputation of his family and only secondarily for his education and that architects trained only their children and relatives.[26] There is, however, no evidence that family tradition ever counted for much in the profession in Greece, and in Rome the professionalism and the intellectual approach of the Greeks prevailed over the traditional lore of the Italian builders.

Architecture as practised in antiquity was based on a wide general education. The fourth-century Greek architect Pythius claimed that an architect should have a complete mastery of all the arts and sciences.[27] Vitruvius, who thought Pythius had overstated his case, requires a knowledge, though not necessarily a profound one, of literature, drawing, geometry, history, philosophy, music, medicine, law and astronomy, a list which includes some subjects outside the normal curriculum of general education.[28] The emperor Constantine, in a constitution of A.D. 334 designed to encourage the young to enter the profession, laid down that they should be eighteen years of age and educated in the liberal arts.[29] The age prescribed is noticeably later than that at which medical studies were begun. Professional training was perhaps less exacting for the architect than for the physician and the preliminary general education more exacting.

The training of an ancient architect was no doubt in essence a system of apprenticeship; but it seems to have had rather more of an intellectual content than such a term might suggest. It included some formal instruction. A treatise like that of Vitruvius seems to imply the existence of oral teaching on the same lines; when Vitruvius, expounding the Doric temple, refers to the doctrine he had received from his teachers we get the impression that architects gave their pupils instruction in the principles of design as well as initiating them in the practical side of their work.[30] At the beginning of the fourth century after Christ we find architectural teaching recognized as a profession in the edict of Diocletian on wages and prices.[31] The small fee which the *architectus magister* is allowed to charge— half that of the grammarian and a quarter of that of the rhetorician—suggests that he did not confine himself to teaching and that he got some help from his pupils in his professional work; but the fact that he is mentioned along with other teachers shows that architectural training had its academic as well as its practical side, and that we can legitimately speak of architectural schools as existing in the ancient world.

In the passage of Cicero referred to at the beginning of this chapter no mention is made of the law, which in modern times has generally been considered one of the learned professions and one which requires a specific training. In Cicero's day the law was hardly a profession; that is to say, it was not, in theory at any rate, a means of making a livelihood.[32] Neither the advocate nor the jurist was supposed to charge a fee for his services; to give such services was part of his duty to his friends or to those who looked to him for protection. Cicero contrasts the Greek *pragmaticus*, the professional giving legal advice to the orator for pay, with the respected and distinguished figure of the Roman jurist, whose opinions were commended by his prestige and position in society.[33]

Though they might not be classed with doctors, architects and teachers, Rome in Cicero's day had its recognized experts in the law; the days were past when, as Cicero recalls, a distinguished Roman might give advice to all who sought it, whether at home or while walking across the forum, not only on civil law but also on betrothing a daughter, buying a property, running a farm or any other matter.[34] The jurist of his day, the *iurisconsultus* or *iurisperitus*, might be an amateur in the sense that he did not exact fees, but he was a professional in the sense that he was an expert in his subject. He was in general distinguished from the advocate, the orator. Of the latter's education we have already spoken. The orator might study law, as Cicero did, but often he dispensed with such training; Cicero writes with indignation of the scandalous neglect of the subject by some advocates.[35] Whereas an English barrister has a thorough training in law and little in the art of advocacy, his counterpart in the ancient world had a thorough training in advocacy and little in law.

Cicero tells how in his boyhood he was made to learn the Twelve Tables by rote.[36] This was presumably a relic of old days when every citizen was expected to know the law, and it ceased to be the practice during Cicero's lifetime. His serious legal education took place after he had assumed the *toga uirilis*, when he attended at the consultations of Scaevola. Scaevola's pupils would do no more than listen while he gave his opinions: the jurist, says Cicero, gives no time specifically to teaching, but supplies the needs of his clients and his pupils at the same time, and this is why the teaching of civil law has always been considered honourable.[37] The pupil would thus hear an experienced jurist's opinions on specific cases, but he would receive no formal or systematic training. Apart from the high social status of the jurists the lack of any comprehensive and systematic treatise on law was an obstacle to any such teaching.[38]

As time went on the law became more of a profession. The distinguished amateurs of the Republican period gave place to paid professionals, and the contrast which Cicero had drawn between the status of the Greek jurist and that of the Roman ceased to be valid.[39] At the same time legal education developed, and we find jurists who specialized in teaching and writing.[40] In the period of the principate there were two schools of law in Rome, each of which had a continuous existence for several generations, to judge by the successions of teachers recorded by the second-century jurist Pomponius.[41] Pomponius followed the history of both schools back to the Augustan age; he supposed their founders to be Antistius Labeo and Ateius Capito, though the schools took their names from two later teachers, Proculus and Cassius, who flourished in the middle years of the first century. Labeo, we are told, divided the year into two halves and spent six months with his pupils and six in writing books.[42] Nothing is recorded of the teaching activity of Capito, but we know that Massurius Sabinus, whom Pomponius counts as Capito's pupil and Cassius's master, depended for his livelihood largely on the contributions of his pupils,[43] while Cassius himself certainly conducted a regular teaching institution, the *schola Cassiana* to which the younger Pliny refers.[44] Textbooks were produced, the earliest being the three books on Civil Law of Sabinus, no longer extant, which probably consisted of lecture notes published after his death.[45] In the second century there were a number of law schools in Rome.[46] One work from this period has survived, the *Institu-*

tiones of Gaius; this is evidently an introduction to law compiled by a teacher for the benefit of his students and, whether published by Gaius or by a pupil after his death, reflects his oral teaching.

Roman law spread to the East, and most of our information about legal training in the later Empire comes from the Greek-speaking lands. Law continued to be taught in Rome, and it was taught in the new Rome, Constantinople, and elsewhere,[47] but the chief centre was Berytus (Beirut).[48] The earliest mention we have of this school is in the early third century, when Gregory Thaumaturgus learned some Latin and some elementary law in Cappadocia with the intention of proceeding to Beirut for further study, though he gave up his plan on meeting Origen at Caesarea.[49] In the fourth century Libanius provides evidence of the popularity of Beirut and of legal study, which he resented as a rival to his own discipline, rhetoric. There had been a time when only the poorer men went to Beirut; now, he complains, it also attracted the wealthy and well-born.[50] A change was taking place in the relations of law and rhetoric; advocates were no longer content to be educated solely in the art of oratory, and the time was to come, in 460, when an imperial enactment laid down that they must pass an examination in law before they could practise in the courts.[51]

At Beirut there was a regular course of study lasting five years, with specific texts assigned to each year. The students may be assumed to have started on the course at about the age of sixteen, after the usual general education in the encyclic arts.[52] In the first year they studied two books of the *Institutiones* of Gaius and four other books, on family and testamentary law. The subjects for study in the next year were legal procedure and the law of property; these were continued into the third year, during which Papinian's *Responsa* were also studied. The fourth year was devoted to the *Responsa* of Paulus, which were studied privately without the help of regular lectures, and the final year to the Imperial Constitutions, also studied by means of private reading. Each year had its name; the first-year students were *dupondii* (recruits); those of the second and third took their names from the authorities they studied and were known as *edictales* and *Papinianistae*. The fourth year were *lytae* (solvers of problems) and the fifth *prolytae*.[53]

The law school at Beirut thus anticipated in some respects the universities of the Middle Ages. We find the same regular course of studies, with prescribed texts, and the slang names for the different years. The *bejauni* or bajans of the medieval universities have their counterpart in the *dupondii*, and the initiatory ragging which was a feature of medieval student life is paralleled in the *ludi* at Beirut condemned by Justinian.[54]

From the end of the fifth century we have a picture of the school of Beirut as seen by one of its students, the Christian Zacharias Scholasticus, who wrote a Life of Severus, later patriarch of Antioch. Both of them went to Beirut to study, Zacharias a year after Severus. As a freshman Zacharias had fears of suffering at the hands of the second-year men, the *edictales*, but in fact there was nothing very dreadful about the ordeal and he merely had to show that he could take some mockery in good part. Severus, though a year senior to him, proved a good friend, and soon the two were spending their spare time together in religious study and exercises. The first two years were taken together by one of the masters, Leontius, a lawyer of great reputation; when the freshmen had finished their day's work the second-year men stayed behind.[55] Classes took place throughout the week except on Saturday afternoons and Sundays.[56] Severus completed his law course by studying the Imperial Constitutions, including those of his own day; he made a comparison of the various commentaries, and when he left he bequeathed his books and his notes to those who came after.[57]

Professional education in the ancient world developed, as we have seen, beyond the stage of apprenticeship and involved a considerable degree of formal academic instruction. It was begun at an early age by modern standards, but not in comparison with what was once the practice in England. In the eighteenth century George Crabbe, the poet, who was originally destined for a medical career, was apprenticed to a country practitioner at the age of thirteen; the leading architect of the last century, Sir Gilbert Scott, left his father's country parsonage for an architect's office in London before he was sixteen; Lloyd George was fifteen when he entered a solicitor's office. Early specialization may have had some disadvantages; Galen thought some of the physicians of his day deficient in literary

I

culture.⁵⁸ But the professional men of antiquity were certainly not ill-educated. We meet with two of them in St Augustine's account of his early days at Carthage, the municipal architect who was able to find the real culprit when Alypius was falsely suspected of theft, and the physician, with his unadorned but lively and impressive manner of speaking, who persuaded Augustine to give up astrology.⁵⁹ Such men might well be thought more useful members of society than the professed guardians of culture, the pedantic grammarians and the vain and pretentious rhetoricians.

chapter 5
Christianity and higher education

It might have been expected that the spread of the Christian religion would have resulted in a transformation or at least a modification of the educational system of the Roman Empire. Christians might well view with disfavour the classics of the grammar school with their false and sometimes immoral stories of gods and goddesses, and reject the rhetoricians' cult of eloquence as mere vanity and worldly ambition; they might also claim that their moral teaching superseded that of the philosophers. Throughout the early Christian centuries voices are heard denouncing secular learning as pernicious or at least unnecessary. But the secular schools survived, and survived unaltered. Even Tertullian, so hostile to pagan culture, did not forbid Christians to send their sons to them,[1] and though he considered teaching in these schools incompatible with Christianity his advice on this point was not widely followed. There must have been many Christian grammarians and rhetoricians teaching the traditional curriculum by the mid-fourth century, when for the first time religion became involved in educational politics under Julian. A teacher of grammar or rhetoric, so Julian argued, ought to honour the gods honoured by the authors he expounded; Christians did not believe what they taught, and therefore they were forbidden to teach in these schools.[2]

This resulted in a curious attempt to provide a Christian alternative to the secular grammar school. Two men called Apollinarius, father and son, the former a teacher of grammar, the latter of rhetoric, set to work at Laodicea to replace the Greek classics by versions of the Scriptures, the historical books of the Old Testament in Homeric hexameters (duly divided into twenty-four books), other parts of the Old Testament in dramatic or lyric metres, and the New Testament in the form of Platonic dialogue.[3] To us this may seem a bizarre and tasteless experiment; yet it could be maintained that the Apollinarii had a juster understanding of the character of the Hebrew scriptures than the allegorizing theologians of the school of Origen. But the new Christian Homer was evidently felt to be only second best in relation to the genuine article. When Julian's ban was lifted with his death and Christians could now teach the pagan classics, the Apollinarii and their works were forgotten. No attempt was made to alter the curriculum or the spirit of the old grammar schools.

With the development in the fourth century of monastic schools we find for the first time an attempt to provide a wholly Christian education; otherwise the faith was taught not in schools but in the home and in the church. The church itself, however, might well be described as an educational institution. Christians referred to their religion as a philosophy,[4] and the church was not unlike a philosophical school. Like the philosophers it taught men to live aright and healed the diseases of the soul,[5] and it claimed to be more successful than they had been; 'We show our wisdom not by our garb but by our attitude of mind; fine words are not ours but fine deeds; we boast that we have attained to what they sought for with every effort but could not find.'[6] Even in minor matters the church recalls the schools of philosophy. Like them it had its 'successions'; as historians of philosophy traced the line of descent from the founders of the schools, so churchmen traced that of the bishops from the apostles. The terms *haeresis* and *secta* which had been used of the philosophical schools found their way into Christian terminology. Like the philosopher in his school the bishop had his chair at the end of the church from which he delivered his instructions; the episcopal throne of today no less than the professorial chair descends from the *thronos* or *cathedra* of the ancient teacher. Inevitably too the Christians had to meet the same charges as the philosophers; when Lactantius says that 'the philosophers of our school' are blamed 'for living otherwise than befits wise men and concealing vices under the cloak of its name',[7] we recognize the familiar charge so often brought against the philosophers.

How did the church set about the task on which the philosophers had long been engaged, of teaching men to live aright? Celsus in his attack on Christianity depicted the Christians as frequenting the marketplaces and begging, avoiding the company of the intelligent and seeking out boys and slaves and ignorant people,[8] in fact proceeding much as the Cynics did. But this kind of activity was not characteristic of the Christians. St Paul had occasionally preached in public, as at Athens, but his usual practice was to use the local synagogue, where it was generally open to him to expound the Scriptures and explain his doctrines; once when he was unsympathetically received by the synagogue he moved to a school, or lecture room, belonging to one Tyrannus.[9] When Christianity broke with Judaism and the synagogue gave place to the church, it was in the churches rather than in public that Christian teaching commonly took place. Indeed the Christians were blamed for avoiding public places, for being a 'tribe that hid in corners and avoided the light'.[10] 'We never,' says the Christian spokesman in Minucius Felix's *Octavius*, 'preach publicly except when questioned.'[11] Christians, as Origen pointed out, examined and tested those who wanted to hear them.[12] None the less there was teaching, or preaching, which was open to the public, though not conducted in the market-places. We hear of discourses given by Polycarp to the general public, and as these were delivered seated they presumably took place within doors.[13] At a later date the sermons of Ambrose which Augustine heard in Milan before his baptism were open to all; Augustine speaks of his expounding the word of truth in public (*in populo*) every Sunday.[14]

It was, however, characteristic of Christianity that candidates for admission to the church had to undergo instruction. There were two stages, the preliminary teaching and testing of the candidate, followed by a more extended course of varying length leading up to baptism. The probationary period before full membership recalls the practice of the Pythagorean school.[15] Like the Pythagoreans too the Christian initiate was required not to reveal the secrets of his religion to outsiders.[16] In practice, however, this cannot have meant much. The doctrines of Christianity soon became well known to the world at large; nor was there anything particularly secret about its worship, even though the unbaptized were excluded from its most solemn rites.[17]

In conducting courses for those seeking admission to the Church the clergy were faced with a difficulty which the philosophers had not experienced. The latter, though they believed in theory that all men had the capacity for virtue, in practice, if we except the Cynics, drew their pupils for the most part from the well educated. The Church on the other hand had room for everybody; it included, as Justin said, not only philosophers and literary men but also craftsmen and those wholly without education.[18] St Augustine had to teach all sorts, 'the learned and the stupid, a fellow-citizen and a stranger, a rich man and a poor, a private citizen and a distinguished man in a position of authority, a person of this or that race, age or sex, one coming from this or that philosophical sect or popular error'; there were ignorant men, well educated men who already knew something of the Christian faith and those educated in grammar and rhetoric only, who would have to unlearn their pride in their oratorical attainments.[19] The model address which Augustine includes in his treatise on catechizing the uninstructed is designed for a candidate without education, but who is a townsman, who could presumably be expected to be more receptive and quick-witted than an applicant from the country.[20] The address, after introductory exhortations and warnings, consists of an outline of sacred history down to the time of writing, followed by further exhortations, after which the candidate is to be asked whether he believes. A different treatment, more doctrinal and less historical, is found in the elaborate Catechetical Oration of Gregory of Nyssa, which is in fact not an address to applicants but a treatise on how to instruct them.[21] Gregory, like Augustine, makes the point that the same method is not suited to all; but he is concerned not with different levels of education, but rather with the different religious background of those who come for instruction. Some would be pagans, some Jews, some Manichees or adherents of various heresies. Gregory assumes a high level of education and an interest in rational argument; his aim is to meet intellectual difficulties and to persuade by finding points of agreement.[22] In the second century Galen and Celsus may have had some justification for saying that the Christians expected their doctrines to be taken on trust, that they said, 'Ask no questions, but believe';[23] in the later fourth century, if all Christian teachers followed the example of Gregory, this charge could no longer be maintained.

Once the catechumen had passed the first stage and had signified his wish to be admitted to baptism he would no doubt be prepared to receive his further instruction more passively. What this was like we can learn from the series of eighteen addresses given in Lent by Cyril of Jerusalem as preparation for baptism, in which after exhorting his hearers to repentance and instructing them on baptism he deals in order with the main articles of the Christian faith.[24]

The regular services of the Church provided for the Christian an instruction which, unlike that which the philosophers gave, continued throughout life. They included readings from the Scriptures and exhortations based on them. 'The memoirs of the Apostles,' says Justin, 'or the writings of the prophets are read, as long as time permits. Then the reader ceases and the president speaks, admonishing us and exhorting us to imitate these excellent examples.'[25] An outsider used, let us say, to the readings from Chrysippus and the moral exhortations of a Stoic teacher would, if he found his way to a Christian meeting, recognize a certain similarity in the method, if not in the content of the teaching.[26] This is not to say that the Church imitated the philosophers; it followed rather the tradition of synagogue worship with its readings from and expositions of the law and the prophets. Nor were the Christian services confined to readings and exhortation; the Christians whose activities Pliny investigated sang 'a hymn to Christ as to a god' and bound themselves by an oath to do no wrong; the readings and sermon described by Justin were followed by the Eucharist.[27] There was, of course, nothing like this in the philosophers' schools; they were content with using the spoken word, and knew nothing of ceremonies 'such as be apt to stir up the dull mind to the remembrance of his duty to God'.[28] Augustine listened to Ambrose's sermons much as a Roman of the first century might have heard the discourses of a Stoic philosopher;

indeed, as he himself admits, he went first in the spirit condemned by Seneca, to enjoy the charms of oratory rather than
to attend to the matter of the sermons.[29] But the parallel with
the philosophers' school breaks down when we read of the
emotion he felt at the sweet sound of the hymns which Ambrose
had introduced to the Church.[30]

If we can judge by Justin's account of Christian worship,
sermons in the second century consisted in the main of exhortation, and this is confirmed by the earliest extant sermon, the
so-called second epistle of St Clement, which probably dates
from this period. From the third century onwards the sermon
often took the form of commentary on the scriptures.[31] Ambrose's exposition of St Luke's gospel is a series of sermons
written up afterwards for publication, and the first fifty-four of
Augustine's treatises on St John's gospel were originally
delivered as sermons in church. In this development of the
sermon we can perhaps see a parallel with the development of
philosophical teaching; moral exhortation was characteristic
of the schools, or at any rate of the Stoic school, in the early
Empire, whereas commentary on texts was characteristic of the
neo-Platonist period. The preacher with his sentence-by-
sentence exposition of the Scriptures certainly reminds us of the
philosopher lecturing on his standard texts, and when Gregory
of Nyssa begins his commentary on the Psalms with an introduction in which he distinguishes the intention of the work, the
order of the Psalms and their usefulness, we recognize the
standard neo-Platonist scheme.[32] When Ambrose in the preface
to his exposition of St Luke claims that the three branches of
philosophy, physical, ethical and logical, are all to be found in
the Old and New Testaments, we can see that the Scriptures,
which to most modern readers seem remote from philosophical
thought as it was developed by the Greeks, could be regarded
as having superseded the standard texts of the pagan schools.

This view, however, was not universally accepted. Philosophy, said Clement of Alexandria, served as a guide to lead the
Greeks to Christ as the law did the Jews,[33] and from the second
century onwards we find men with a philosophical training
turning to the new religion. Pantaenus came to Christianity
from Stoicism, Justin after sampling various schools,[34] and the
apologists Athenagoras and Aristides are described as philo-

sophers. In fourth-century Rome Marius Victorinus and Manlius Theodorus were converted to Christianity from Platonism, and according to St Augustine there were many other such cases both among his contemporaries and a little before his time.[35] Such men would bring to Christianity something of their old habits of thought; if philosophy had brought them to Christ they might well suppose that it could perform the same function for others. This was the principle that guided the teaching of Origen.

Origen taught in what is known as the 'catechetical school' of Alexandria. The term *katechesis*, which originally meant no more than oral instruction, was commonly used for instruction in the Christian faith, and in particular for the instruction given to those preparing for baptism. But the school at Alexandria, though it may have been intended for this limited purpose, grew into something more, into a kind of Christian university.

It was started by Pantaenus, who was succeeded by Clement and then Origen; Origen was followed by his former assistant Heraclas, and the school appears to have had a continuous existence at least until towards the end of the fourth century when Didymus, the blind scholar then in charge of the school, died.[36] This continuity implies that the school had some form of organization, but all that can be said on this point is that it was to some extent under ecclesiastical control at least from the time of Origen. Origen himself was put in charge of it by Demetrius, bishop of Alexandria,[37] and Didymus is said to have succeeded to the school 'with the approval of the bishop Athanasius and the other wise men in the church of God'.[38]

The men who conducted the school were well educated in Greek learning, including philosophy. Pantaenus was an ex-Stoic; Clement, as his writings show, was well-versed in contemporary Greek culture. Origen received a philosophical education under Ammonius Saccas, Plotinus's teacher, and was familiar with the chief writers of the Platonist and Pythagorean schools, as well as with the Stoics.[39] Heraclas had five years of philosophical training, probably under Ammonius.[40] The education given in the school was an adaptation to Christian purposes of the contemporary Greek system; it included philosophy and the *enkuklios paideia* which was regarded as a necessary preliminary to philosophy, and it added Christian doctrine as the final stage. Thus philosophy was no longer the crown of education; it was now to take second place to theology. As Origen puts it, 'after the young have been first trained in general education and philosophical thought, I would try to lead them higher', to the profundities of Christian doctrine.[41]

Origen had already begun teaching grammar when he was put in charge of the catechetical school in his eighteenth year. As his hearers increased in number he gave up his teaching of grammar as inconsistent with the work of religious instruction.[42] Even so he found the burden too great and took on Heraclas as an assistant, putting him in charge of what may be called a lower school while he himself was responsible for the upper.[43] His course included dialectic, arithmetic, geometry and astronomy, followed by philosophy.[44] After he left Alexandria he taught at Caesarea, and Gregory Thaumaturgus, who studied under him there, has left an interesting, if somewhat wordy, account of his teaching. A few extracts will show how he handled philosophy:

> He required us to study philosophy by reading all the existing writings of the ancients both philosophers and religious poets, taking every care not to put aside or reject any (for we were not yet able to exercise judgment), apart from the writings of the atheists who rejecting the common notions of mankind deny the existence of god and of providence . . . but with all the rest we were to be conversant and familiar, not preferring any one type or any philosophical theory, nor on the other hand rejecting any whether Greek or non-Greek, but giving an ear to all . . .

> He guided us to them all, desiring us to leave none of the Greek doctrines untried; and he himself accompanied us, leading the way and guiding us by the hand as if on a journey, in case he should come across anything misleading or unsound or sophistical, when with all the skill that came from long converse with words, familiar with and experienced in everything, he could remain aloft in safety himself, while he stretched out a saving hand to rescue as it were those who were drowning. He selected everything that was useful and true in each philosopher and set it

before us, but condemned what was false, particularly what pertained to piety on the part of man . . .

For us there was nothing forbidden, nothing hidden, nothing inaccessible. We were allowed to learn every doctrine, non-Greek and Greek, both spiritual and secular, both divine and human; with the utmost freedom we went into everything and examined it thoroughly, taking our fill of and enjoying the pleasures of the soul.[45]

Origen's philosophical programme was, it would appear, identical with that of the neo-Platonist teachers. He excluded the Epicureans (the atheists 'who deny the existence of god and of providence') as the neo-Platonists did, and like them he admitted philosophers of all other schools.

It might well have been expected that schools modelled on that of Origen would supersede the existing institutions of higher learning, that the secular studies of the ancient world would be incorporated, as was to happen later in the Middle Ages, in a Christian university. In fact the pagan schools continued to flourish, and they outlived the catechetical school, which may well not have maintained for long the character which Origen gave it.[46] It was quite common for Christians to study under non-Christian teachers. Origen himself, as we have seen, was a pupil of Ammonius Saccas; Synesius (though it is not certain that he came of a Christian family)[47] studied under Hypatia and always spoke of her with respect. Basil and Gregory of Nazianzus pursued the regular course of secular studies in Athens in the middle of the fourth century, when the city still maintained its pagan traditions to a large extent. There were two ways, says Gregory, known to us: that which led to our sacred buildings and the teachers there and that which led to the pagan teachers.[48] The two ways were to survive and to remain to a large extent independent of one another, even when the teachers of the secular subjects were no longer pagans.

In the Latin-speaking West things were rather different. Education tended to be confined to grammar and rhetoric; there was, after Porphyry, little teaching of philosophy in Rome and probably none in the provinces. St Augustine was self-taught in the liberal arts (apart, of course, from grammar and rhetoric) and in philosophy. In spite of this he had a strong interest in all branches of secular learning, and through-out his life was concerned with the problem of their relation-ship to higher studies. In his *De Ordine* his attitude is not unlike that of Origen. He regards secular learning as of value not only from the utilitarian point of view but also as a foundation for future study; he maintains that no one should approach theological problems without a knowledge of both dialectic and mathematics, or at least of one of the two.[49] Later in life, after he had become a bishop, his attitude to secular learning was less favourable. In *De Doctrina Christiana* he allows that it has its uses within limits, and can help towards the understanding of the Scriptures. But its value is small compared to what is to be found in the sacred writings. 'Whatever a man has learned from other sources, if it is harmful, is condemned there [in the Scriptures]; if it is useful, it is found there.'[50] As for philosophy, it can be used if true; as the people of Israel despoiled the Egyptians of gold and silver, so the man who leaves the gentiles with Christ as his leader can take from them valuable treasure in the shape of moral precepts and even certain theological truths.[51] Augustine had no desire to abolish the secular schools. He assumed their existence, but he regarded them as of minor importance. All was to be subordinated to the study of the Bible, the new classic, the textbook of the Christian scholar.[52]

In the early Christian centuries specialist theological schools, schools for the study of the Scriptures intended for the clergy, existed only in a rudimentary state. Informal teaching would be given by any bishop or churchman of sufficient authority to attract disciples. Thus Jerome studied under the leading theologians of the Greek-speaking world, Apollinarius of Laodicea, Gregory of Nazianzus and Gregory of Nyssa.[53] At Alexandria, however, there was what may be called a school of theology in the final stage to which the secular curriculum already described led up. Theological teaching would consist of expositions of the Scriptures. Eusebius describes Pantaenus as interpreting the treasures of the sacred doctrine orally and in writing.[54] His writings have perished; but some of his teaching survives in his pupil Clement, and it is clear from one reference in Clement that, as we should expect, it included the interpreta-tion of the Scriptures.[55] We know from Gregory Thaumaturgus that Origen expounded the prophets when at Caesarea, and he wrote commentaries on Isaiah and Ezekiel which doubtless embodied the substance of his oral teaching.[56] While at Alexandria he began his commentary on St John's gospel, at the request of his pupil Ambrosius;[57] this too was no doubt based on the teaching he had been giving in his school. He shared with the neo-Platonists a tendency towards prolixity in commentary. In the thirty-second book of his work on St John he reached only the thirteenth chapter of the gospel, and he required thirty books to cover a third of the prophet Isaiah.[58]

St Augustine for all his interest in the theory of education had no plans for reorganizing the educational system. In *De Doctrina Christiana* he evidently had the clergy in mind, but he did not think in terms of educational institutions designed for their benefit. It was only in the sixth century that the church authorities in the West began to be concerned at the lack of regular theological schools. Cassiodorus, in conjunction with Pope Agapetus, planned to establish such schools in Rome, his models being the school of Alexandria, by then defunct but still remembered, and that 'said to flourish even now among the Hebrews' (that is, the Syriac-speaking Nestorian Christians) at Nisibis.[59] The plan came to nothing, but the scheme which Cassiodorus drew up for his monks at Vivarium shows what his ideas on education were. He divides learning into two branches, sacred and secular, clearly distinguished from one another. The latter comprises the traditional liberal arts, the former the study of the Bible, doctrine and church history. Theology is now fully recognized as an independent discipline, with its own textbooks and aids to learning. It has not permeated and transformed the educational system; it has become in effect the course of study for a profession, that of the Christian minister.

chapter 6
The survival of the ancient educational tradition

The Byzantine Empire

In the year 425 the Imperial University of Constantinople was founded.[1] It consisted of twenty grammarians, ten Greek and ten Latin; eight rhetoricians, five Greek and three Latin; one philosopher and two lawyers. They were to teach in the Capitolium and each had a room allotted to him there.[2] The mathematical arts were not represented (unless, as is possible, they were taught by the philosopher), nor was the study of medicine; otherwise the recognized ancient disciplines were combined in a single institution which may not unjustly be called the first of the medieval universities. This university lasted, with periods of decline and temporary extinction, until the capture of Constantinople in 1453.

Separate from the university was the Patriarchal School, which probably also dated from the fifth century.[3] This was primarily a theological school, but it also provided a secular education preparatory to theology. There were three theological professors, who taught respectively the gospels, the epistles and the psalms, and a 'master of the rhetoricians'. While theology was taught at the church of St Sophia, there were a number of subordinate schools attached to other churches, and of one of these, that at the church of the Holy Apostles, we have a description dating from about 1200.[4] Round a cloister was the primary school where reading, hymn-singing and elementary arithmetic were taught. In another part of the buildings more advanced instruction was given to students of all ages, in grammar, rhetoric, dialectic, arithmetic, geometry, music (theoretical) and medicine.

The educational system of later antiquity continued with little change in the Byzantine Empire. There was a period of decline in the later sixth century, but higher education revived under the emperor Heraclius (610–41), who brought Stephanus from Alexandria to Constantinople, where he expounded Plato and Aristotle as well as the mathematical subjects.[5] But philosophical teaching seems to have been extinct by the end of the seventh century, when one Ananias of Schirak came to Constantinople to study the subject, but could find no teachers.[6] In the ninth century, after the end of the iconoclastic controversy, there was a revival of secular learning thanks to the encouragement and support of Bardas, uncle of the emperor Michael III. In 863 he refounded the university under Leo, known as the philosopher, or the mathematician, who taught in the Magnaura Palace with three subordinate teachers of geometry, astronomy and grammar.[7]

According to Anna Comnena intellectual activity, though not entirely extinguished, was in a state of decline from the reign of Basil II (963–1025) to that of Constantine IX (1042–55).[8] In the latter reign, however, in 1045, the university was reconstituted by the emperor with two branches, a law school under Xiphilinus and a school of philosophy under Michael Psellus with a teacher of grammar, Nicetas, under him.[9] There was no rhetorician on the establishment and Psellus himself, a gifted and versatile man, combined rhetorical with philosophical teaching.[10] He attracted pupils from far and wide. Celts and Arabs came to hear him; he was known and admired, he claimed, by Persians and Ethiopians; he had one student who came from Babylonia.[11] He held the title of 'chief of the philosophers' (*hupatos ton philosophon*) and on his retirement to a monastery in 1054 he was succeeded in this office by John Italus. Italus lacked Psellus's literary culture, but was a keen dialectician and, in spite of his irascibility and unstable temperament, a popular teacher.[12] His teaching of philosophy aroused the suspicions of the Church and in 1081–2 he was tried for heresy and condemned; he was succeeded by Theodore of Smyrna, after whom the post of *hupatos ton philosophon* was vacant for half a century.

In the twelfth century the university declined in importance. This was the flourishing period of the Patriarchal School when, among other noted scholars, Eustathius, the Homeric commentator and future archbishop of Thessalonica, taught there. In 1204, with the Latin capture of Constantinople, Nicaea became the imperial capital. It does not, however, seem to have become much of an intellectual centre; Gregory of Cyprus, who went there in search of learning, found no one able to teach him more than grammar and poetry.[13] But with the recovery of Constantinople in 1261, when George Acropolites began to teach philosophy there, the old capital became once more the centre of higher studies.

Though advanced education was concentrated in the imperial capital, there would be schools, whether monastic or private, elsewhere in the Empire where a knowledge could be acquired at least of grammar and sometimes of other subjects. Leo the philosopher studied rhetoric, philosophy and arithmetic at Andros.[14] During the Latin occupation of Constantinople Nicephorus Blemmydes acquired his education in grammar at Prusa, went on to study poetry, rhetoric and elementary logic at Nicaea, and learned mathematics and more advanced logic at Scamander.[15] In the fourteenth century Thessalonica was a flourishing intellectual centre. This was the home of Triclinius, known to classical scholars for his work on the Greek dramatists, and rhetoricians and philosophers were to be found there as well as grammarians.[16] A common practice, however, for those born outside Constantinople was to move there for higher studies after a grammar school education. As a writer of the twelfth century puts it, 'when my father, devoted to learning and to his children, had brought me from Asia to Byzantium for the sake of study at the age of puberty, he handed me over to the masters of the liberal arts and the philosophers, since I had already laid the foundations of grammar and of verse composition'.[17]

Throughout the history of the Byzantine Empire the general scheme of education remained the same. After learning to read, write and count the boy went on to grammar and then to rhetoric. The maintenance of classical standards of spelling and pronunciation must have become more difficult as time went on, and the course in grammar was probably rather longer than had been usual in the classical period. Psellus, an unusually gifted man, who completed his primary education at the early age of eight, did not proceed from grammar to rhetoric until he was sixteen, and George Acropolites finished with grammar at the same age.[18] On the other hand, Theodore Metochites was only thirteen when he passed on from grammar to rhetoric, and Nicephorus Blemmydes had completed his rhetoric course at sixteen.[19] After rhetoric came logic and then mathematics. The Greek equivalent of the Latin term *quadrivium (he mathematike tetraktus)* is found in the eighth century,[20] and the four subjects, arithmetic, geometry, music and astronomy, sometimes with the omission of music, appear regularly in accounts of Byzantine education.[21] There does not seem to have been much specialization in teaching. In the university as reorganized by Bardas there were, as we have seen, specialist teachers of geometry and astronomy, but Psellus taught all the liberal arts other than grammar in the eleventh century, and in the thirteenth George Acropolites combined the teaching of mathematics and of rhetoric with that of Aristotelian philosophy.[22]

The course in logic which was included in the regular secondary education might be followed later by further philosophical study. Teaching was also available in medicine, and law, and these subjects were not always studied merely for professional purposes; the scholar and patriarch Photius had studied medicine as well as grammar, rhetoric and philosophy,[23] and Psellus's education included some study of law and of theology.[24] The last subject however was not normally pursued by laymen, but was primarily a professional study for the clergy. It might follow a secular education in the liberal arts, but there were those who rejected secular studies altogether and pursued nothing but sacred learning.[25]

Grammar, as in the classical period, involved the study of both language and literature, and the two sides of the course were often distinguished, the term *grammatike* or *orthographia* being applied to the first and poetry (*poiesis*) to the second.[26] The teacher of grammar distinguished dialects and dealt with pronunciation, accentuation, accidence and syntax.[27] Dionysius Thrax remained the standard authority, but as time passed the basic doctrine was swollen with elaborate commentary and

K

new textbooks were produced which themselves became the subject of commentary. In an educational dialogue probably of the eleventh century the teacher invites his pupil to learn 'how Dionysius was expanded by Theodosius; Horus and Herodian also wrote textbooks on grammar, and it was expounded by Heliodorus and one Georgius and in greater detail by Choeroboscus'.[28]

Reading of the poets began, as it always had done, with Homer. Other authors studied were the three Attic tragedians, Aristophanes, Hesiod, Pindar and Theocritus,[29] and in the case of the four dramatists it was usual to read three plays of each. Commentary, as is shown by Eustathius's exposition of Homer, tended to run to excessive length. Some teachers made use of allegorical interpretation; Nicetas, Psellus's colleague, we are told, unlike most teachers, did not confine himself to explaining the words and metre, but displayed the hidden meaning beneath the surface and 'entered into the inmost sanctuary'.[30]

In his autobiography Nicephorus Blemmydes described himself as having studied 'the progymnasmata of Aphthonius and the rhetoric of Hermogenes'.[31] These were evidently the two main textbooks of the rhetoric school. Aphthonius's work has been mentioned in an earlier chapter; Hermogenes was a second-century rhetorician who abandoned sophistic declamation for writing on rhetorical theory and added new refinements to traditional doctrine. Both were furnished by the Byzantine teachers with prolegomena and explanatory comment; inevitably too new outlines of rhetoric and expositions of its separate branches were produced.[32] The progymnasmata probably constituted the main, perhaps the sole, exercises in composition of the Byzantine student of rhetoric; the old type of speechmaking on historical and judicial themes seems to have died out.

Mathematical teaching like that of other subjects was based on the old textbooks, in arithmetic Nicomachus and Diophantus, in geometry Euclid and in astronomy Aratus.[33] Teaching, at any rate at certain periods, was limited in scope. According to Theodore Metochites (*c.* 1260–1332) there had been a lack of mathematical teachers for many years, and only those parts of Euclid and Nicomachus that were considered of use for philosophy were studied. Theodore eventually found someone to teach him, and studied the syntaxis of Ptolemy, after which he proceeded to Euclid and other authorities.[34] Theodore himself wrote an introduction to Ptolemaic astronomy, and several of his contemporaries shared his mathematical interests. John Pediasimus wrote scholia on Greek mathematical works and George Pachymeres compiled a handbook to the quadrivium.[35] The monk Maximus Planudes, known for his new and enlarged version of the Greek anthology, had mathematical interests; he wrote on the Arabic or, as he called them, Indian, numerals and rewrote some lines of Aratus in the interests of scientific accuracy.[36]

Philosophy began with Aristotelian logic. The usual practice seems to have been to go through the *Isagoge*, the *Categories* and *De Interpretatione* as part of the trivium and postpone the *Analytica* until after the quadrivium,[37] though George Acropolites expounded the *Analytica* before proceeding to rhetoric and there appear to have been some who dealt with the whole of Aristotelian philosophy before the quadrivium.[38] Philosophical teaching in general was based on Aristotle and his commentators, and teachers who like Psellus proceeded to Plato and the neo-Platonists were rare. According to Psellus the philosophers of his youth 'stood only at the outer door of the Aristotelian doctrines and merely repeated the Platonic allegories, without any understanding of their hidden meaning'.[39] He himself, so he claims, without having had any masters worth mention, studied Aristotle and Plato, and from them went on to Plotinus, Porphyry, Iamblichus and Proclus.[40] His successor John Italus also expounded Plato and the neo-Platonists, though he paid more attention to Aristotle.[41] While Aristotle was regarded as unexceptionable, Platonism was considered dangerous and laid its adherents open to the charge of heresy and paganism. Psellus was accused of being too much of a Platonist to be a Christian, though he himself saw no incompatibility between the faith and Platonism;[42] John Italus, as we have seen, was condemned for heresy, and in the last years of Byzantine civilization Gemistus Plethon was with some justice believed to be attempting to revive neo-Platonist paganism.

Numerous Byzantine commentaries on Aristotle, largely

derived from those of late antiquity, survive to show that the methods of the philosopher's classroom remained unchanged. But the good teacher did more than dictate his comments on the standard texts. Psellus did his best to arouse the interest of his students and to keep their attention. He was not always successful. He complained that because he made learning easy and attractive they did not value it. They arrived late, they failed to turn up if it rained; when they did come their minds were on the theatre rather than on their studies.[43] When he invited questions they would try to catch him out or say what first came into their minds without taking trouble to prepare their questions.[44] 'One of you says "What business of mine is it to know the causes of earthquakes?", another "What's the point of my learning why seawater is salt, and how does it help me to earn a living?".'[45] But he had his responsive pupils such as John Patricius who, although interested in practical affairs and drawn to the study of law, made a point of omitting no branch of philosophy and asked intelligent questions if there was anything he did not understand.[46]

In medicine Byzantium preserved and handed on the science of the ancient world as embodied in the encyclopaedic work of the fourth-century physician Oribasius and of followers of his such as Paul of Aegina (seventh century).[47] Alexandria remained the centre for medical teaching until the Arab conquest, but in the fifth century a leading physician Agapius was brought from there to teach at Constantinople, and medical training continued to be available there[48] until the fourteenth century. Teaching then came to an end, and for the last century or so of Byzantine civilization medical practice was in the hands of the Jews.

The destruction of Beirut by earthquake in the mid-sixth century brought an end to the law school there and left Constantinople as the only centre for legal education in the Greek Empire.[49] After Justinian's codification of the law in 534 the curriculum consisted of the Institutes, the Digest and the Codex; twenty-six digests out of fifty were lectured on, the rest being studied by the pupils on their own. The lawyers continued to use the Latin texts until the death of Justinian, and consequently it was found necessary to dictate a translation or paraphrase, after which the teacher made his comments on the passage dictated and asked and answered questions. Public teaching of law seems to have ceased about the time of Justinian's death and to have given place to private teaching by practising barristers. But the re-establishment of the university in 1045 brought into existence a state school of law, with a competent lawyer in Xiphilinus to direct it. Xiphilinus had the title of *nomophulax*; he had a salary and official robes and rooms were provided for his teaching.

Theology continued to be taught on traditional lines; it was based on the Scriptures and the Fathers and little influenced by secular philosophy. Intellectually the eastern theologians were hardly equal to those of the West, as was noted by George Scholarius in the fifteenth century when there was considerable contact between Byzantium and the West. The Latin theologians, he observed, were more thoroughly educated than the Greeks; 'they have to be philosophers and dialecticians first before they begin theology'.[50] Byzantium produced no synthesis like that of the Latin churchmen between faith and reason, between Christianity and Aristotelian philosophy.[51] There was indeed a greater degree of intellectual activity and original thought in western Europe in the Middle Ages than in the Byzantine Empire. The fact that so much of the ancient heritage was lost in the West and had to be recovered seems to have provided a stimulus which was absent in the East where the tradition of higher education remained unbroken.

While Greek learning was maintained and preserved in the Byzantine Empire some part of it passed to the Arabs and was absorbed into Islamic civilization. As the Romans had learned from the Greeks and had adopted and adapted their culture, so did the Arabs. But there were differences. The Arabs did not learn Greek and take over the Greek educational system. They did not, as the Romans did, look to the masterpieces of Greece to provide models in poetry and prose; unlike the Romans they already had a literature of their own when they came into contact with the Greeks, and though it may have been under Greek influence that they developed the study of grammar and rhetoric, Greek theory and scholastic practice were of little relevance to their literature. Nor did the Arab world adopt Roman law. Arab borrowings from Greece were in science and philosophy. They adopted the medicine, the mathematics and the philosophy of the Greek world of late antiquity. In the case of philosophy there was, as in Byzantium and western Europe, some conflict with religion. Islam had its revealed religion and its sacred text. There were those who reconciled the teachings of Mohammed with those of the Greek philosophers, but on the whole Islam was less receptive of secular philosophical influences than was Christianity, and its educational system was more exclusively religious than that of Byzantium or of western Europe after the twelfth century.

The translation of Greek works into oriental languages began in late antiquity, when Syriac versions were made of Christian writings and of Aristotelian and medical texts. After the rise of Islam and the Arab conquests there was extensive translation into Arabic both from Syriac versions and direct from the Greek. After the foundation of Baghdad the work of translation enjoyed official support. The caliph Al-Ma'mūn (812–33) founded in Baghdad a 'House of Wisdom' with a library, as a centre for translators. The chief translator Hunain b. Ishāq was a competent linguist who used the best manuscripts available, and as a medical practitioner had a particular interest in Galen. As a result of his work and that of a number of other translators the standard texts in philosophy, mathematics and medicine became available in Arabic.

The Arab scholars accepted the general scheme of contemporary Greek science, the four mathematical subjects and the Aristotelian disciplines of logic, physics, metaphysics and ethics. According to the fourteenth-century writer Ibn Khaldūn logic comes first, followed in order by arithmetic, geometry, astronomy and music, and then physics (under which he includes medicine) and metaphysics.[52] But these studies did not obtain a secure place in the Arab educational system. The Madrasa, or colleges, taught Islamic theology and law, and their recognition of Greek philosophy did not go further than the *Isagoge*; philosophy was for the most part taught privately, or acquired from books, rather than transmitted, as in the Greek world, in regular schools. The best illustration of how it could be acquired is in the autobiography of the philosopher Avicenna (980–1037). He had already studied the Koran, Arabic literature and Muslim law when a philosopher arrived at his home town. His father invited the philosopher to stay in his house and under him Avicenna read the *Isagoge*, studied the simpler parts of logic and began Euclid and the Almagest of Ptolemy. The philosopher, whose capacity was limited, left and Avicenna continued with his reading unaided. He went on to natural science, metaphysics and medicine. At the age of sixteen he had read all the books on medicine and began to practise. Aristotle's Metaphysics he found difficult, but he read it forty times until he knew it by heart, and with the aid of a book by al-Fārābī which he acquired he eventually mastered it. In later life he gave instruction privately while holding various official posts. His follower al-Juzjani used to visit his house, read the Almagest with him and heard his lectures on logic, and at a later stage of his life he would teach a band of students who assembled at his house after the day's work was over.[53] In this sort of unofficial way Greek learning and thought was handed on among the Arabs. They preserved what they had taken over from the Greeks and added something of their own. In medical science, mathematics and Aristotelian philosophy they were ahead of western Europe until the revival of intellectual life in the twelfth and thirteenth centuries, when the learning of the Arab world along with that of Byzantium passed by means of translations to the universities of the West.

The Middle Ages in the West

In the West education declined with the collapse of Roman civilization in the fifth and following centuries. In Italy, however, there was something of a revival under the Ostrogoth Theodoric (493–526) and his successor Athalaric.[54] In this period Cassiodorus testifies to a widespread interest in secular learning;[55] we hear of schools of rhetoric and law at Rome and of a grammarian and rhetorician teaching at Milan.[56] In this period, too, we have the literary activity of Boethius. Whether, as has been suggested,[57] Boethius himself studied in Alexandria or not, the scheme of study represented by his works, completed or projected, was that of the Greek schools of later antiquity. He did not deal with grammar and rhetoric, which had long had a secure place in Roman education, but he covered the quadrivium, and in philosophy began by translating Porphyry's *Isagoge* and went on to the Organon, from which he would have proceeded to the rest of the Aristotelian corpus and finally to Plato if he had been able to complete his project. This was the order followed in the Greek schools, and Boethius's intention of reconciling Aristotle and Plato[58] was in line with what had long been their aim. His work has all the appearance of a scholastic programme; it seems designed to provide texts for a complete course of higher education. Yet Boethius himself was not a teacher, and there were, so far as we know, no philosophic schools in contemporary Rome which could use his works as textbooks. At the time his work can have had little influence. Eventually, however, it was to be of immense importance. It could indeed be argued that Boethius set the tone for the whole of medieval thought, both by what he wrote and by what he did not write, by the fact that he translated Aristotle's logical works but went no further.

Secular education, confined in the main no doubt to grammar and rhetoric, survived to a limited extent in Italy. In Gaul and other provinces it faded away with the decay of the municipalities which had supported it. Education was left in the hands of the Church. The monasteries were the main educational centres until the rise of cathedral schools in the eleventh and twelfth centuries, and the teaching they provided was of course primarily religious. The age of Charlemagne saw an advance in education, and advance, then as later, meant the recovery of the heritage of antiquity. It was Charlemagne's deliberate policy to encourage education; he summoned Alcuin from York to take charge of his palace school and to advise on educational matters; he decreed that schools should be established in all monasteries and cathedrals. The Carolingian renaissance was followed by a certain decline in the tenth century, but at the end of that century we find Gerbert (Pope Silvester II) studying and teaching not only grammar and rhetoric but also logic and mathematics. With the twelfth century came a second renaissance. Guibert of Nogent (1053–1124) records that when he began to study grammarians were so scarce that there were virtually none in small towns and very few in the cities, and even these were of meagre attainments; later in his life, in the early twelfth century, grammar was so flourishing and the schools so numerous that its study was available to anyone.[59] This was the great age of cathedral schools. The cathedrals were in the main centres of population and open to new ideas; their schools were progressive by contrast with the conservative monastic schools.[60]

In the twelfth century students would move from one centre to another to study under some famous master; Abelard went wherever he heard that the study of dialectic was flourishing.[61] In the latter part of the twelfth century the various schools of Paris developed into the university. With the establishment of this and other universities higher education became concentrated in certain centres and regulated by statute. Some universities specialized in particular subjects, Bologna in law, Salerno and Montpellier in medicine. Others embraced all the recognized branches of learning. In these the arts faculty, as its name indicates, comprised the seven liberal arts with the addition of an increasing quantity of Aristotelian philosophy and science; above the arts faculty were the higher faculties of medicine, law and theology. The scheme of study was essentially that of classical antiquity; the difference was that the schools of the ancient world were now combined in a single institution and that courses were regulated, students examined and degrees conferred.

The curriculum fixed in antiquity remained unchallenged so far as concerned the liberal arts. Cassiodorus had included them in his *Institutiones*; Rabanus Maurus in the early ninth century and Hugo of St Victor in the twelfth recognized their value for the education of the clergy.[62] But though accepted in theory the arts had little place in monastic education; grammar, it is true, was essential for the understanding of Latin, but the chief use of mathematics was for the calculation of the date of Easter. The Carolingian renaissance was primarily literary in character, and it is not until Gerbert that we find any serious teaching of mathematics.

The philosophers, according to Rabanus Maurus, need not be shunned if, like the Platonists, they say what is agreeable to the Christian faith.[63] This, however, was simply taken from St Augustine and was of little relevance to the ninth century. When philosophy (as opposed to the elementary logic which formed part of the trivium) made its way into the educational system it was that of Aristotle, not Plato. Aristotle was at first regarded with suspicion by the Church authorities; in 1210 and

1215 lectures on his Metaphysics and physical works were forbidden at Paris.[64] Thanks, however, to the work of the Dominican theologians in reconciling his philosophy with orthodox Christianity he became the accepted authority in the universities. By the middle of the thirteenth century nearly all his works were studied at Paris, and a century or so later inceptors in arts had to take an oath to teach no doctrine inconsistent with Aristotle.[65]

Theology was considered to be the queen of sciences, the crown of education. 'If believers,' wrote Abelard, 'are allowed to read works on the liberal arts and the books of the ancients it is . . . that we may be able to grasp whatever concerns the understanding or the beauty of Holy Scripture, or the defence or support of its truth.'[66] Abelard was one of the chief creators of a new theology in which reason was applied to doctrinal questions, and the impressive work of Albertus Magnus and Thomas Aquinas enhanced the status of the subject. Yet in the later Middle Ages its position in education was not quite as strong as might be thought. It had its rivals in the secular subjects of law and medicine, and not a few churchmen preferred the study of canon law to that of theology. Moreover, many university students failed to proceed beyond the faculty of arts, and there the curriculum was entirely secular.[67]

Grammar inevitably came first in the order of studies, if only because Latin was the medium of higher education and an adequate command of the language was necessary for any further study. Next came dialectic and rhetoric and then the quadrivium. This was the order followed by Gerbert at Rheims, though he read the poets, who had presumably been neglected in the earlier stage of grammatical instruction, as a preparation for rhetoric.[68] In the twelfth century there seems to have been no regular curriculum or established order of studies. John of Salisbury studied logic at Paris; then he went to Chartres where he spent three years studying grammar and the quadrivium, after which he returned to Paris to attend lectures on logic and theology from one master and then on theology from another. From about the middle of the twelfth century logic became the all-absorbing interest of the schools and ousted the humanistic studies represented by grammar and rhetoric. We meet with a number of complaints about the neglect of the latter subjects.

Peter of Blois writes of students disputing on profound philo-sophical and scientific subjects without learning the elementary disciplines,[69] Giraldus Cambrensis of those who neglect gram-mar and rhetoric and hurry on to logic.[70] John of Salisbury, after describing the methods of his masters in grammar, writes:

> Afterwards when . . . men preferred the appearance of philosophers to the reality and teachers of the arts promised to impart the whole of philosophy to their hearers in less than three, or even two, years, they retired defeated before the attack of the ignorant mob; and from then on less time and care has been spent on the study of grammar;

and he goes on to write scornfully of how 'boys of yesterday today turned masters, who yesterday were being caned in school and are now teaching robed in the master's chair' run down the study of grammar.[71] The prevailing passion for logic and the rediscovery of the complete Aristotle led to the neglect not only of grammar and rhetoric but also of the quadrivium. At Paris from the thirteenth century the arts faculty was dominated by Aristotelian philosophy and science, though at Oxford the old scheme still had some validity and the seven arts were not completely ousted.[72]

In grammar the standard textbooks were the works of Donatus and Priscian dating respectively from the fourth and the sixth centuries. Donatus's *Ars Minor*, an elementary work on the parts of speech in the form of question and answer, was used in the earlier stages; at the universities Donatus's 'Barbarismus' (the third book of his *Ars Major*) and Priscian's lengthy treatise were the textbooks. At the end of the twelfth century and the beginning of the thirteenth two new Latin grammars appeared, both in Latin hexameters, the *Doctrinale* of Alexander of Villedieu and the *Graecismus* of Eberhard of Béthune, which owed its name to the fact that it included explanations of some Greek words; the former became the standard textbook of Europe in the fourteenth and fifteenth centuries.[73] Latin was now a language which had to be acquired by those who were to use it. No doubt it was acquired to some extent by using it and hearing it used; the rule was that nothing but

Latin must be spoken in schools and colleges. But use was certainly made of the vernacular in teaching. At the end of the tenth century Aelfric wrote a Latin grammar in Anglo-Saxon. 'Construing', that is, word-for-word oral translation of the original, was in use in schools, and in England from the Norman Conquest to the mid-fourteenth century it was done into French. Then a grammar school master called John Cornwaile introduced the use of English and by 1385 it had become the universal medium.[74] Whatever the methods used the medieval teachers succeeded in giving their pupils, with their diverse linguistic background, an adequate command of the language, and though there were departures from classical usage, grammatical correctness was maintained in writing Latin, though not always in speaking it.[75]

The first reading book was the 'Distichs of Cato', a series of moral maxims in verse dating from late antiquity. Next might come the fabulists Aesop and Avianus and the 'Eclogue' of Theodulus, a ninth-century 'amoebaean' poem in which the contestants expound respectively pagan and Christian stories. There appears to have been no generally accepted programme for more advanced reading. In the fourth, fifth and sixth centuries a number of poems had been written on Christian themes in the classical metres, and some of these, for example the epic poems of Juvencus and Sedulius, seem to have been consciously designed to provide an alternative to the traditional texts of the grammar schools.[76] These works continued to be popular, but they never ousted the pagan classics. Gerbert lecturing at Rheims read Virgil, Statius, Terence, Juvenal, Persius, Horace (Satires) and Lucan with his students.[77] A list of authors in verse and prose dating from the twelfth century includes the same writers and adds Ovid and a number of Christian poets, and in prose Cicero (*De Amicitia* and *De Senectute*), Sallust and Boethius.[78] Another document, belonging to the end of the twelfth century, lays down that after the early reading books the student should 'read the satirists and writers of history, so that even when young he may learn to avoid vices and desire to imitate the noble deeds of heroes'. From the *Thebaid* he should proceed to the *Aeneid* and then go on to Lucan and Juvenal. He should read all Horace's works and Ovid's elegies and *Metamorphoses* and in particular his *Remedia*

Amoris. There follows a list of books which one might call recommended (in some cases with considerable reserve) rather than prescribed: the *Fasti*, the *Achilleid*, the *Eclogues* and *Georgics*, Sallust, Cicero (*De Oratore, Tusculans, De Amicitia, De Senectute, De Fato, De Natura Deorum, De Officiis*), Martial, Petronius, Symmachus, Solinus, Sidonius, Suetonius, Quintus Curtius, Pompeius Trogus (i.e. Justin), Crisippus [*sic*], Livy and Seneca (Letters, *Naturales Quaestiones, De Beneficiis*, tragedies and declamations).[79] These lists are too comprehensive to enable us to judge how much the average student actually got through. Nor did practice always agree with the precepts of the educationalists. Roger Bacon quotes Boethius (that is, the thirteenth-century *De Disciplina Scholarium* which went under the name of Boethius) as recommending that schoolboys should begin by reading Seneca, but, he says, 'that is not how they are taught; they are brought up on the foolish tales of Ovid and other poets'.[80] The pagan poets survived the competition not only of Christian poets but also of pagan moralists.

After the flourishing period of medieval humanism in the twelfth century the study of literature was in decline. The 'arts' ousted the 'authors'. Literary study was limited to a grammar school course which normally ended at the age of fourteen and cannot have been carried very far. In the French universities of the thirteenth and fourteenth centuries no classical Latin texts were prescribed.[81] Grammar in the universities meant not, as it had meant in classical times, the study of both language and literature, but that of language divorced from literature, of Donatus and Priscian but not of Virgil and Horace.

The fullest account we have of teaching in a medieval grammar school is that given by John of Salisbury of the method followed by his masters at Chartres, William of Conches and Richard l'Évêque, and before them by Bernard of Chartres.[82] Teaching consisted of three parts, lectures on authors, grammatical instruction and composition. In lecturing on texts the masters of Chartres pointed out grammatical figures, rhetorical colours, and sophistical quibbles; they showed where the section prescribed for reading had a bearing on other branches of learning and pointed to examples of brilliance or propriety and of metaphorical usage. Passages were committed to memory and recited on the following day. In the evening a class called 'declinatio' was held, which was 'so replete with abundance of grammar that if anyone spent a whole year on it, provided he was reasonably intelligent, he would have command of the principles of speaking and writing and could not fail to know the meaning of phrases in common use'. In teaching composition the masters provided models for imitation and pointed out their virtues and their faults. The pupils wrote exercises in prose and in verse every day, and learnt by comparing their work with that of their fellows.

The procedure is much the same as it was in the time of Quintilian, on whom John draws extensively in describing it. In one respect, however, there is innovation: verse composition has now become part of grammar school teaching. The rules of Latin metre had been taught as part of grammar in late antiquity, but there is no firm evidence that grammar school boys were then made to compose verses. When this exercise was first introduced is not clear, but we find it in use in the school of York under Alcuin's master Aelbert,[83] and the ready command of the classical metres shown by so many writers from the time of Charlemagne must have been the result of practice at school in the art of verse making.

The textbooks for rhetoric are given in a twelfth-century source as *De Inventione, Ad Herennium, De Oratore* and the Greater Declamations ascribed to Quintilian,[84] but of these only the first two were in general use. Gerbert, teaching rhetoric at Rheims, after his preparatory course in Latin poetry passed his pupils on to a 'sophist' with whom they were exercised in *controversiae*.[85] This was perhaps the last time rhetoric was taught as in the schools of the classical period; if the *controversiae* declaimed at Rheims were of the old type they were not of much relevance to the Middle Ages. Classical rhetoric declined. It was neglected in the French universities;[86] at Bologna in the thirteenth century student opinion had no use for Ciceronian rhetoric and it was not the subject of ordinary lectures.[87] A new rhetoric, however, developed more suited to contemporary needs, the *ars dictaminis*, which gave rules for the composition of letters and official documents and which was particularly associated with Buoncampagno, who taught at Bologna in the first half of the thirteenth century. In addition to this specialized teaching there was training in the writing of

Latin such as that provided at Chartres, where orators as well as poets were read as models. In the later Middle Ages grammar and rhetoric tended to be combined, in the sense that poetry and prose were studied together; at Bologna in 1324 a doctor in grammar was appointed to lecture on Cicero and Ovid's *Metamorphoses*, and at Oxford in 1431 the *Metamorphoses* and Virgil's works appear along with Aristotle and Cicero as text-books in rhetoric.[88]

Of the subjects which formed the quadrivium music was of small importance. It was unknown in Italy when Gerbert was studying and equally unknown in France when he began to teach it, no doubt using Boethius's treatise as his textbook.[89] The subject appears in the curricula of Oxford and Cambridge, but we hear nothing of it at Paris.[90] Though it was to a large extent neglected in arts courses it was taught in a different way as part of elementary education. The seven-year-old schoolboy in Chaucer's Prioress's Tale learns

> Swich maner doctrine as men used there,
> This is to seyn, to singen and to rede,
> As smale children doon in hir childhede.[91]

The practical training given in the monasteries and cathedral song schools was of more significance than the faint survival of theoretical music as one of the liberal arts.

In addition to his treatise on music Boethius had handed down to the Middle Ages a work on arithmetic (derived from Nicomachus of Gerasa) and a translation of Euclid;[92] if he also wrote, as he is said to have done, a textbook of astronomy, it has not survived. Mathematical knowledge remained at a low level until the end of the tenth century, but revived with Gerbert. In the twelfth century there was an increased interest in the subject shown in the appearance of a number of trans-lations of Arabic mathematical works,[93] but in the next century it tended to be pushed out of the university curricula by Aris-totle. In the fourteenth and fifteenth centuries some Euclid was included in the courses of the northern universities, and at Bologna in the fourteenth century there was a four-year course in astrology which included some arithmetic and geometry.[94]

Logic, or dialectic, had a place in the trivium and it also served as the first stage in a course of Aristotelian philosophy.

Its recognition as part of the trivium ensured it a place in medieval education, and its establishment there opened the way to the higher stages of Aristotelianism. When Gerbert lectured on logic he read, in Boethius's translation, the *Isagoge*, the *Categories*, *De Interpretatione* and Cicero's *Topica* with Boethius's commentary, as well as Boethius's independent logical works.[95] This, apart from Boethius's independent works, formed the normal course in logic until the twelfth century, the *logica vetus*. To judge by the practice of Byzantium[96] this 'old logic' constituted what was considered appropriate to the trivium, while the rest of the Organon belonged properly to a course in philosophy, though this distinction can hardly have been specifically recognized in the West at a time when philosophical courses were non-existent.

Logic was already flourishing when Abelard was a student, and in the first half of the twelfth century the widespread interest in the subject led to the rediscovery of the *Analytica*, *Topica* and *Sophistici Elenchi*, the 'new logic', as it was called. The old translations by Boethius began to circulate and a new version of the whole of the Organon was made about 1128. The rest of Aristotle followed. Translations appeared whether from Arabic or from the original Greek. The Metaphysics and the Physics first became available in the second half of the twelfth century, and *De Caelo*, *De Generatione*, *De Animalibus*, *De Anima*, and finally the Ethics, Politics, Poetics and Rhetoric in the thirteenth century.[97] These translations became the set texts of the universities. The arts faculties of the later Middle Ages were in the main schools of Aristotelian science and philosophy. They did not go beyond Aristotle to Plato. Certain Platonic works were known in translation in the Middle Ages, but they had no place in university curricula. Plato did not, in England at any rate, gain a footing in the universities until the nineteenth century.

The medical science of the medieval universities was, of course, Greek in origin, but in the main it came via the Arabs. Towards the end of the eleventh century one Constantinus Africanus translated a number of medical works, Greek and Arabic, which became the textbooks of the medical faculties with, at a later date, translations of works by Avicenna and Averroes. Little, if any, practical training was involved; all was theoretical and derived from books. The revival of Roman Law as an academic study dates from the first three decades of the twelfth century when Irnerius taught at Bologna. Some law had been taught before in conjunction with grammar and rhetoric; now law became a professional subject to which grammar and rhetoric were preparatory. Bologna was the leading school of law, and it was probably there that lectures were first given on the whole of the corpus of civil law.[98] The method of teaching was as follows. The lecturer gave a summary of each title and expounded the purport of the law; then he read the text with a view to correcting it, then repeated its contents. Next he solved apparent contradictions and added any general legal principles, distinctions or problems arising out of the law, with their solution. If the law deserved it there was an evening session at which there was a more detailed discussion of some particular question; and in Lent there were disputations at which a doctor maintained a thesis against all comers.[99]

According to a fourteenth-century writer the trivium is sufficient preparation for theologians, but the more proficient a man is in the arts the better theologian he is, 'because it is the theologian alone who disputes on any subject'.[100] In fact the characteristic feature of medieval theology was that its exponents were proficient in the arts and approached theology well trained in logical argument. The basic text in teaching was, of course, the Bible. To the Bible the commentators added the opinions of the Fathers. These were sometimes contradictory; their contradictions had to be resolved, and this led to theological discussion and the appeal to reason as well as authority. In the twelfth century Abelard deserted the old method of scriptural commentary to lecture on fundamental problems of the faith, and in response to requests from his students wrote an introduction to theology.[101]

The standard theological textbook from about the middle of the twelfth century was the *Sentences* of Peter Lombard, a collection of the opinions of the Fathers on various points of doctrine with answers to the questions arising from their divergences. In theological courses the study of the *Sentences* came after that of the Bible. At Paris, the great centre of theological teaching, four years were spent on the Bible and two on the *Sentences*, after which came the baccalaureat; the

L

bachelor lectured for two years on the Bible, after which he was allowed to lecture on the *Sentences*.[102]

The method of Peter Lombard, the resolving by dialectic of contrary opinions, was embodied in that characteristic feature of the medieval universities, the disputation, in which one participant maintained an opinion and another raised objections, while the master determined the question. This exercise developed from the problems raised in connection with the reading of texts and the questions put by the master or his pupils. A respondent would be appointed to give a solution and to answer any objections raised by others, and by the thirteenth century this had developed into a regular academic exercise.[103] 'The key to wisdom lies in constant questioning. . . . Doubt leads us to enquire and by enquiring we come to perceive the truth.' So wrote Abelard.[104] It sounds like a return to Socrates, or at least to Carneades. But whatever may have been the case with Abelard and his pupils the disputations as finally established did not necessarily encourage doubt. The student was expected to know not only the arguments but also the answers to them. And he had to observe the rules of the game, to argue according to Aristotelian logic. The time came when men began to regard the game as barren and pointless and to look for guidance and inspiration elsewhere than in the Organon.

The Renaissance did not bring a sudden change to the educational system. The general pattern long remained the same, and Aristotle continued to be the accepted authority in the universities. The main change, apart from an advance in scholarship, was a shift of emphasis from philosophy to literary study, which resulted in the extension of the grammar school course and a relative decline in the importance of the universities. The intellectual system known as scholasticism, which was essentially derived from antiquity, was, paradoxically, challenged by the movement which is commonly thought of as a return to the ancient world.[105] The Renaissance was a return to the ancient world, but to aspects of it not represented in the schools of the later Middle Ages, to the practical morality of men like Cicero, to a philosophy which did not merely sharpen one's wits but made one a better man. Paradoxically too the Renaissance, which brought to western Europe the knowledge of Greek and of Greek literature, was also a movement away from Greece. For medieval education, although conducted in Latin, was essentially Greek in character. The curriculum was that of the Greek schools of later antiquity, and the scholastic philosophers with their love of subtle dialectic argument are more Greek than Roman. Scholasticism flourished in northern Europe and was relatively weak in Italy. The Renaissance was primarily an Italian movement, and it was only natural that it should bear the stamp of ancient Rome. Humanist education, with its emphasis on literature, oratory and morality, can be thought of as a return to Rome.

It was a return to Rome, but to a Rome whose education, as we have seen, was based on the study of Greek as well as of Latin. As the Romans in the days of Cicero and Quintilian had studied Greek literature so did the schoolboys of Renaissance Europe. While the authority of Aristotle was superseded with the rise of experimental science, the *doctrina duplex* of the Romans as revived at the Renaissance survived until, belatedly it might be said, the vernacular literatures claimed a place in the curriculum and the descendants of the ancient *grammatici* began to retreat before the English, French, German and other *grammatici*.

Notes

Notes to chapter 1

1 Solon, fr. 27; Hippocrates VIII, p. 636 (Littré); Aristotle, *Pol.* VII. 1336b (*ad fin.*); Philo, *de Opificio Mundi* 35–6 (I. 25–6); Macrobius, *Comm. Somn. Scip.* I. 6. 70–4.

2 Quintilian I. 1. 15.

3 Aristotle, *Pol.* 1336b (*ad fin.*).

4 *Ibid.* 1339a.

5 See F. Kühnert, *Allgemeinbildung und Fachbildung in der Antike* (Berlin, 1961).

6 In the third century B.C. study of the encyclic subjects preceded the *ephebia* (Teles, p. 50 Hense). In the second and first centuries, when it no longer involved serious military training, the *ephebes* were required to attend classes in grammar, rhetoric, mathematics and philosophy. *I.G.* II². 1006. 17–20; 1008. 56; 1009. 35; 1011. 22; 1028. 34–5; 1029. 21; 1032. 32; 1039. 17, 45–8; 1040. 27; 1043. 42–3.

7 Plato, *Rep.* VI. 537b.

8 Plato, *Rep.* VI. 497e–498a (Cornford's translation, adapted).

9 Athenaeus II. 59d–f (fr. II Kock).

10 Plato, *Rep.* VII. 536d; *Laws* VII. 817e–818a.

11 D. L. IV. 10; Stobaeus II. 31. 22, 27, 28, 111. The inscription said to have been put up in the Academy *ageometretos medeis eisito* (Philoponus, *in Arist. de Anima, C.A.G.* XV. 117. 27; Elias, *in Arist. Cat., C.A.G.* XVIII. 1. 111. 18) points in the same direction.

12 D.L. VII. 32, 129.

13 D.L. X. 2, 14.

14 See De Witt, *Epicurus and his Philosophy* (Minneapolis, 1954), pp. 68, 93. (But De Witt quotes no evidence for his statement that the Epicureans established elementary schools of their own.)

15 Cicero, *Fam.* XIII. 1. 2.

16 Cicero, *Ac. Pr.* II. 8.

17 Isocrates, *Ant.* 264–6.

18 Seneca, *Epp.* 88. 1–2. (We ought to have learnt them, not to go on learning them.)

19 Seneca, *Epp.* 88. 20.

20 Plutarch, *Mor.* 7c–d. *Cf.* Philo, *De Congressu* 3 (1. 520); Maximus Tyrius XXXVII. 3; Lactantius, *Div. Inst.* III. 25; Clemens Alexandrinus, *Strom.* 1. 30.

21 Sextus Empiricus treated dialectic as part of philosophy and omitted it when he directed his destructive criticism against the liberal arts.

22 Isocrates, *Ant.* 87, 93.

23 Quintilian I. 12. 12.

24 Pliny, *Epp.* V. 8. 8.

25 Cicero, *Brut.* 306; *De Am.* 1.

26 Gellius XVIII. 4. 1.

27 *Vita Persii*; Persius V. 30–40.

28 Plutarch, *Mor.* 37b–f. A character in Lucian has nearly finished a course in Peripatetic philosophy at the age of eighteen. *Philopseudes* 14.

29 Galen V. 41 (references here and elsewhere are to Kühn's edition); Philostratus, *Vit. Ap. Ty.* I. 7; Seneca, *Epp.* XLIX. 2.

30 Quintilian XII. pr. 3.

31 A. Birley, *Marcus Aurelius* (London, 1966), pp. 120–1.

32 Lucian, *Herm.* 2, 13.

33 Quintilian I. 10. 2 f. *Cf.* Apuleius, *Flor.* 20.

34 D.H., *Comp. Verb.* 25, 206; Theon, *Prog.* 1.

35 Lucian, *Rhet. Praec.* 14.

36 Galen XIX, p. 9.

37 *F. Gr. Hist.* II. 90. 132; Plutarch, *Mor.* 736d.

38 Philo, *De Congressu* 14 (I. 530); Eusebius, *H.E.* VI. 18. 3; Gregory Thaumaturgus, *In Orig. Or.* 6–15 (*P.G.* 10. 1050–1103).

39 Augustine, *Conf.* IV. 16. 30.

40 *S.I.G.* 577, 578; E. Ziebarth, *Aus den Griechischen Schulwesen* (Leipzig-Berlin, 1909); M. P. Nilsson, *Die Hellenistische Schule* (München, 1955), pp. 42–6.

41 *S.I.G.* 672; Polybius XXXI. 31. 1.

42 *I.G.* XII. 9. 234. 8–13, 235. 10–11.

43 Strabo XVII. 1. 8; *O.G.I.* II, p. 453.

44 This privilege was enjoyed by the philosopher Hermias and, after his death, by his sons. Suidas *s.v.* Aidesia.

45 Suetonius, *Vesp.* 18.

46 Dio Cassius LXXII. 31.3. For the philosophical schools, see p. 78.

47 Strabo IV. 1. 5; Pliny, *Epp.* IV. 13. 1.

48 Suetonius, *Vesp.* 18.

49 Juvenal VII. 186–7.

50 Suetonius, *Gr.* 23.

51 Juvenal VII. 157; Libanius, *Or.* XXXI. 19.

52 Augustine, *Conf.* V. 12. 22; *A.P.* IX. 174 (Palladas), which shows that payment (of a grammarian) might be by the year or by the month. The former seems to have been usual in the case of rhetoricians. Libanius, *Or.* XXXI. 19.

53 Philostratus, *Vit. Soph.* II, 21 (604), I. 21 (519).

54 Suetonius, *Gr.* 7.

55 Juvenal VII. 217.
56 T. Frank, *An Economic Survey of Rome* V (Baltimore, 1940), pp. 344–7. The teacher of mathematics (*geometres*) gets the same as the grammarian.
57 *Cod. Theod.* XIII. 3. 11. At Trier only 50 per cent higher.
58 McCrum and Woodhead, *Select Documents of the Principates of the Flavian Emperors* (Cambridge, 1961), No. 458.
59 *Cod. Theod.* XIII. 3. 1, 3, 10, 16, 18; *Digest* XXVII. 1. 6. 1, 5, 8, L. 4. 18. 30.
60 *Cod. Theod.* XIII. 3. 16; *Digest* XIII. 1. 6. 5, 7, 8, L. 5. 8; *Cod. Just.* X. 42. 6.
61 *Digest* L. 5. 2. 8.
62 McCrum and Woodhead, *Select Documents of the Principates of the Flavian Emperors*, No. 458.

Notes to chapter 2

1 Sextus Empiricus, *Adv. Math.* I. 41.
2 Suetonius, *Gr.* 4.
3 Aurelius Opilius, Antonius Gnipho, Ateius Philologus (*ibid.* 6, 7, 10). But with the possible exception of Gnipho these men did not teach both subjects concurrently. One of Ausonius's Bordeaux professors, Nepotianus, was both grammarian and rhetorician. Ausonius V. 15.
4 Suetonius, *Gr.* 4.
5 Strabo XIV. 1. 48.
6 Persius started grammar at the age of eleven or twelve (*Vita Persi*). In the fourth century twelve was the recognized age for beginning the subject. Oribasius, *Synopsis ad Eustathium* V. 14 (*Corpus Medicorum Graecorum* VI. 3, p. 158). Jullien (*Les Professeurs de littérature dans l'ancienne Rome* (Paris 1885), p. 138) notes that in Ovid, *Met.* VIII. 241–3, Perdix begins his lessons with Daedalus at twelve.
7 Strabo XII. 3. 16.
8 Cicero, *Q.F.* II. 4. 2.
9 Suetonius, *Gr.* 16.
10 Gellius VII. 6. 12, XX. 6. 1. Libanius was aged twenty when he read the *Acharnians* with a grammarian. *Or.* I. 9. He describes his teacher as a *grammatistes*, but see P. Wolf, *Vom Schulwesen der Spätantike. Studien zu Libanius* (Baden-Baden, 1952), pp. 32–3.
11 Plato, *Prot.* 338e–339a.
12 Plato, *Hipp. Min.* 363a–c.
13 Aristophanes, fr. 222 Kock (from the *Daitales*).
14 Clemens Alexandrinus, *Strom.* I. xvi. 79. *Cf.* Schol. Vat. Dion. Thr. p. 164 Hilgard (*Gr. Graeci* III); Schol. Lond. *ibid.* p. 448. Another candidate for the title of the first *grammatikos* was Antidorus of Cumae. *Gr. Graeci* III, pp. 3, 7, 448. See R. Pfeiffer, *History of Classical Scholarship* (Oxford, 1968), pp. 157–8.
15 Athenaeus XI. 489a.

16 Dionysius Thrax I (*Gr. Graeci* ed. Uhlig I, p. 5); Sextus Empiricus, *Adv. Math.* I. 250.

17 *Ibid.* 79, 248.

18 [Plato], *Axiochus* 366E.

19 Quintilian I. 4. 2.

20 Tacitus, *Dialogus* 29. 1.

21 Quintilian I. 1. 13.

22 Paulinus of Pella, *Eucharisticus* 75–80. But his grandfather Ausonius had difficulties with his Greek. Ausonius V. 8. 13–16.

23 Augustine, *Conf.* I. xiv. 23.

24 This is Quintilian's recommendation (I. 1. 12–14). He seems to imply that it was normal practice.

25 Jullien, *Les Professeurs de littérature dans l'ancienne Rome*, p. 170. The separation of the two professions was probably not quite as complete as Jullien maintained. Two of Ausonius's Bordeaux professors were *grammatici Latini et Graeci*. Ausonius V. 21.

26 Petronius 46. 5.

27 Suetonius, *Gr.* 2.

28 Strabo XIV. 1. 48.

29 Cicero, *Arch.* 1. See *Greece and Rome* XV (1968), pp. 19–20.

30 Cicero was an *adulescens* when he heard him. *Brut.* 207.

31 Suetonius, *Gr.* 3. Suetonius gives no date, but seems to be speaking of the late Republican period.

32 *Ibid.* 7.

33 Cicero, *De Or.* III. 48.

34 Quintilian I. 4. 1.

35 Language and literature were no doubt studied concurrently. The grammarian Diomedes divides his material into three books *ut secundum trina aetatis gradatim legentium spatia lectio probabiliter ordinata crimen prolixitatis euadat taediumque permulceat. Gr. Lat.* ed. Keil, I, p. 299. This seems to imply a three-year course corresponding to the normal period of time spent in the grammar school.

36 Quintilian I. 4. 6–29.

37 Seneca, *Epp.* XCV. 65.

38 Quintilian I. 6. 45.

39 *Ibid.* I. 8. 5; Pliny, *Epp.* II. 14. 2; *A.P.* IX. 168, 173, 174. 1–2.

40 Plato, *Laws* VII. 811a.

41 In *Ox. Pap.* VI 930 a mother writes that she has asked her son's teacher what the boy was reading and he replied 'to zeta' (the sixth book, probably of the *Iliad*).

42 Horace, *Epp.* II. 2. 41–2 (Howes' translation).

43 *Ibid.* I. 2. 1–31.

44 For specific evidence that Cicero read Homer as a boy, see *Q.F.* III. 5–6. 4.

45 Plato, *Laws* VII. 810E–811A.

46 Quintilian I. 8. 7. *Cf.* Ovid, *Trist.* II. 370; Statius, *Silv.* II. 1. 114.

47 Ausonius XVIII. 22. 46–7.

48 The selection of Aristophanic plays is thought to have been made by the

grammarian Symmachus *c.* A.D. 100. See n. 10 for Libanius's reading of Aristophanes.
49 Statius, *Silvae* V. 3. 146–58. For Hesiod, see also Cicero, *Fam.* VI. 18. 6.
50 Suetonius, *Gr.* 1.
51 Suetonius, *Gr.* 2. 8.
52 Horace, *Epp.* II. 1. 69–71.
53 *Ibid.* 50–61.
54 Suetonius, *Gr.* 24.
55 Quintilian I. 8. 8. See Colson's note on I. 8. 8–12. Phaedrus (III *epilogus* 33–5) quotes a line from Ennius which he had read as a boy. But this *sententia*, as Phaedrus calls it, could well have been a copybook maxim of the primary school.
56 Suetonius, *Gr.* 16.
57 It will be seen that I do not agree with Jacques Perret, who attributes the recognition of Virgil to the influence of Seneca. *Virgile, l'homme et l'oeuvre* (Paris, 1952), p. 148.
58 Quintilian I. 8. 5.
59 Seneca quotes seventy-three times from the *Aeneid*, twenty-nine times from the *Georgics* and eight times from the *Eclogues*, that is, in proportion to the length of the works, about equally from all three. *Epp.* CVIII. 24 provides evidence of study of the *Georgics* by grammarians.
60 The fact that Servius begins his commentary with the *Aeneid*, and then goes on to the *Eclogues* and *Georgics*, suggests that this was the normal order in teaching. Donatus, however, took the works in order of composition.
61 Petronius 118. 5 (see 99. 2 for Eumolpus as a teacher); Quintilian I. 8. 6; Juvenal VII. 226–7.
62 Quintilian X. 1. 98.
63 Ausonius XVIII. 22. 56–60.
64 Gellius XX. 10. 2.
65 *Vita Lucani.*
66 Marrou's statement (*History of Education in Antiquity*, p. 277) that in Rome every successful poet was studied in the schools in his lifetime is not borne out by the passages to which he refers.
67 Dionysius Thrax 1 (*Gr. Graec.* I, p. 5).
68 Cicero, *De Or.* I. 187; *Div.* I. 34; Nepos *ap.* Suet. *Gr.* 4; Quintilian I. 4. 2.
69 Quintilian I. 4. 4.
70 Quintilian II. 5. 3.
71 Gellius XVIII. 4. 2. *Cf.* III. 1. 5, IV. 15.
72 Ausonius XVIII. 22. 61–3.
73 Plato, *Prot.* 325E.
74 Plato, *Laws* VII. 810e–811a.
75 Cicero, *Tusc.* II. 27; *cf.* III. 3. See also, for reciting from memory, Seneca, *Ben.* V. 25. 6.
76 Xenophon, *Symp.* III. 5; Augustine, *De Anima et eius Origine* IV. vii. 9 (a friend of Augustine believed to be able to recite Virgil backwards).
77 For dictation, see Horace, *Sat.* I. 10. 74, *Epp.* I. 1. 55, I. 18. 13, II. 1.

69–71; Persius I. 29; Beudel, *Qua ratione Graeci liberos docuerint* (Münster, 1911), p. 30. For copying out, see *C. Gloss. Lat.* III. 381. 58–60. On the other hand, the schoolboy in Lucian (*Amores* 44) is accompanied to school by attendants carrying 'books recording the great deeds of the past'.

78 Thus a grammarian describes himself on his tomb as *lector eorum/more incorrupto qui placuere sono. Anth. Lat.* II. 2. 1012, 1–2. Atticus's biographer records that *erat in puero praeter docilitatem ingenii summa suauitas oris ac uocis, ut non solum celeriter acciperet quae tradebantur sed etiam excellenter pronuntiaret.* Nepos, *Att.* 1.

79 Dion. Thr. 2 (*Gr. Graec.* I, p. 6); Ausonius XVIII. 22. 47–50 (Evelyn-White's translation).

80 Quintilian I. 8. 1–2. See XI. 3. 36–8 (directions for reading the opening of the *Aeneid*).

81 Quintilian I. 8. 2–3.

82 *enarrationem praecedit emendata lectio.* Quintilian I. 4. 3. *Cf.* Schol. Vat. Dion. Thr. p. 169 Hilgard (*Gr. Graec.* III); Schol. Lond. Dion. Thr. *ibid.* p. 453. Marrou (*History of Education in Antiquity*, p. 279) makes *praelectio* precede reading. This is true in that the word *praelectio* could be applied to the reading through of a passage beforehand to show how it should be done (Quintilian II. 5. 4), and this the master did, though not always (*ibid.* I. 2. 12). But *praelectio* in the sense of *enarratio* followed reading.

83 *Gr. Lat.* (ed. Keil) III. 459–515.

84 Quintilian I. 8. 13–17.

85 *Ibid.* 18–21.

86 Seneca, *Epp.* LXXXVIII. 6–8; Sext. Emp., *Adv. Math.* I. 255, 261–2.

87 Juvenal VII. 233–6; *cf.* Augustine, *De Ordine* II. 12. 37.

88 Suetonius, *Tib.* 70. 3.

89 Gellius IV. 1, VI.17, XVIII. 4. 2, XX. 10; Augustine, *Conf.* I. ix. 15.

90 Schol. Vat. Dion. Thr. p. 170 Hilgard (*Gr. Graec.* III).

91 *pueri cum essemus ... sine iudicio mirabamur; inspicere autem uitia nec per magistros nec per aetatem licebat.* Macrobius, *Sat.* I. 24. 6.

92 Augustine, *De Utilitate Credendi* vi. 13.

93 Ps.-Longinus, *De Sublimitate* 6.

94 Suetonius, *Gr.* 4; Quintilian I. 9. 6; II. 1. 1–3. The exercises mentioned by Suetonius do not correspond exactly with the recognized progymnasmata, but are clearly of the same type.

95 Marrou (*History of Education in Antiquity*, p. 172) supposes that this division applied also to the Greek schools. But there is no hint of it in the Greek writers of progymnasmata, who include Quintilian's contemporary Theon. They treat the whole series of exercises as a continuous course and as the first stage of rhetorical teaching.

96 Quintilian II. 1. 2. In the Augustan age the grammarian Verrius Flaccus set his pupils exercises in composition and awarded prizes for the best performance. Suetonius, *Gr.* 17.

97 Suetonius, *Rhet.* 1 (*Gr. et Rhet.* 25); *Gr.* 4.

98 Augustine, *Conf.* I. xvii. 27. Colson (on Quintilian I. 9. 2) takes Augustine's exercise as an example of paraphrase, which Quintilian mentions as an early progymnastic exercise. (So also Beudel, *Qua ratione Graeci*

liberos docuerint, pp. 53-4.) But paraphrase, which was done in connection with ordinary reading, would probably not call for special mention.

99 Quintilian II. 1. 6; Sextus Empiricus, *Adv. Math.* I. 98.

100 Quintilian II. 1. 13.

101 Quintilian II. 1. 4.

102 Juvenal VII. 226-7; *C. Gloss. Lat.* 380. 66-7. Marrou (*History of Education in Antiquity*, p. 274) is surely wrong in describing, on the basis of this passage, a school as a shop shut off from the forum by a curtain.

103 Juvenal VII. 237-41.

104 Cicero, *Fam.* IX. 18. 4; Augustine, *Conf.* VIII. vi. 13.

105 Ausonius V. 22. St Augustine (*Sermo* 178. 8) refers to a man so poor that he was *proscholus* to a grammarian. He was a Christian, the grammarian a pagan. *melior ad uelam* [the curtain separating the schoolroom from the vestibule] *quam in cathedra*. This man can hardly have been a teacher; at any rate he did not, like Cicero's *hypodidascalus* (see n. 104), have a seat by the master. *C. Gloss. Lat.* III, p. 646, refers to an assistant teacher in what is apparently a primary school. There is also evidence for pupil teachers. *Ibid.* 382. 35-42, 646.

106 Here I draw on one of the colloquia in the 'Hermeneumata pseudo-Dositheana', a collection of bilingual phrase books dating from the early third century. The colloquium in question (*C. Gloss. Lat.* III. 379-84) describes a day in a school which, unlike that of two other colloquia (*ibid.* 376-9 and 645-7), appears to be the school of a grammarian, though certain features, such as the mathematics lesson by a pupil teacher, suggest that of a *grammatistes*. The Greek version of the Hermeneumata is thought to be the original. (See Marrou, *History of Education in Antiquity*, p. 428.)

107 *C. Gloss. Lat.* III. 381. 20-52.

108 *Ibid.* 381. 58-65.

109 *C. Gloss. Lat.* III. 381. 66-75.

110 *Ibid.* 382. 24-5.

111 Seneca, *Contr.* I. pr. 2. Does this mean, as Jullien supposed (*Les Professeurs de littérature*, p. 177) that there were more than two hundred boys in the school? It is not impossible. Comparable numbers were handled, with the aid of monitors or pupil teachers, by masters of schools in early nineteenth-century England.

112 *C. Gloss. Lat.* III. 382. 48-71.

113 *Ibid.* 384. 11-29.

114 Though as St Augustine remarked, *aliud est esse arte aliud gente securum*. His pronunciation was criticized in Italy. *De Ordine* xvii. 46.

115 *non modo quae diserta sed uel magis quae honesta sunt discant*. Quintilian I. 8. 4. *ex magnitudine rerum spiritum ducat* [*animus*] *et optimis imbuatur. Ibid.* 5. See also for the moral influence of poetry, Plutarch, *De Audiendis Poetis*, and Horace, *Epp.* II. 1. 126-31. But one has one's doubts. Ausonius's *Cento Nuptialis* was the work of a grammarian. *Torquet ab obscenis?*

116 *propterea paruuli* [*Vergilium*] *legunt ut uidelicet poeta magnus omniumque praeclarissimus atque optimus teneris ebibitus animis non facile obliuione possit aboleri.* Augustine, *C.D.* I. 3. This type of education, of course, survived with little change until not so very long ago. The author's grandfather, who was at an

unreformed grammar school in the 1860s, returned on his retirement to the classics of his schooldays, which were also those of the Roman Empire: Virgil, Horace and Homer.

117 Quintilian I. 4. 5.

118 Cicero, *Brut.* 46, quoting the authority of Aristotle. For discussions of Corax and Tisias and the origins of rhetoric, see S. Wilcox in *Harvard Studies* 53 (1942), pp. 121–55, and G. A. Kennedy in *A.J.P.* 80 (1959), pp. 169–78; also Kennedy's *The Art of Persuasion in Greece* (London, 1963), pp. 26–70.

119 Plato, *Phaedr.* 267a, 273a; Aristotle, *Rhet.* II. 24. 11.

120 Plato, *Gorgias* 452e, 454b.

121 Aristotle, *Soph. El.* 34. 183b.

122 Plato, *Phaedr.* 267c; Aristotle, *Rhet.* II. 24. 11; Cicero, *Brut.* 46; D. L. IX. 53.

123 Plato, *Phaedr.* 266e–267c.

124 In his *Synagoge Technon*. See Cicero *Inv.* II. 6.

125 Isocrates, *Soph.* 19; *Panath.* 1. Some professed to teach political oratory. *Ibid. Soph.* 9.

126 *Ibid.* 10.

127 *Vita Isocr.* (*Biographi Graeci Minores*, ed. Westerman, p. 257); Plutarch, *Mor.* 837B–E.

128 Plutarch, *Mor.* 837C. Marrou (*History of Education in Antiquity*, p. 377) argues that one hundred was the total number of pupils Isocrates had in his lifetime and that therefore his school was small and select. (See R. Johnson in *A.J.P.* 78 (1957), pp. 297–300, for further arguments in support of this view.) This seems hardly consistent with Isocrates's own statements about the number of his pupils and the wealth they brought him. (*Ant.* 5, 87, 219.) Whether it is reliable or not the Life of Isocrates attributed to Plutarch clearly meant that he had a hundred at one time, just as Philostratus did when he similarly described Chrestus as having a hundred pupils. *Vit. Soph.* II. 11. (591).

129 For an attempt to reconstruct his methods of teaching, see R. Johnson, *A.J.P.* 80 (1959), pp. 25–36.

130 Isocrates, *Ant.* 187–92; *Soph.* 14–18.

131 Cicero, *Inv.* II. 7; *Biographi Graeci Minores*, p. 258; Plutarch, *Mor.* 838E; Quintilian II. 15. 4.

132 Isocrates, *Panath.* 200. Other teachers used Isocrates's works as models. *Ibid.* 16.

133 Quintilian II. 4. 41–2.

134 Cicero, *Brut.* 38; Quintilian X. 1. 80.

135 For a fuller treatment, see my *Rhetoric at Rome* (London, 1953).

136 Suetonius, *Rhet.* 1 (*Gr. et Rhet.* 25).

137 Tacitus, *Dial.* 34. 1–2.

138 Cicero, *Cael.* 9; Quintilian V. 7. 7; Tacitus, *Dial.* 2. 1. Tacitus himself had a number of aspiring orators attached to him. Pliny, *Epp.* IV. 13. 10.

139 Cicero, *De Or.* I. 14.

140 Suetonius, *Rhet.* 2 (*Gr. et Rhet.* 26); Quintilian II. 4. 42.

141 Suetonius, *Rhet.* 1 (*Gr. et Rhet.* 25); Cicero, *De Or.* II. 2.

142 Cicero, *De Or.* III. 93–5.

143   Cicero, *Brut.* 310.

144   Cicero, *Q.F.* III. 3. 4. Only Cicero's nephew is mentioned, but it is generally assumed that the two cousins were taught together.

145   It may be significant that two rhetoricians of Greek birth, Cestius and Argentarius, declaimed only in Latin. Seneca, *Contr.* IX. 3. 13. Dionysius of Halicarnassus is a distinguished example of a Greek who came to Rome (in 30 B.C.) to teach (Greek) rhetoric.

146   Suetonius, *Rhet.* 5 (*Gr. et Rhet.* 29); Cicero, *Phil.* II. 43; Seneca, *Contr.* IX. 3. 13. The identification of Sextus Clodius with Seneca's Clodius Sabinus, though probable, is not certain. Arellius Fuscus declaimed *suasoriae* in Greek as well as in Latin. Seneca, *Suas.* IV. 5.

147   Suetonius, *Vesp.* 18; Philostratus, *Vit. Soph.* II. 8 (580), 10 (588–9), 13 (594), 16 (596), 23 (627).

148   Pliny, *Epp.* VI. 6. 3.

149   Gellius IX. 15. 2; Philostratus, *Vit. Soph.* II. 10 (589).

150   This is the impression one gets from *Cod. Theod.* XIII. 3. 11 and from Ausonius's poems on the Bordeaux professors. A Greek rhetorician at Gades is mentioned on an inscription of uncertain date (*C.I.L.* II. 1738). Latin rhetoricians were to be found in the East, though as the case of Lactantius shows (Jerome, *Vir. Ill.* 80) there was little demand for their services.

151   Quintilian I. 2. 15; X. 5. 21. *Cf.* Juvenal VII. 151; Libanius, *Or.* 51. 15; Philostratus, *Vit. Soph.* I. 25 (531) (Polemo appreciably increased the population of Smyrna by attracting students from outside).

152   *Ibid.* II. 11 (591).

153   Libanius, *Or.* I. 37; *Epp.* 405. 4, 6; *Or.* I. 104 (but according to *Or.* I. 101 he started with fifteen). The school day of a rhetorician normally ended at midday. *Ibid.* 108; Augustine, *Conf.* VI. 11. 18.

154   Libanius, *Or.* 43. 8; Augustine, *Conf.* V. 12. 22.

155   Pliny, *Epp.* II. 18. 2.

156   Augustine, *Conf.* V. 8. 14.

157   Philostratus, *Vit. Soph.* II. 21 (604).

158   Quintilian II. 2. 14.

159   See *C. Ph.* LXIII (1968), p. 42.

160   Seneca, *Contr.* I. pr. 24; Quintilian I. 2. 23–4; Libanius, *Epp.* 139.

161   Cicero, *De Or.* I. 138–45, translated by E. N. P. Moor (1892).

162   Quintilian I. pr. 7. See *C. Ph.* LXIII (1968), p. 42.

163   *Rhetores Latini Minores* (ed. Halm) 81–134.

164   See the works of Rutilius Rufus (*R.L.M.* 3–21), based on a work by Gorgias, the younger Cicero's teacher at Athens; of Aquila Romanus and Julius Rufinianus and the anonymous *Carmen de Figuris* (*R.L.M.* 22–47, 63–70).

165   Quintilian II. 1. 2, 10. 2, 11. 1–2.

166   See the *Progymnasmata* of Hermogenes (authenticity disputed), Aphthonius, Theon, Nicolaus Sophistes and Libanius, the first three in Vol. II and the fourth in Vol. III of Spengel's *Rhetores Graeci*, the last in Vol. VII of Foerster's edition of Libanius.

167   Quintilian I. 9. 5; Suetonius, *Rhet.* 1 (*Gr. et Rhet.* 25); *Rhetores Graeci* (Spengel) II. 101 (Theon), III. 459 (Nicolaus).

168 Diomedes, *Gr. Lat.* (Keil) I. 310.
169 E. Ziebarth, *Aus der Antiken Schule*, 2nd edn (Berlin, 1913), p. 37.
170 Called *prosopopoiia* by Theon. Hermogenes distinguishes *prosopopoiia* (personification of a thing) from *ethopoiia* (of a person).
171 See *R.E.* I. 2798. Aphthonius's schemes were not original. That recommended for the chria is found as early as the first century B.C. (*ad Herennium* IV. 56–7).
172 See Theon's Introduction, p. 64 Spengel (but chria later appears in its usual place). Quintilian's order is (1) fable, (2) chria and allied exercises, (3) narratives (I. 9. 2–6). See also *Rhetores Graeci* (Spengel) III. 459.
173 Quintilian II. 4. 26. See Colson on I. 9. 3. for the possible identification of this exercise with the *aetiologia* mentioned, according to some manuscripts, there and in Suetonius, *Gr.* 4.
174 Suetonius, *Rhet.* I (*Gr. et Rhet.* 25).
175 Cicero, *De Or.* I. 155.
176 Quintilian X. 5. 2. Pliny (*Epp.* VII. 9. 1–2) recommends the practice.
177 *Rhetores Graeci* (Spengel) II, pp. 71–2 (Theon); Quintilian II. 4. 12; *cf.* II. 6, where, however, Quintilian may be referring to more advanced work.
178 Quintilian II. 5. 3.
179 Libanius, *Or.* 31. 8; P. Wolf, *Vom Schulwesen der Spätantike, Studien zu Libanius* (Baden-Baden, 1952), p. 20.
180 Libanius, *Epp.* 894; Wolf, *op. cit.* p. 64.
181 Quintilian II. 5. 6–13. Asconius's commentary on Cicero's speeches (written between A.D. 54 and 57) might seem to suggest that the speeches were read in schools. But there is no evidence that Asconius was a teacher of rhetoric (his commentary was written for the benefit of his sons), and his treatment is historical rather than rhetorical.
182 *Ibid.* 5. 2.
183 *Ibid.* 5. 2–3, 17.
184 Gellius I. 4, XI. 13.
185 Augustine, *De Cura pro Mortuis Gerenda* XII. 13. The *rhetorici Ciceronis libri* referred to are no doubt the two books of *De Inventione*.
186 *usitato discendi ordine. Conf.* III. iv. 7. *Cf. De Beata Vita* 4 (*in schola rhetoris illum librum Ciceronis . . . accepi*).
187 Tacitus, *Dial.* 35.4.
188 Suetonius, *Rhet.* 1 (*Gr. et Rhet.* 25).
189 Cicero, *De Or.* II. 100.
190 Cicero, *De Inv.* II. 153–4; *cf. ad Her.* I. 19.
191 Seneca, *Contr.* I. pr. 12.
192 Seneca, *Contr.* I. 5, 6, 7; [Quintilian], *Decl. Maj.* II; Libanius, *Decl.* 49.
193 Libanius's declamations include eleven *suasoriae* and eleven mythological or historical *controversiae*; the rest are either *controversiae* with no specific setting, or speeches which do not come into either category. Aristides's school declamations (*Or.* 29–39) are all *suasoriae*. In Sopatros's *Diaeresis Zetematon* (*Rhetores Graeci* ed. Walz, VIII (1835), pp. 2–385), which is evidently based on school teaching (he taught at Athens in the fourth century), *controversiae* with a historical setting are very much in the minority, but still more numerous than in the corresponding Latin collections.

194   See the various themes mentioned in the course of Philostratus's Lives of the Sophists.

195   *Ox. Pap.* 2400.

196   Lucian, *Rhet. Praec.* 18.

197   See S. F. Bonner, *Roman Declamation* (Liverpool, 1949), pp. 51–2.

198   In the *Declamationes Minores* the master's comments are given under the heading 'Sermo'.

199   Pollux VIII. pr. *Cf.* Seneca, *Contr.* I. pr. 21, III. pr. 11, VII. pr. 1; Philostratus, *Vit. Soph.* I. 21 (519); Eunapius, *Vit. Phil.* 489.

200   Quintilian I. 2. 23–4, II. 7. 1, X. 5. 21; Juvenal VII. 160–1. *Sexta quaque die* could also mean 'every fifth day'. See C. L. Howard in *C.Q.* VIII (1958), p. 6; he is, however, surely wrong in interpreting this particular phrase to mean 'every Friday'. A school programme based on the week seems most unlikely in Roman schools at this date. It has been supposed that parents were invited to be present on these occasions, but the passages quoted in support (Quintilian II. 7. 1, X. 5. 21; Persius II. 45–7) hardly justify this inference. The Persius passage seems to refer to a recitation by the boy at home (like that in Herondas III. 31–6). Juvenal VII. 165–6 suggests, if anything, that parents did not hear their sons declaim.

201   Seneca, *Contr.* IX. 2. 23.

202   Quintilian II. 7. 1, X. 5. 21.

203   Juvenal VII. 152–3. I suggested another interpretation of these lines in *C. Ph.* LXIII (1968), pp. 42–4; but see *ibid.* pp. 295–6.

204   Jerome, *c. Rufin.* I. 30; Libanius, *Progymnasmata, Chriae* 3.

205   Pliny, *Epp.* II. 18. 1, 3. 5–7.

206   Seneca, *Contr.* I. 1. 21, II. 3. 19, VII. 2. 9; Petronius 6. 2; Tacitus, *Dial.* 20. 5.

207   Quintilian III. 8. 51, VI. 2. 17; and, for the practice of usually not speaking as advocate, [Quintilian], *Decl. Min.* CCLX (*sermo*), CCCXIII (*sermo*), CCCXXXI (*sermo*).

208   Seneca, *Contr.* IX. pr. 5; Quintilian II. 2. 9–12.

209   See S. F. Bonner, *Roman Declamation* (Liverpool, 1949), chs. V and VI, for a discussion of the laws in declamations.

210   Quintilian IV. 2. 29, V. 13. 42; Seneca, *Contr.* IX. pr. 2, X. 5. 12.

211   Cicero, *De Or.* I. 149.

212   Seneca, *Contr.* IX. pr. 1–5; *cf. ibid.* III. pr. 12.

213   Tacitus, *Dial.* 35. 2.

214   Petronius 4. 1–2.

215   Quintilian II. 10. 1–6.

216   *Ibid.* 8.

217   Augustine, *De Util. Cred.* vii. 16.

218   Juvenal VI. 158–60; Libanius, *Or.* XXV. 47.

219   See Quintilian II. 8. 7 (*nonnulli rus fortasse mittendi*).

220   Quintilian VIII. pr. 27. 31, X. 3. 10–16.

221   *hai tessares methodoi,* Nicolaus Gerasinus (*c.* A.D. 100), *Intr. Arithm.* I. 4. 1.

222   Plato, *Theaet.* 145a; *Prot.* 318e.

223   Diels, *Vorsokratiker* I. 432 (Nicolaus Gerasinus, *Intr. Arithm.* I. 3. 4).

224   Proclus, *In Euc.* I, p. 65, Friedlein.

225 Plato, *Laws* VII. 817e–819d.

226 Isocrates, *Ant.* 261–8.

227 Cicero, *De Rep.* I. 30; Quintilian I. 10. 34. Quintilian himself argues, not very convincingly, that mathematics is useful to an orator.

228 Plato, *Rep.* VII. 522e.

229 Augustine, *Conf.* XIII. 20. 22; *cf. De Ordine* II. 12. 35.

230 Classed with the *notarius*, or shorthand teacher, by Martial and distinguished from the *ludi magister* (X. 62. 4). In the Edict of Diocletian the *calculator* (the same word transliterated in the Greek version) is recognized as distinct from other teachers. T. Frank, *An Economic Survey of Rome*, Vol. V, pp. 344–5.

231 Horace, *A.P.* 326–30.

232 Petronius 58. 7.

233 See Vitruvius I. 4 for its use to architects.

234 Stobaeus, *Eclogae* II. 31. 114. Sir Thomas Heath was surely wrong when he said that Euclid's *Elements* cannot have been meant for schoolboys because of its theoretical character and its aloofness from anything in the nature of practical geometry. *The Thirteen Books of Euclid's Elements* (Cambridge, 2nd edn, 1908), p. vi.

235 Plato, *Rep.* VII. 525c.

236 Simplicius, *in Arist de Caelo* II. 12 (p. 488 Heiberg); *Academicorum Index Herculanensis*, ed. Mekler (Berlin, 1902), pp. 15–16; Proclus, *In Euc.* I, p. 67.

237 Aristotle, *Metaph.* I. 9. 27 (992a).

238 Iamblichus *in Nicom. Arithm.* 20. 11 (Pistelli) refers to *hoi peri Eukleiden*, his pupils, that is. See also n. 234.

239 Lucian, *Nigr.* 2.

240 T. L. Heath, *History of Greek Mathematics* (Oxford, 1921), II. 528.

241 *Ibid.* II, p. 532.

242 Proclus, *In Euc.* I, p. 65. Aristotle (*Meteor.* I. vii. 344b) refers to *hoi peri Hippokraten*, i.e. his pupils.

243 D.L. IV. 29; Teles, p. 50 Hense.

244 O. Kern, *Die Inschriften von Magnesia am Meander* (Berlin, 1900), No. 107; A. Dumont, *Mélanges d'archéologie et d'épigraphie* (Paris, 1892), p. 435, 100x.

245 *I.G.* II². 1006. 18, 1008. 56, 1009. 35.

246 Cicero, *Tusc.* I. 5.

247 Cicero, *Off.* I. 19.

248 Cicero, *Tusc.* V. 113.

249 See Quintilian I. 10. 39.

250 Vitruvius IX. 1. 16. *Cf.* Hyginus, *Astr.* pr. '. . . ne nihil in adolescentia laborasse dicerer et imperitorum iudicio desidiae subirem crimen hoc uelut rudimento scientiae nisus scripsi ad te.' Seneca, *Ben.* III. 5, provides further evidence of Roman study of astronomy.

251 Jullien, *Les Professeurs de littérature dans l'ancienne Rome*, p. 349.

252 Heath, *History of Greek Mathematics* I. 359. *Cf.* Martianus Capella VI. 587. 'quod nunquam fere accidit Romuleis ut potero uocibus intimabo.'

253 Quintilian I. 10. 35, 46. *Cf.* Seneca, *Epp.* 88. 10–13; Columella I. pr. 3–5.

254 T. Frank, *An Economic Survey of Rome* V. 346–7.
255 *Historia Augusta*, M. *Antoninus* 2. 2. Cicero, *Tusc.* V. 113.
256 Quintilian I. 4. 4.
257 H. Weinhold, *Die Astronomie in der antiken Schule* (München, 1912), p. 85. Seneca, *Epp.* 88. 14–17; Sextus Empiricus, *Adv. Math.* V. Vitruvius (IX. 6. 2) refers to a school of astrology founded by Berosus at Cos.
258 Hipparchus, *In Arati et Eudoxi Phaenomena Commentarium* I. 1. 7.
259 Marrou (*History of Education in Antiquity*, pp. 184–5) seems to me to exaggerate the extent to which the teaching of astronomy through Aratus was in the hands of grammarians. (See also Weinhold, *Die Astronomie in der antiken Schule*, pp. 25, 32, 34–5, 39.) There is some evidence that grammarians concerned themselves with Aratus (Maass, *Commentariorum in Aratum reliquiae*, (Berlin 1898), pp. 80, 342), and one of his commentators ('Anonymus I') appears to have been a grammarian (*ibid.* pp. 91, 95). But Attalus and Achilles were astronomers (according to Suidas Achilles wrote *peri sphairas*, though Maass identifies him with an Achilles included in a list of grammarians (*ibid.* p. XVII)); so evidently was the scholiast who sent his commentary to one Julianus (*ibid.* p. 555).
260 *Ibid.* pp. 27–75.
261 *Ibid.* pp. 315–33.
262 *Ibid.* pp. 338, 341.
263 Quintilian I. 10. 3, 39.
264 *Ibid.* 39–45, 49.
265 Vitruvius IX. 1. 16.
266 Cicero, *Tusc.* V. 64. *Cf. N.D.* II. 48 and passages quoted by Pease *ad loc.*
267 Aristophanes, *Nub.* 177–8.
268 Martianus Capella VI. 579.
269 Daremberg and Saglio, *Dictionnaire des antiquités grecques et romaines* II. 2. 1545.
270 Cicero, *Tusc.* V. 113.
271 See *R.E.* VII. 1427; Weinhold, *Die Astronomie in der antiken Schule*, pp. 41–4, 58–9.
272 See Cicero, *De Rep.* I. 22.
273 Maass, *Commentariorum in Aratum reliquiae*, p. 95; Geminus, *Elementa Astronomiae* V. 69.
274 Maass, *Commentariorum in Aratum reliquiae*, p. 561.
275 Cicero, *Tusc.* I. 4.
276 Aristophanes, *Nub.* 961–9.
277 Aristotle, *Pol.* VIII. iv. 1339b; *cf.* vi. 1341a.
278 *Ibid.* iv. 1341a, vii. 1341b.
279 *Ibid.* v. 1340b.
280 *S.I.G.*³ 959, 960.
281 *S.I.G.*³ 578. See Ziebarth, *Aus den griechischen Schulwesen*, p. 48; Nilsson, *Die hellenistische Schule*, pp. 45–6. At Teos the lyre player teaches the younger boys *ta mousika* (perhaps musical theory) in addition to lyre playing, the older ones *ta mousika* only.
282 Lucian, *Amores* 44.

283 Macrobius, *Sat.* III. 14. 7.
284 Cicero, *De Or.* III. 86–7. See G. Wille, *Musica Romana* (Amsterdam, 1967), p. 350.
285 Horace, *Odes* IV. 6. 31–2; Quintilian I. 10. 22–8. Some orators kept their voices in training by singing scales (Seneca, *Contr.* I. pr. 16), though Quintilian says there is no time for this (XI. 3. 22).
286 Suetonius, *Titus* 3. 2.
287 Suetonius, *Nero* 20. 1.
288 Augustine, *De Musica* I. 5–8.
289 Aristides Quintilianus I. 4 (p. 6 Meibom); Alypius, *Introductio Musica* (p. 1 Meibom).
290 Martianus Capella III. 326; Augustine, *De Ordine* II. 14. 40. But Augustine dealt with rhythm in his *De Musica*, and, though he planned further books on melody, never completed them.
291 Plato, *Rep.* III. 398d–399c.
292 Plato, *Prot.* 326a–b; *Rep.* III. 401d–402a.
293 Plutarch, *Mor.* 1146a–b.

Notes to chapter 3

1 Porphyry, *Vit. Pyth.* 37; Iamblichus, *Vit. Pyth.* 81.
2 D.L. VIII. 10; Iamblichus, *Vit. Pyth.* 30, 71–4; Gellius I. 9. 3–4. Apollonius of Tyana revealed certain doctrines to his disciples after a four-years' silence. Philostratus, *Vit. Ap. Ty.* I. 16.
3 D.L. VIII. 13, 19; Iamblichus, *Vit. Pyth.* 68–9, 107; Porphyry, *Vit. Pyth.* 34. There were, however, various traditions about the Pythagorean food rules. Guthrie, *History of Greek Philosophy* I (Cambridge, 1962), pp. 187–91.
4 Iamblichus, *Vit. Pyth.* 100, 149.
5 *Ibid.* 68, 94, 188; Porphyry, *Vit. Pyth.* 19.
6 Porphyry, *Vit. Pyth.* 40. According to Iamblichus (*Vit. Pyth.* 164–6) these exercises were part of the training of the memory.
7 Porphyry, *Vit. Pyth.* 33; Iamblichus, *Vit. Pyth.* 110–14.
8 *Ibid.* 96–9.
9 Polybius II. 39. 1–4; Porphyry, *Vit. Pyth.* 54–5; Iamblichus, *Vit. Pyth.* 248–51 (based on Aristoxenus); Guthrie, *op. cit.* I, pp. 178–81.
10 Porphyry, *Vit. Pyth.* 58; Iamblichus, *Vit. Pyth.* 252–3; D.L. VIII. 45.
11 Fragments of Middle Comedy show that Athenian audiences of the fourth century were familiar with the peculiar habits of Pythagorean devotees. See the passages quoted by Burnet, *Early Greek Philosophy* (3rd edn), p. 94, n. 3. See Theocritus XIV. 5, with Gow's note, for a 'Pythagorist' pale and barefooted, who claims to be an Athenian.
12 Cicero, *N.D.* I. 10; D.L. VIII. 46.
13 Plato, *Apol.* 33a; *cf.* 19d.
14 *Ibid.* 30a; *Theaet.* 149a–f.
15 Xenophon, *Mem.* I. 1. 10.
16 Plato, *Symp.* 222b.

17 Plato, *Phaed.* 118.

18 Julian, *Letter to Themistius* 264c-d (Wright's translation).

19 D.L. III. 7. See R. E. Wycherley in *Greece and Rome* IX (1962), pp. 1-21, for the topography of the Athenian schools.

20 D.L. VI. 13.

21 Cicero, *Fin.* V. 2; Apuleius, *De Plat.* I. 4; D.L. III. 5.

22 Plutarch, *Mor.* 603b.

23 D.L. IV. 1.

24 Wilamowitz, *Antigonos von Karystos* (Berlin, 1881), excursus 2; Gomperz, *Greek Thinkers* (E.T., 1901-12) II, p. 272, III, p. 308 (criticizing Wilamowitz); G. C. Field, *Plato and his Contemporaries* (London, 1930), p. 34; Boyancé, *Le Culte des Muses chez les Philosophes Grecs* (Paris, 1937), pp. 261-2; Marrou, *History of Education in Antiquity* (E.T., 1956), p. 67.

25 D.L. VI. 69; Aeschines, *In Timarch.* 10.

26 D.L. III. 41-3.

27 D.L. IV. 3; Plutarch, *Mor.* 603b.

28 Cicero, *Fin.* V. 2.

29 D.L. IV. 19; *Academicorum Index Herculanensis*, ed. Mekler (Berlin, 1902), p. 54.

30 D.L. IV. 60.

31 Cicero, *Fin.* V. 4. *Cf. ibid.* 8, which shows that the scene is the Academy.

32 Plutarch, *Sull.* 12; Appian, *Mithr.* 30; Cicero, *Brut.* 306.

33 Cicero, *Fin.* V. 1.

34 Horace, *Epp.* II. 2. 45.

35 If this is so, Propertius's *stadiis Platonis* (III. 21. 25. *stadiis* is a generally accepted emendation for *studiis*) is also a conventional phrase.

36 Cicero, *Att.* V. 10; *Tusc.* V. 22.

37 D.L. V. 51-3.

38 *Ibid.* 39.

39 D.L. V. 38; Athenaeus XIII. 610e-f; Pollux IX. 42. W. S. Ferguson, *Hellenistic Athens* (London, 1911), pp. 104-7.

40 *Digest* 47. 22. 4.

41 Wilamowitz, *Antigonos von Karystos*, p. 271. *Cf.* J. W. Jones, *Law and Legal Theory of the Greeks* (Oxford, 1956), p. 165; Boyancé, *Le Culte des Muses chez les Philosophes Grecs*, pp. 315-16.

42 Athenaeus XI. 508f-509a.

43 Cicero, *Fin.* V. 3; D.L. X. 10.

44 *Ibid.* 16-21.

45 Cicero, *Fin.* V. 3.

46 Cicero, *Fam.* XIII. 1; *Att.* V. 11. 6.

47 D.L. VII. 184, 185.

48 For the heads, see *Index Stoicorum Herculanensis*, ed. Traversa (Genova, 1952).

49 *Academicorum Index Herculanensis*, p. 67; D.L. IV. 32, 60. Diogenes, ignoring Socratides, says that Lacydes was the first to resign.

50 *Academicorum Index*, pp. 38-9.

51 *Ibid.* p. 67. What happened when Lacydes resigned is not clear. According to Numenius (*ap.* Eusebius, *Praep. Ev.* XIV. 6) he was succeeded

by Euandros. Diogenes Laertius says that Lacydes handed over the school to Telecles and Euandros (IV. 60). The *Academicorum Index* (p. 93) after recording his retirement gives a list of his pupils which includes Telecles and Euandros.

52 *Academicorum Index*, p. 91.
53 D.L. V. 51–3, 62.
54 *Ibid.* 70.
55 D.L. X. 17 and 20.
56 *I.G.* II.² 1099 (A.D. 121).
57 D.L. V. 70.
58 *Ibid.* 4.
59 *Ibid.*; Athenaeus XII. 547e.
60 *Ibid.* 547f.
61 *Ibid.* V. 186a–b.
62 Athenaeus XII. 547d–f.
63 Plutarch, *Mor.* 26b, 53c.
64 Aristoxenus, *Harm.* II. 30–1. Aristotle, according to Aristoxenus, often used to tell the story of this lecture.
65 Plato, *Epp.* VII. 341c–d.
66 Cherniss, *The Riddle of the Early Academy* (Berkeley, California, 1945), p. 64.
67 *Academicorum Index*, pp. 15–16.
68 Athenaeus II. 59d–f (fr. 11. Kock).
69 D.L. IV. 16. According to another account Xenocrates was lecturing on a different topic, but changed to Sophrosyne when Polemo came in. Val. Max. VI. 9 *ext.* 1.
70 D.L. IV. 28.
71 Cicero, *Fin.* II. 2. *Cf. N.D.* I. 11; *Tusc.* I. 8; *Fin.* V. 10; Plutarch, *Mor.* 634a.
72 Cicero, *Fin.* II. 2.
73 Cicero, *De Or.* I. 102.
74 Cicero, *Tusc.* IV. 8.
75 Cicero, *Tusc.* I. 7–8, V. 11; *De Fato* 4.
76 Quintilian III. 1. 14; Gellius XX. 5. 1–6.
77 Cicero, *De Or.* III. 141; *Tusc.* I. 7; Quintilian III. 1. 14. According to Cicero in *De Oratore* he was already engaged in teaching and *mutauit totam formam disciplinae suae*.
78 D.L. V. 3. Xenocrates appears to have taught rhetoric. See Alexis *ap.* Athenaeus XIII. 610e.
79 Cicero, *Fin.* V. 10; *Or.* 46. *Cf. De Or.* III. 80; *Tusc.* II. 9; D.L. V. 3; Quintilian XII. 2. 25.
80 Strabo XIII. 54.
81 In 86 B.C. Sulla brought them to Rome. Plutarch, *Sulla* 26. According to Athenaeus Ptolemy Philadelphus bought them from Neleus and took them to Alexandria. Athenaeus I. 3b.
82 D.L. X. 6 (*mustike sundiagoge*).
83 Cicero, *Fin.* I. 65. *Cf. Ac. Pr.* II. 115; D.L. X. 17.
84 D.L. X. 18; Cicero, *Fin.* II. 101; Philodemus, *A.P.* XI. 44. Philodemus's

words suggest a yearly celebration, but Epicurus's will makes it clear that it was a monthly one.

85   Philodemus, *peri parrhesias*, ed. Olivieri (Leipzig, 1914), fr. 45; Lucretius III. 15, V. 8, V. 51; Cicero, *Tusc.* I. 48; Plutarch, *Mor.* 1117b.

86   Numenius, *ap.* Euseb., *Praep. Ev.* XIV. 5.

87   D.L. X. 120.

88   Cicero, *Fin.* II. 20.

89   Crönert in *S.B. Berl. Acad.* XLI (1900), p. 947.

90   See Philodemus, *peri parrhesias, passim.* De Witt's attempt (*C. Ph.* XXXI, 1936, pp. 205–11) to extract from this treatise evidence for a hierarchical organization in Epicurean groups is not altogether convincing.

91   Cicero, *Tusc.* III. 13; *De Or.* I. 43.

92   Cicero, *Fin.* IV. 79.

93   Cicero, *Tusc.* II. 26.

94   See W. Jaeger, *Aristotle* (E.T., 1934), pp. 111–16.

95   D.L. VII. 6–9; *S.V.F.* I. 435–45; Plutarch, *Cleomenes* II. 2, XI. 2.

96   Crönert in *S.B. Berl. Akad.* XLI (1900), pp. 942–59; Usener, *Kleine Schriften* III (Leipzig, 1912–13), pp. 188–92 (= *Rh. Mus.* LVI 1901, pp. 145–8); *R.E.* XX. 1, pp. 63–73.

97   Athenaeus V. 211a–d.

98   *S.E.G.* 1. 368; *cf. I.G.* VII. 2849 (the philosopher Xenocrates of Macedonia honoured at Haliartus).

99   Lucretius V. 20–1.

100   Cicero, *Fin.* II. 49. *Cf. ibid.* 81, 115; *Tusc.* V. 28; D.L. X. 9; De Witt, *Epicurus and his Philosophy*, pp. 329–31.

101   Cicero, *Fin.* I. 25; D.L. IV. 43.

102   Plutarch, *Mor.* 1100d; Athenaeus XII. 547a; Sextus Empiricus, *Adv. Math.* II. 25; Aelian, *V.H.* 9. 12.

103   Suetonius, *Rhet.* 1.

104   Plutarch, *Cat. Maj.* 22. 4.

105   Cicero, *Ac. Pr.* II. 5; *Tusc.* I. 81; *Rep.* I. 34.

106   Cicero, *Fin.* II. 24; *De Or.* I. 75; *Brut.* 101; *De Or.* III. 78; *Brut.* 114; *De Or.* I. 227–30. For Stoics who flourished in the second half of the second century and the early first, see Cicero, *Brut.* 94, 117, 175, 206; *De Or.* I. 67, III. 78.

107   Though Cicero's statement in *Pro Caelio* 41 that the Stoics *prope soli iam in scholis sunt relicti* is not to be taken too literally.

108   Cicero, *Fam.* XIII. 1. 2; *Fin.* I. 16; *N.D.* I. 93.

109   Cicero, *Brut.* 306.

110   Cicero, *N.D.* I. 59. Perhaps Cicero is here drawing on his own experience, though he makes Cotta the recipient of the advice.

111   In *Brut.* 309 he mentions Diodotus after Philo. In *Ac. Pr.* II. 115 he says he heard Diodotus *a puero.*

112   Cicero, *Brut.* 315; *Fin.* I. 16; *Ac. Pr.* II. 4. 11; *Fin.* V. 8; *Tusc.* V. 21.

113   Plutarch, *Cic.* 4. 4; Cicero, *N.D.* I. 6, II. 88; *Div.* I. 6, II. 47.

114   Cicero, *Brut.* 131.

115   Cicero, *Fin.* II. 44.

116 Cicero, *Tusc.* IV. 6–7. For Roman Epicureans, see Momigliano in *J.R.S.* XXXI (1941), pp. 149–57.

117 *I.G.* II². 3897, as restored by A. E. Raubitschek in *Hesperia* XVIII (1949), pp. 96–103.

118 Cicero, *Fin.* II. 119. *Cf. Fam.* VI. 11. 2. See also Cicero, *In Pisonem* ed. R. G. M. Nisbet (Oxford, 1961), p. 187.

119 Cicero, *Pis.* 68; *A.P.* XI. 44. For the Villa of the Papyri, see Nisbet, *op. cit.* Appendix IV.

120 *Catalepton* 5, 8.

121 Cicero, *Ac. Pr.* II. 11.

122 *Ibid.*; Plutarch, *Brut.* 2. 3.

123 Plutarch, *Crassus* 3. 3; Cicero, *Fin.* V. 8; *De Or.* I. 104.

124 Cicero, *Brut.* 309; *Tusc.* V. 112–13; *Ac. Pr.* II. 115; *N.D.* I. 6; *Fam.* XIII. 16. 4; *Att.* II. 20. 6.

125 Plutarch, *Cat. Min.* 4. 1, 10. 1, 16. 1; Strabo XIV. 5. 14.

126 Plutarch, *Cat. Min.* 65. 5, 66. 4–67. 2, 69. For philosophers and other learned Greeks in the household of Augustus, see G. W. Bowersock, *Augustus and the Greek World* (Oxford, 1965), pp. 30–41.

127 Strabo XIV. 5. 13.

128 Cicero, *De Or.* III. 43.

129 *Ibid.* I. 45–7, 82, III. 68, 75.

130 Cicero, *Fin.* V. 1–5.

131 We hear of reports from Leonides and Herodes (Cicero, *Att.* XIV. 16. 3, XV. 16a) and Plutarch knew of letters from Cicero to Herodes (*Cic.* 24. 6). Cicero junior saw a lot of 'Epicrates, princeps Atheniensium, Leonides et horum ceteri similes' (*Fam.* XV. 21. 5).

132 *Ibid.* XII. 16. 1–2.

133 *Ibid.* XVI. 21. 1–6.

134 Horace, *Epp.* II. 2. 43–6.

135 See E. Fraenkel, *Horace* (Oxford, 1957), p. 8. Four hundred years later it was still a painful experience for students to leave Athens. Greg. Naz., *Or.* XLIII. 24 (*P.G.* 36. 529).

136 Plutarch, *Brut.* 24. 1.

137 Dio Cassius XLVII. 49.

138 Petronius, *Sat.* 71. 12.

139 *I.G.* II². 1099.

140 Dio Cassius LXXII. 31. 3; Lucian, *Eun.* 3; *cf.* Tatian, *ad Graecos* 19.

141 Eusebius, *Praep. Ev.* XIV. 5–9.

142 D.L. X. 9.

143 Seneca, *N.Q.* VII. 32. 2.

144 Damascius, *Vit. Isid.* 151.

145 Galen (XIX. 50) refers to the establishment of the *diadochoi* by M. Aurelius, but the term was used earlier. *Stoicorum Index* 53; *I.G.* III. 661, 1441.

146 Philostratus, *Vit. Soph.* II. 2 (566).

147 Lucian, *Eun.* 3.

148 *Ibid.* 12.

149 Alexander Aphrodisias, *De Fato* 1.

150 Porphyry, *Vit. Plot.* 15, 20.
151 Philostratus, *Vit. Ap. Ty.* IV. 17.
152 Lucian, *Nigrinus* 12–16.
153 *Ibid.* 13.
154 Gellius XVIII. 2. 2.
155 Philostratus, *Vit. Ap. Ty.* I. 7.
156 Galen V. 41–2.
157 Tacitus, *Agr.* 4. 3–4. In Strabo's time Romans had recently taken to going to Massilia for study. Strabo IV. 5 (181).
158 Tacitus, *Annals* XVI. 32; Juvenal III. 116–17; Friedländer, *Roman Life and Manners* (E.T., 1965) III. 260–2.
159 Seneca, *Tranqu.* 14.
160 Tacitus, *Ann.* XVI. 34.
161 Lucian, *De Mercede Conductis* 36.
162 Lucian, *Hermotimus* 16.
163 Sextus Empiricus, *Adv. Math.* I. 331.
164 Plutarch, *Mor.* 434d.
165 Lucian, *Alex.* 25; *cf.* 38, 44–5, 47.
166 *Acts* 17. 18.
167 Longinus *ap.* Porph. *Vit. Plot.* 20.
168 References to Epicureans and Epicureanism in other Christian writers do not mean a great deal. The words came to be little more than terms of abuse which were freely applied to heretics. See R. Jungkurtz in *Journal of Ecclesiastical History* XVII (1966).
169 Julian, *Epp.* 89b (Bidez), 301c.
170 Augustine, *Contr. Acad.* III. 42.
171 *Idem, Epp.* CXVIII. 21. The disappearance of Chrysippus's works is a sign of the failure of the Stoic school to survive.
172 Porphyry *ap.* Euseb. *Praep. Ev.* X. 3 (Prosenes a Peripatetic at Athens); Eusebius, *H.E.* VII. 32. 6 (Anatolius, bishop of Laodicea from *c.* 270, a distinguished Peripatetic whom the Alexandrians wanted to make head of the school there).
173 Hierocles *ap.* Phot. cod. 251, 461a.
174 Cicero, *Tim.* 1. Another contemporary Pythagorean was Vatinius (*Vat.* 14).
175 Seneca, *Epp.* CVIII. 17.
176 Plutarch, *Mor.* 727b.
177 Philostratus, *Vit. Ap. Ty.* I. 7.
178 *Ibid.* I. 18, IV. 37.
179 *Ibid.* I. 7.
180 *Ibid.* I. 8.
181 *Ibid.* I. 13.
182 *Ibid.* I. 15.
183 Cicero, *Tusc.* V. 113.
184 Seneca, *Epp.* LXIV. 2, CVIII. 18.
185 *Idem, De Ira* III. 36.
186 Justin, *Dial. cum Tryph.* 2; *cf.* Lucian, *Herm.* 14.
187 Epictetus III. 22. 45.

188 Cicero, *Off*. I. 148.
189 Epictetus III. 22.
190 Gellius XII. 11. 1. But in VIII. 3 Gellius describes how Peregrinus rebuked a young Roman for his inattention in Gellius's presence, which seems to suggest something like a class as conducted by Epictetus. Julian (*Or*. VII. 204a) describes how he was invited to hear a Cynic discourse.
191 Epictetus III. 22. 17.
192 Julian, *Or*. VI. 187d.
193 Lucian, *Bis Acc*. 6.
194 Dio Chrys., *Or*. XXXII. 9; *cf. ibid*. XXXIV. 2; Lucian, *Fug*. 12-21.
195 Cicero, *Fin*. III. 4.
196 Cicero, *Tusc*. III. 2. *Cf*. Lucretius III. 319-22 for a similar view expressed by an Epicurean. The Sceptic Sextus Empiricus, however, argues that there is no art of living and that it cannot be taught. *Pyrrh*. III. 23-30 (239-73).
197 Plutarch, *Mor*. 796d.
198 Seneca, *Epp*. LII. 9, 11; Lucian, *Jup. Trag*. 4, 27.
199 Lucian, *Nigr*. 26; Symmachus, *Relationes* V.
200 Lucian, *Nigr*. 25, *Herm*. 9, *Eun*. 3; Justin, *Dial. cum Tryph*. 2.
201 Plutarch, *Mor*. 39b-c, 41c, 42c, 45d, 45f-46a, 46c.
202 Gellius XIX. 6. 2.
203 *Idem* I. 9. 8-10. *Cf*. Lucian, *Dial. Meretr*. 10. 4.
204 Gellius XVII. 20. 1.
205 Epictetus, *Ench*. 49 (Matheson's translation). *Cf. Discourses* II. 21. 10-11, III. 21. 7.
206 Fronto, p. 154 Naber.
207 Epictetus I. 10. 8.
208 *Ibid*. I. 26. 13; *cf*. I. 26. 1.
209 *Ibid*. II. 6. 23, I. 7. 32, II. 13. 21, 17. 27.
210 *Ibid*. 19. 5-10, 21. 10.
211 *Ibid*. I. 23, II. 20.
212 Pliny, *Epp*. I. 10. 7.
213 Seneca, *Suas*. II. 12.
214 Seneca, *Epp*. CVIII. 13-14.
215 Musonius *ap*. Gell. V. 1; Epictetus III. 23; Plutarch, *Mor*. 79c, 41c-e.
216 Seneca, *Epp*. CVIII. 6-12. *Cf*. Quintilian V. 11. 39 for the use of quotations from poetry by philosophers.
217 Epictetus III. 6. 10, 23. 29.
218 *Idem* I. 7. 32. But this mode of address is not found in Musonius's discourses as preserved by Stobaeus.
219 *Idem* II. 27. 37. Th. Colardeau, *Étude sur Épictète* (Paris, 1903), pp. 101-2.
220 Plutarch, *Mor*. 42f-43d.
221 *Ibid*. 43e. For the invitation of questions, *cf*. Cicero, *Fam*. IX. 26. 3.
222 Seneca, *Epp*. CVIII. 3.
223 Gellius I. 26.
224 Musonius III, p. 8 (Hense), IV, p. 13, XVII, p. 88.

225 Epictetus I. 13. 1, 14. 1.
226 *Idem* III. 6. 1, 8.
227 Musonius XVI, p. 81.
228 Epictetus I. 15. 1–6.
229 *Idem* III. 22. 1.
230 *Idem* I. 2. 26, 30.
231 *Idem* I. 11. 1 f., 14. 1 f., II. 24. 1 f., III. 1 f.,7. 1 f. Similarly Musonius questions one of his hearers. V, pp. 20–1 (Hense).
232 Epictetus III. 1. 10–11.
233 *Idem* II. 14. 17–22.
234 Plutarch, *Mor.* 717a–b; Porphyry, *Vit. Plot.* 2, 15; *idem. ap.* Euseb. *Praep. Ev.* X. 3; Marinus, *Vit. Procl.* 23; Proclus, *In Rem Publicam* (ed. Kroll), I, pp. 69–70.
235 Plutarch, *Mor.* 720c; Gellius VII. 13. *Cf.* XV. 2. 2–3 (a weekly philosophic dinner-party held by a group of students at Athens).
236 Plutarch, *Mor.* 673a.
237 Persius V. 41–4.
238 Musonius XVIIIa, XVIIIb.
239 Seneca, *Epp.* CVIII. 14, 23.
240 Lucian, *Nigr.* 27–8.
241 Plutarch, *Mor.* 70e.
242 *Hist. Aug., Marc. Ant.* II. 6.
243 Seneca, *Epp.* CVIII. 13–23.
244 Lucian, *Dial. Meretr.* 10. But another reason is alleged: the philosopher is a paederast.
245 Musonius XII; Dio Chr. VII. 133f.
246 Epictetus, *Ench.* 33. 8. The neo-Platonist Olympiodorus requires complete chastity in a philosopher. *In Phaed.* A. III. 5.
247 Plutarch, *Mor.* 37d–e; *cf. ibid.* 5b.
248 Persius V. 30–40 (Gifford's translation).
249 Epictetus, III. 21. 8–9.
250 Lucian, *Herm.* 80–2.
251 Seneca, *Epp.* CVIII. 4.
252 Musonius XVI. For parental opposition to the study of philosophy, *cf.* Epictetus I. 26. 5.
253 Plutarch, *Mor.* 7d–e.
254 Compare also what Seneca says of Attalus, how he commended *castum corpus, sobriam mensam* (*Epp.* CVIII. 14), with the phrase in the Catechism 'to keep my body in temperance, soberness and chastity'.
255 Nepos, fr. 40 Malcovati.
256 Seneca, *Epp.* XXIX. 1–9.
257 Lucian, *Symp. Cf. Icar.* 21, 29–31; *Pisc.* 34; Athenaeus XIII. 565d–f.
258 See Marrou, *History of Education in Antiquity* (E.T.), p. 33.
259 D.L. VII. 129; Cicero, *Tusc.* IV. 72, *Fin.* III. 68, *N.D.* I. 79, with Pease's note.
260 Plutarch, *Mor.* 11d–f.
261 Porphyry, *Vit. Plot.* 15.
262 Cicero, *Tusc.* IV. 70; Plutarch, *Mor.* 752a–b; Lucian, *Am.* 23–4, 54;

Dial. Meretr. 10. 4; *Fug.* 18; Athenaeus V. 182a, 187c–f; XI. 506e, 508d; XIII. 563d–e, 564f, 565d–f; Origen, *c. Cels.* VII. 49; Tatian, *c. Graec.* 19.

263 Lucian, *Bis Acc.* 7–8.

264 Dio Chrys. XXVII. 7–9.

265 Porphyry, *Vit. Plot.* 2.

266 Eunapius, *Vit. Soph.* 456–7.

267 See J. Bidez, *Vie de Porphyre* (Gand, 1913), pp. 103–4.

268 Symmachus, *Relationes* V.

269 J. Bidez in *R.E.G.* XXXII (1921), p. 31.

270 Eunapius, *Vit. Soph.* 458–9. See also the letters falsely attributed to Julian (74–9 Wright; 34, 40, 41, 53, 60, 61 Hertlein) for the extravagant veneration accorded to Iamblichus by his followers.

271 Eunapius, *Vit. Soph.* 461–2, 465, 469, 474–5. Praechter in *Genethliakon Carl Robert* (Berlin, 1910), p. 109.

272 Ammianus XXV. 3. 23.

273 Marinus, *Vit. Procl.* 29.

274 Olympiodorus, *In Alc.* 140–1. A. Cameron (*Proc. Cam. Phil. Soc.* N.S. 15, 1969) argues that Olympiodorus's words date from *c.* 560, after the closing of the Athenian school in 529, that the confiscations referred to were those of that year and that these had only been partial and had left some of the property intact.

275 Damascius, *Vit. Isid.* 158; Suidas 1709 (Plato).

276 Marinus, *Vit. Procl.* 19, 22.

277 *Ibid.* 27–9.

278 *Ibid.* 23.

279 *Ibid.* 22.

280 Damascius, *Vit. Isid.* 221, 229–30.

281 Aeneas, *Theophrastus* (*P.G.* 85, 877).

282 *Cod. Just.* I. 5. 18. 4.

283 Malelas, p. 451 Dindorf. See Gibbon, *Decline and Fall*, ed. Bury, IV, p. 283 n.

284 Agathias, II, p. 227 Dindorf.

285 *Ibid.* pp. 231–3.

286 See A. Cameron in *Proc. Cam. Phil. Soc.* N.S. 15, 1969, pp. 7–29.

287 Synesius, *Epp.* LIV, CXXXV.

288 Suidas, s.v. Aedesia.

289 Damascius, *Vit. Isid.* 54.

290 Aeneas of Gaza, *Theophrastus* (*P.G.* 85. 876).

291 *P.G.* 85. 1028–9. Whether any such discussion actually took place is doubtful.

292 Damascius, *Vit. Isid.* 292. See H. P. Saffrey, *R.E.G.* LXVII (1954), pp. 399–400, and, for Ammonius's paganism, *P.G.* 85. 1021.

293 According to Busse (*Davidis Proleg. et in Porph. Isag. Comm., C.A.G.* XVIII. 2, p. vi) it is more likely that David was a pupil of Elias and Elias of Olympiodorus than that they were co-pupils of Olympiodorus. *Cf.* R. Vancourt, *Les derniers commentateurs alexandrins d'Aristote. L'école d'Olympiodore, Étienne d'Alexandrie* (Lille, 1941), p. 6.

294 M. Meyerhof in *S.B. Preuss. Akad. Wiss., Phil.-hist. Kl.* 23 (1930),

M

pp. 389–429. At one time the school was reduced to one teacher with two pupils, but the two carried on the tradition and each in turn had two followers.

295 Porphyry, *Vit. Plot.* 9. Plotinus planned to found a Platonic community in Campania; the emperor Gallienus showed some interest in the project, but it came to nothing. *Ibid.* 7, 12.

296 *Ibid.* 7.

297 *Ibid.* 1.

298 *Ibid.* 4, 5.

299 *Ibid.* 14.

300 See Plotin, *Enneades*, ed. E. Bréhier, intr. pp. xxviii–xxix.

301 Porphyry, *Vit. Plot.* 18.

302 *Ibid.* 13.

303 *Ibid.* 3.

304 Socrates, *H.E.* I. 17.

305 Julian, *Epp.* 89b (Bidez), 301c.

306 Marinus, *Vit. Procl.* 9; Damascius, *Vit. Isid.* 79.

307 Marinus, *Vit. Procl.* 13; Damascius, *Vit. Isid.* 36. See also *Vit. Procl.* 12 and *Vit. Isid.* 42 for teaching of Aristotle by Plutarchus and Marinus.

308 Suidas, s.v. Hypatia.

309 Themistius, *Or.* XX. 234d–235a.

310 Damascius, *Vit. Isid.* 36, 58.

311 Eunapius, *Vit. Soph.* 500.

312 Marinus, *Vit. Procl.* 26.

313 See the heading to his commentaries on Aristotle's *Analytica Posteriora, de Generatione et Corruptione* and *De Anima.* That on the *Categories* has no reference to John's own contribution; that on the *Meteorologica* has no reference to Ammonius.

314 The commentaries of Elias on Porphyry's *Isagoge* and Aristotle's *Categories* and of David on the *Isagoge* were published by pupils from lecture notes. See Busse's edition of Elias (*C.A.G.* XVIII. 1), p. vii and the heading to David's *Prolegomena.*

315 Marinus, *Vit. Procl.* 12.

316 Proclus's commentary on the *Cratylus* survives only in extracts. It seems more likely that these are from a book by Proclus than from lecture notes of a pupil.

317 Schemmel in *Neue Jahrbücher* 11 (XXI) (1908), p. 509; Ammonius, *In Cat. proem.* (*C.A.G.* IV. iv, p. 6); Simplicius, *In Cat. proem.* (*C.A.G.* VIII, pp. 5–6).

318 Proclus, *In Alc.* 11. According to *Proleg. Plat. Phil.* (Plato, ed. Hermann, VI, Leipzig, 1892, p. 219) Iamblichus selected twelve dialogues.

319 *Proleg. Plat. Phil.* pp. 219–20.

320 Ammonius, *in Isag.*, *C.A.G.* IV. 3, p. 21.; John Philoponus, *In Cat.*, *C.A.G.* XIII. 1, p. 7; Olympiodorus, *In Cat.*, *C.A.G.* XII. 1, p. 1.

321 The prolegomena and commentaries on the *Isagoge* by both Elias and David are also divided into *praxeis.* On Olympiodorus's teaching, see R. Vancourt, *Les derniers commentateurs alexandrins d'Aristote*, pp. 8 f.

322 That of Westerink (Amsterdam, 1954).

323 Themistius, *Anal. Post. Paraphr.*, *C.A.G. V.* 1, p. 1. *Cf. Or.* 294d. See Schemmel in *Neue Jahrbücher* 11 (XXI), 1908, pp. 155–7.
324 Themistius, *Or.* 20d. 294b; Himerius, *Or.* VII. 13; Greg. Naz., *Or.* XLIII. 14 (*P.G.* 36. 513). Gregory of Nyssa disputed on fate with a pagan philosopher at Constantinople. *P.G.* 45. 148.

Notes to chapter 4

1 Cicero, *De Officiis* I. 150.
2 Celsus, *De Medicina* I. pr. 6–8.
3 Plato, *Meno* 90b; *Prot.* 311b.
4 Celsus I. pr. 8.
5 Strabo XII. 8. 20.
6 Galen II. 220–1; Ammianus Marcellinus XXV. 16. 18.
7 Pliny, *N.H.* XXIV. 12–17.
8 See examples given in Daremberg and Saglio, *Dictionnaire des antiquités grecques et romaines*, art. Medicus.
9 Littré, *Hippocrate*, Paris 1839–61, IV. 628–30.
10 See n. 3.
11 Littré, *Hippocrate* IV. 634–5.
12 Galen XIX. 59; Rufus, *De Corporis Humani Appellationibus*, 1–10.
13 V. Rose, *Anecdota Graeca et Graeco-Latina* II (Berlin, 1870), pp. 244–5.
14 Galen X. 5; XIII. 599.
15 Littré, *Hippocrate* IX. 206.
16 *Ibid.* IX. 243. We learn from Plato's *Laws* (IV. 740b–c) that doctors also had slave assistants who were used to treat slaves. *Cf.* Galen X. 4.
17 Philostratus, *Vit. Ap. Ty.* VIII. 7. 14; Martial V. 9.
18 Littré, *Hippocrate* IV. 630, IX. 218.
19 Pliny, *N.H.* XXVI. 11; Galen II. 280–1.
20 See n. 5.
21 Galen XIX. 15, 19, 21. Some of Galen's MSS were lost when the temple was burnt. *Ibid.* II. 216, XIX. 19.
22 Rufus, *De Corporis Humani Appellationibus* 1–10, 127. *Cf.* Galen XIV. 627–30 for anatomical demonstrations.
23 Galen, XIX. 57–8.
24 M. Meyerhof in *S.B. Preuss. Akad. Wiss., Phil.-hist. Kl.* 23 (1930) p. 399. According to another source the presented books numbered sixteen. *Ibid.* pp. 395–7. Similarly in the law school at Beirut the students were on their own in the later part of their course. See p. 116.
25 See *Architectural History* 6 (1963), pp. 9–22.
26 Vitruvius VI. pr. 6.
27 *Ibid.* I. 1. 12.
28 *Ibid.* I. 1.
29 *Cod. Theod.* XIII. 4. 1.
30 Vitruvius IV. 3. 3. *Cf.* VI. pr. 5, X. 11. 2.
31 T. Frank, *Economic Survey of Ancient Rome* V, pp. 346–7.
32 Cicero classes the services of a jurist as *beneficia*; but he admits they could

be profitable. *Off.* II. 65. According to F. Schulz, *History of Roman Legal Science* (Oxford, 1946), pp. 43, 49, in Cicero's day there were minor jurisconsults who demanded a fee for their services.

33 Cicero, *De Or.* I. 198.
34 *Ibid.* III. 133.
35 *Ibid.* I. 185–203.
36 Cicero, *Leg.* II. 59.
37 Cicero, *Brut.* 306, *Orat.* 142–3. According to Schulz, *History of Roman Legal Science*, p. 57, the lawyer's pupils lived in his house. This seems to be contradicted by Cicero, *Leg.* I. 13, where Atticus says to Cicero 'a primo tempore aetatis iuri studere te memini cum ipse etiam ad Scaeuolam *uentitarem*'.
38 Cicero, *De Or.* I. 186–90. Cicero himself wrote *de Iure Ciuili in Artem redigendo*. Gellius I. 22. 7.
39 Schulz, *History of Roman Legal Science*, pp. 103–4.
40 *Ibid.* pp. 119–21.
41 *Digest* I. 2. 2. 47–53.
42 *Ibid.* 47.
43 *Ibid.* 48.
44 Pliny, *Epp.* VII. 24. 8.
45 Schulz, *History of Roman Legal Science*, pp. 156–8.
46 Gellius XIII. 13. 1.
47 Justinian (Constitutio *Omnem*, 7) imposed penalties on those who taught law elsewhere than at Beirut, Rome and Constantinople. Alexandria and Caesarea are specifically mentioned.
48 See P. Collinet, *Histoire de l'école de droit de Beyrouth* (Paris, 1925).
49 Gregory Thaumaturgus, *In Originem Oratio* 5 (*P.G.* X. 1065–8).
50 Libanius, *Or.* 62. 21–3 (IV. 356–8 Förster). *Cf. Or.* 2. 44, 48. 22; *Epp.* 1170 (I. 253, III. 438–9, XI. 257 Förster).
51 *Cod. Just.* II. 7. 11.
52 Zacharias Scholasticus, *Life of Severus* (*Patrologia Orientalis* II. 11.); Collinet, *Histoire de l'école de Beyrouth*, pp. 48–9, 112–13.
53 Constitutio *Omnem*; Collinet, *Histoire* 233–8.
54 Constitutio *Omnem* 9.
55 *Patrologia Orientalis* II, pp. 46–8.
56 *Ibid.* p. 53.
57 *Ibid.* p. 91.
58 Galen XIX. 9.
59 Augustine, *Conf.* IV. 3. 5, VI. 17. 15.

Notes to chapter 5

1 Tertullian, *De Idolatria* 10.
2 Julian, *Epp.* 61 (Bidez).
3 Socrates, *H.E.* II. 46. III. 16; Sozomen, *H.E.* V. 18 (*P.G.* 67. 361–4, 417–20, 1269–72). Similar attempts to classicize the Scriptures have been made in modern times, for example George Buchanan's version of the Psalms in Latin lyric metres and James Duport's in Homeric hexameters.

4 *E.g.* Melito in Eusebius,*H.E.* IV. 26. 7; Justin, *Dial. cum Tryph.* 8.
5 Origen, *c. Celsum* III. 54.
6 Minucius Felix, *Oct.* 38.
7 Lactantius, *Op. Dei* I. 2.
8 Origen, *c. Cels.* III. 50.
9 *Acts* 19. 8.
10 *Latebrosa et lucifugax natio.* Minucius Felix, *Oct.* 8.
11 *Ibid.* 19.
12 Origen, *c. Cels.* III. 51.
13 Eusebius, *H.E.* V. 20. 6.
14 Augustine, *Conf.* VI. 4. *Cf. ibid.* 6 and V. 23.
15 It is not, of course, peculiar to the Pythagoreans. It is found in the Essene community as described by Josephus (*Bell. Jud.* II. 8. 7).
16 Origen (*c. Cels.* I. 7) draws the parallel with the Pythagoreans.
17 See A. D. Nock, *Conversion* (Oxford, 1961 edn.), p. 214.
18 Justin, *Apol.* II. 10.
19 Augustine, *Cat. Rud.* 12, 13, 23.
20 *Ibid.* 24.
21 *P.G.* 45. 9–113.
22 *Ibid.* 12.
23 R. Walzer, *Galen on Jews and Christians* (Oxford, 1949), p. 15; Origen, *c. Cels.* I. 9.
24 *P.G.* 33. 369–1060.
25 Justin, *Ap.* I. 67 (tr. Henry Bettenson).
26 See Nock, *Conversion*, p. 203.
27 Pliny, *Epp.* IX. 96. 7; Justin, *Ap.* I. 67.
28 From 'Of Ceremonies' in the Book of Common Prayer.
29 Augustine, *Conf.* V. 23.
30 *Ibid.* IX. 14.
31 This survives to the extent that it is still usual to base a sermon on a scriptural text.
32 *P.G.* 44. 431.
33 Clement, *Strom.* I. 5. 28.
34 Eusebius, *H.E.* V. 10. 1; Justin, *Dial. cum Tryph.* 2. *Cf.* Clement, *Strom.* VI. 167.
35 Augustine, *De Vera Relig.* 23. *Cf. Epp.* cxviii. 21, 33.
36 Eusebius (Rufinus), *H.E.* XI. 7. The successions given by Philip of Side (*P.G.* 39. 229) are not, however, regarded as altogether reliable. See G. Bardy in *Vivre et penser*, 1942, pp. 81–4.
37 Eusebius, *H.E.* VI. 3. 8, VI. 14. 11; Jerome, *De Viris Illustr.* 54.
38 Eusebius (Rufinus), *H.E.* XI. 7.
39 Porphyry *ap.* Eusebius, *H.E.* VI. 19. 6–8. It appears from *ibid.* VI. 19. 13 that Origen's philosophical studies were undertaken after he had begun teaching.
40 *Ibid.*
41 Origen, *c. Cels.* III. 58.
42 Eusebius, *H.E.* VI. 2. 15, 3. 1, 3. 3, 3. 8.
43 *Ibid.* VI. 15.

44 *Ibid.* VI. 18. 3; Gregory Thaumaturgus, *In Origenem Oratio* 6–15 (*P.G.* 10. 1068–96).
45 Gregory Thaumaturgus, *In Origenem* 13–15 (*P.G.* 10. 1088–96).
46 G. Bardy, *Vivre et penser*, 1942, p. 109. But Bardy probably goes too far when he says that after the departure of Origen '*seule subsiste l'humble école catéchétique*'. Heraclas, who still studied philosophy as bishop of Alexandria (Eusebius, *H.E.* VI. 19. 13–14), is likely to have continued on Origen's lines.
47 See H.-I. Marrou in *Paganism and Christianity in the Fourth Century*, ed. A. Momigliano (Oxford, 1963), pp. 140–2.
48 Gregory Nazianzenus, *Or.* XLIII. 21 (*P.G.* 36. 513).
49 Augustine, *De Ordine* II. 46. 44, 18. 47. At the end of his life Augustine thought he had gone too far and allowed too much importance to secular studies. *Retractationes* I. 3. 2.
50 Augustine, *De Doctr. Christ.* II. 42. 63.
51 *Ibid.* II. 40. 60. 'Spoiling the Egyptians' comes from Origen, but Augustine's attitude to pagan philosophy is less sympathetic than Origen's.
52 See Peter Brown, *Augustine of Hippo* (London, 1967), p. 263.
53 See P. Courcelle, *Les Lettres grecques en occident* (Paris, 1948), pp. 38–9.
54 Eusebius, *H.E.* V. 10. 4.
55 Clement, *Eclogae* 56. *Cf.* Eusebius, *H.E.* VI. 13. 2. See Bousset, *Jüdisch-Christlicher Schulbetrieb in Alexandria und Rom* (Göttingen, 1915), pp. 190 f. for Clement's debt to Pantaenus.
56 Gregory Thaumaturgus, *In Origenem* 15 (*P.G.* 10. 1093); Eusebius, *H.E.* VI. 32. 1.
57 *Ibid.* 23. 1–3.
58 *Ibid.* 32. 1.
59 Cassiodorus, *Institutiones* I. pr. 1.

Notes to chapter 6

1 For general accounts of Byzantine education, see F. Fuchs, *Die höheren Schulen von Konstantinopel im Mittelalter* (= *Byzantinisches Archiv*, Heft 8) (Leipzig-Berlin, 1926); Georgina Buckler, 'Byzantine Education' in *Byzantium*, eds. Baynes and Moss (Oxford, 1948); J. M. Hussey, *Church and Learning in the Byzantine Empire 867–1185* (Oxford, 1937); R. Browning, 'Byzantinische Schulen und Schulmeister' in *Das Altertum* IX (1963), pp. 105 f.
2 *Cod. Theod.* XIV. 9. 3. This may have been a refoundation of an older institution rather than a completely new foundation.
3 See R. Browning in *Byzantion* XXXII (1962), pp. 167–202; XXXIII (1963), pp. 11–40.
4 Translated and edited by Glanville Downey in *Trans. Am. Philosophical Soc.*, N.S. 47 (1957).
5 See H. Usener, *Kleine Schriften* (Leipzig, 1912), III, p. 251.
6 *Byzantinische Zeitschrift* VI, p. 579.
7 *P.G.* 109. 200.
8 Anna Comnena, *Alexiad* V. 8. 2. *Cf.* Psellus, *Chronographia* III. 3 (few learned men under Romanus III (1028–34)).

9 *Mesaionike Bibliotheke*, ed. K. N. Sathas (Venice, 1872–4) IV. 433, V. 90, 93.

10 Psellus, *Chronographia* VI. 41; *De Operatione Daemonum accedunt inedita opuscula*, ed. J. F. Boissonade (Nürnberg, 1838, repr. Amsterdam, 1964), p. 145.

11 *Mesaionike Bibliotheke* V, p. 508.

12 Anna Comnena, *Alexiad* VIII. 9. 1. See also P. E. Stephanou, *Jean Italos, philosophe et humaniste* (Rome, 1949).

13 *P.G.* 142. 24.

14 *P.G.* 109. 206.

15 Nicephorus Blemmydes, *Curriculum Vitae et Carmina*, ed. A. Heisenberg (Leipzig, 1896), pp. 2–6, 55.

16 See O. Tafrali, *Thessalonique au quatorzième siècle* (Paris, 1913), p. 150.

17 *P.G.* 140. 363.

18 *Mesaionike Bibliotheke* V. 12, 28; *P.G.* 140. 1051.

19 *Mesaionike Bibliotheke* I, p. πζ; Nicephorus Blemmydes, *Curriculum Vitae*, p. 2.

20 *Nicephori Archiepiscopi Constantinopolitani Opuscula Historica*, ed. C. de Boor (Leipzig, 1880), pp. 149–50.

21 *Ibid.*; *Le Muséon*, N.S. III (1902), p. 109; Psellus, *Scripta Minora*, ed. E. Kurtz, I (Milan, 1936), p. 109; *Byzantinische Zeitschrift* II (1893), pp. 97–9; Nicephorus Blemmydes, *Curriculum Vitae*, p. 5; *Trans. Am. Philos. Soc.* N.S. 47 (1957), pp. 895–6 (without astronomy).

22 *P.G.* 142, 25.

23 *Ibid.* 105. 509.

24 *Mesaionike Bibliotheke* V. 60; Psellus, *Chronographia* VI. 42.

25 *E.g.* John the Psichaite. *Le Muséon* N.S. III (1902), p. 109.

26 *P.G.* 99. 117, 105. 509, 109. 206, 142. 24; *Mesaionike Bibliotheke* V, p. 14.

27 *Ibid.* p. 91.

28 *Byzantinische Zeitschrift* II (1893), p. 97. Theodosius wrote Canons of declensions and conjugations (in *Gr. Graeci* I. 3). Horus was a grammarian of Constantinople who flourished in the fifth century; for Herodian's grammatical works see *Gr. Graeci* III. 1 and 2; Heliodorus (seventh century) wrote a commentary on Dionysius Thrax (*Gr. Graeci* I. 3). Choeroboscus (later sixth century) commented on Theodosius (*Gr. Graeci* IV. 2).

29 Nicetas also expounded Epicharmus, Archilochus, and Nicander. *Mesaionike Bibliotheke* V. 92. Eustathius's commentary on Dionysius Periegetes's geographical work indicates that this was a school text.

30 *Mesaionike Bibliotheke* V. 92.

31 Nicephorus Blemmydes, *Curriculum Vitae*, p. 2.

32 There are a number of Byzantine works on rhetoric in Walz's *Rhetores Graeci*.

33 Nicephorus Blemmydes, *Curriculum Vitae*, p. 5; *P.G.* 142. 25.

34 *Mesaionike Bibliotheke* I, pp. πέ–ρια.

35 *Cambridge Medieval History* IV. ii (1957), p. 275.

36 L. D. Reynolds and N. G. Wilson, *Scribes and Scholars* (Oxford, 1968), pp. 65, 182.

37   Nicephorus Blemmydes, *Curriculum Vitae*, pp. 2, 5–6, 55.
38   *P.G.* 142. 25; *Byzantinische Zeitschrift* II (1895), p. 99.
39   Psellus, *Chronographia* III. 3 (trans. E. R. A. Sewter).
40   *Ibid.* VI. 37–8.
41   Anna Comnena, *Alexiad* V. 8. 6, VIII. 9. 1.
42   C. Zervos, *Un philosophe néoplatonicien du xiᵉ siècle. Michael Psellos* (Paris, 1920), pp. 215–18.
43   Psellus, *De Operatione Daemonum*, pp. 135–9, 140–4, 146.
44   *Ibid.* pp. 142, 149.
45   *Ibid.* p. 150.
46   Psellus, *Scripta Minora*, pp. 146–8.
47   See *Cambridge Medieval History* IV. ii, pp. 288–92.
48   It was available outside Constantinople during the Latin conquest. Nicephorus Blemmydes, whose father was a physician, studied medicine, theoretical and practical, for seven years. *Curriculum Vitae*, p. 3.
49   See *Cambridge Medieval History* IV. ii, pp. 55–70.
50   *P.G.* 161. 41.
51   See L. Bréhier in *Byzantion* III (1926), p. 84.
52   Ibn Khaldūn, *The Mugaddimah, An Introduction to History*, trans. by F. Rosenthal (New York, 1948), III, pp. 111–12.
53   See Avicenna's Autobiography, continued by al-Juzjani, in A. J. Arberry, *Avicenna on Theology* (London, 1951). Al-Ghazali (A.D. 1058–1111) was self-taught in philosophy. W. Montgomery Watt, *The Faith and Practice of Al-Ghazali* (London, 1953), p. 30.
54   See R. Pierre Riché, *Éducation et culture dans l'occident barbare* (Paris, 1962), pp. 62–8.
55   Cassiodorus, *Inst.* I. pr. 1.
56   Cassiodorus, *Varia* IX. 21; Ennodius, CCXIII (*Carmina* I. 2); CCXXXIV (Carmina II. 104); III (*Dictiones* 7); LXXXV (*Dictiones* 9).
57   By P. Courcelle, *Les Lettres grecques en occident*, pp. 268–300.
58   *Comm. in Arist. de Interpr.* II. pr. (*P.L.* 64. 433).
59   *P.L.* 156. 844, 681.
60   G. Paré, A. Brunet and P. Tremblay, *La Renaissance du XIIᵉ siècle. Les écoles et l'enseignement* (Paris–Ottawa, 1933), p. 18.
61   *P.L.* 178. 115.
62   *Ibid.* 107. 393–404, 176. 768.
63   *Ibid.* 107. 404–5.
64   Lynn Thorndike, *University Records and Life in the Middle Ages* (New York, 1944), pp. 26–8.
65   *Ibid.* pp. 64–5; H. Rashdall, *Universities of Europe in the Middle Ages*, ed. Powicke and Emden (Oxford, 1936), I, p. 369.
66   *P.L.* 178. 979.
67   Rashdall, *Medieval Universities* III. 444–52.
68   *P.L.* 138. 103.
69   *Ibid.* 207. 313–14.
70   Giraldus Cambrensis, *Opera*, Vol. IV, ed. J. S. Brewer (1873), p. 7 n.; *cf.* II, pp. 348–51.
71   John of Salisbury, *Metalogicus* I. 24–5.

72 Rashdall, *Medieval Universities* III. 152–5.

73 L. J. Paetow, *The Arts Course at Medieval Universities* (Champaign, Illinois, 1910), pp. 33–8.

74 Higden, *Polychronicon* (ed. Churchill Babington, 1869) II, pp. 158–61.

75 See Giraldus Cambrensis, *Opera* II. 344–8.

76 F. J. E. Raby, *Christian Latin Poetry* (Oxford, 1927), pp. 18, 108.

77 *P.L.* 138. 103.

78 Conrad of Hirschau, *Dialogus super Auctores sive Didascalon*, ed. G. Schepss (Würzburg, 1884). Conrad regards Horace as primarily the author of the *Ars Poetica*, and has considerable reserves about Ovid's works other than the *Fasti*, *Ex Ponto* and *Nux*.

79 C. H. Haskins, *Studies in the History of Mediaeval Science* (Harvard, 1927), pp. 351–76.

80 Roger Bacon, *Opera quaedam hactenus inedita*, ed. J. S. Brewer (1859), pp. 54–5.

81 Paetow, *The Arts Course at Medieval Universities*, p. 11.

82 John of Salisbury, *Metalogicus* I. 24.

83 F. J. E. Raby, *Secular Latin Poetry in the Middle Ages* (Oxford, 1934), I, p. 178.

84 C. H. Haskins, *Studies in the History of Mediaeval Science*, p. 374.

85 *P.L.* 138. 103.

86 Paetow, *The Arts Course at Medieval Universities*, p. 69.

87 Thorndike, *University Records*, p. 45.

88 Paetow, *The Arts Course at Medieval Universities*, pp. 60, 61.

89 *P.L.* 138. 102, 103.

90 Rashdall, *Medieval Universities* I, p. 450; III, pp. 155. 290.

91 Chaucer, *Prioress's Tale*, 1689–91.

92 The one that survives may not be genuine.

93 Heath, *History of Greek Mathematics* II, p. 367.

94 *Ibid.* pp. 368–9; Rashdall, *Medieval Universities* I, pp. 248–9; Thorndike, *University Records*, pp. 281–2.

95 *P.L.* 138. 102–3.

96 See p. 135

97 Rashdall, *Medieval Universities* I, pp. 361–2.

98 Rashdall, *Medieval Universities* I. 123.

99 Rashdall, *Medieval Universities* I. 218–19; Thorndike, *University Records*, p. 67.

100 *Ibid.* p. 226.

101 *P.L.* 178. 979–80; Paré, Brunet and Tremblay, *La Renaissance du XIIe siècle*, pp. 256–7.

102 Rashdall, *Medieval Universities* I, pp. 474–7.

103 A. G. Little and F. Pelster, *Oxford Theology and Theologians c. A.D. 1282–1302* (Oxford, 1934), pp. 28–32.

104 *P.L.* 178. 1349.

105 See David Knowles, *The Evolution of Medieval Thought* (London, 1962), p. 339.

Index